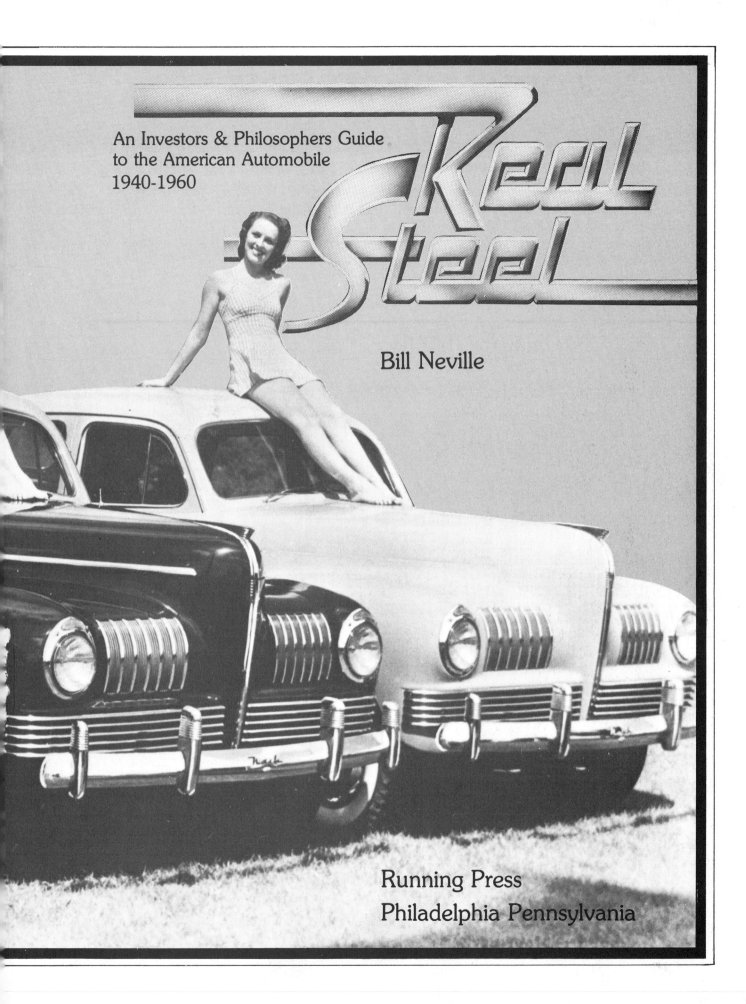

An Investors & Philosophers Guide
to the American Automobile
1940-1960

Real Steel

Bill Neville

Running Press
Philadelphia Pennsylvania

Acknowledgements

Special thanks to the Free Library of Philadelphia for the unlimited use of its superb Automotive Reference Collection, and in particular to Miss Mary Cattie and Mrs. Dolores Axam, who cheerfully and tirelessly assisted me in its use. A friendlier, more diligent staff cannot be found.

Library of Congress Cataloging in Publication Data

Neville, Bill, 1945-
   Real steel.

   Bibliography: p.
   Includes index.
   1. Automobiles--Collectors and collecting.
I. Title.
TL7.A1N48   629.22'22'0973   75-17045
ISBN 0-914294-27-X lib. bdg.
ISBN 0-914294-26-1 pbk.

Printed in the United States of America

Distributed in Canada by Van Nostrand Reinhold Ltd., Ontario

Library of Congress Catalog Card Number 75-17045

ISBN 0-914 294-26-1 trade paper

ISBN 0-914 294-27-X library edition

Art Direction by Jim Wilson
Cover Design by Louis Brooks
Cover Photography by Bill Neville
Interior Graphics and Design by Tom Fetterman
Rear Cover Photo by Bob Callahan

Type: Haas Helvetica & I.T.C. Souvenir, Composition by Alpha Publications, Inc.
Cover printed by Harrison Color Process Lithographers
Real Steel printed and bound by Port City Press

This book may be ordered directly from the publisher. Please include 25¢ postage.
Try your bookstore first.

Running Press, 38 South Nineteenth Street, Philadelphia, Pennsylvania 19103

Premise

This book is being assembled because there is a need to combine four basic ingredients of car-collecting for the growing number of antique buffs, car lovers, investors and collectors. Only obtainable cars, indicative of several similar models, will be presented. Pictures obviously serve to identify these specimens and, moreover, to convey the aesthetic qualities that make these cars popular and valuable. A second need is fulfilled by the mood and analysis presented in writing for each car: the author believes that even for the most calculating investor, it is not best to buy a car just because it looks good on paper. If a proper understanding of the true vitality of the American Dream is cultivated, then it is so much easier to buy and appreciate a good car.

It is necessary to know certain basic specifications, thirdly, to define and maintain the automobile. Some cars have a good deal of value primarily on the strength of extraordinary mechanical refinements. The section on specifications and measurements serves to clarify these examples. Finally, the collector needs a true dollar picture of the car as an investment. The actual cost of each car will thus be represented graphically in a manner which shows present value plotted with previous value and potential worth. As a point of comparison, the original price of each car will be pinpointed on the graph.

Of the many automobiles chosen for **Real Steel**, selections of virtually every body style available from the late thirties to the mid-sixties are included, with a wide range of prices to satisfy the collector on any budget. Many others could have been included, but they would only have served to second the existing categories. The trick is to be able to identify the conceptual pieces and to profit by putting them in their proper places.

Contents

Introduction

With automobiles, as with everything we pursue, order fulfills function. In deciding which cars to illustrate in this book, I paid particular heed to several forms of order. Primarily, I was concerned with categorical beauty, availability of the samples and a varied but acceptable price range. Since these concepts are mutable, you will find your own areas of interest according to your own tastes and pocketbook. However, the trend of popularity over the years can be broken down to a guide that is generally acceptable as a hierarchy of values. Most will agree, for instance, that a four-door sedan is less appealing than a two-door coupe or hardtop. Perhaps this is because stylists generally start out with the freedom of expression that is best embodied in a two-door version, and then extended to other applications. The 1953 Loewy Studebaker is an excellent example of such function. The completed hierarchy of body styles goes something like this:

1. Convertible

2. Two-door hardtop/coupe

3. Station wagon

4. Four-door sedan

Keep in mind this is a general guide subject to the occasional insertion of a unique body style (Ford retractable hardtop) or a particularly pleasing adaptation of a lesser body style (Chevrolet Nomad).

Furthermore, certain names inspire almost instant success. Fords have always been tremendously popular. Until recently, any model Ford over 20 years old has brought a higher price than its Chevrolet or Plymouth counterpart. The Packard name has always been symbolic of quality and respect. It's not that all Packards ever built are such impressive automobiles (indeed, the last ones were Studebakers in disguise); it's just the charisma of the name. Cadillac, on the other hand, has built quality automobiles as long as anyone; but the late ones, at least, are slower to be accepted as collectors' choices.

It seems also true that any car no longer produced goes through a latent period of mourning to emerge as an extremely valuable collector's prize. Perhaps the feeling of individuality that comes from owning a car that the Joneses can't simply go out and duplicate comes into play here.

At any rate, there is a tremendous amount of ego present in the automobile, and depending on your individual tastes, you will gravitate toward the material personification of that beauty. It is for this reason that I cannot break down the manufacturers into a hierarchy similar to that of body styles. That and the fact that the last few years have seen a trend toward a more universal acceptance of beauty for its own sake, rather than for name's sake.

One distinction that can still be observed is that the car-producing corporations have always introduced similar models in different lines: the 1953 Buick Skylark and 1953 Cadillac Eldorado represent two attempts to achieve the same end. They were both successful and therefore have relatively similar values, the margin of difference being arbitrary, but perhaps going to Cadillac on the strength of the name.

The Pontiac Safari was that division's version of the Chevrolet Nomad. The Nomad has always been tremendously popular, with the Safari only recently being collected in earnest. This is where it pays to identify collective trends in cars. A purist always knew the Safari would catch up to the Nomad in value. The decision became one of time v. storage costs, rather than "will it or won't it."

Even more recently in the era of the super cars, or muscle cars, if you prefer, the original GTO inspired a trend that is already nostalgic (due to government pollution restrictions), but certainly it is not the solitary example of this category. The Chevelle SS, the Olds 4-4-2 and even the Buick GS Stage I, to mention only General Motors counterparts, are beginning to share this limelight. The other corporations had their Mustangs and Road Runners; so a puzzle begins to fall into place just by thinking about these concepts.

In this book I have tried to avoid the inclusion of too many examples of any one particular mood of expression, but I do mention similar cars as a guide for the novice. It is always best to form a categorical picture in your mind to help piece things together. In this way, you are in the ballpark with any car you are thinking about and can, therefore, gain the necessary confidence.

Finally, when you have this confidence you will need the money to purchase your gem. I have tried to steer away from very old, very expensive, and very rare cars, so that anyone who wishes will be able to find and afford what he decides is desirable. That is not to say that some cars are not already expensive; but relative to, say, a Deusenberg, they are all priced very low.

II. Condition

Now that you know the market, it is very important to understand the role that condition, or state of repair, plays in buying cars for profit. There is really only one rule of thumb to follow, but a good familiarity with cars is required to be successful. Simply stated, if you know why you are buying a car, whether it is valued for its mechanical excellence or its classical simplicity, or any blending of ingredients, those points of interest are the ones that should be in good condition.

For example, a woody has appeal for the wooden body; one with much wood rot is far less valuable than one with good wood but perhaps poor mechanics or metal. Or maybe you've found an Avanti that is desirable for its body style while its supercharger is a problem that detracts from the value, but can be repaired or even discarded without totally ruining the effectiveness of the car. The body, though, is fiberglass and if cracked, cut or damaged represents a serious confrontation with the law of diminishing returns. Never buy a car beneath its present value if it is in need of more dollar input than its value will represent when completed! That sounds quite simple, but it has befuddled many a wide-eyed car nut. The best advice is to stay calm and observe, as an estimator does, what is needed to make the prospective car right. If you can do this within a margin of profit, you will be a success. One thing is for sure: old cars never go down in value, so even if you've made a marginally poor choice, time is in your favor. The longer you own it, the more valuable it becomes.

The charts in this book give two levels of value. They show a high value, for a car that is in excellent condition, and a low value, for one that is sound and solid but needs attention. Since the latter is the type of car you are most likely to find, it is assumed that you will put some effort into it and sell it at the higher value, or that you have bought it beneath even the low figure and can make a profit by turning it over "as is." How you keep and sell depends on your heart a lot, but it is best to leave your heart at home when buying a car.

One final note on condition — and this goes back to understanding categories. Many cars share similar components. If damage to these parts exists, it is usually a simple matter to seek out replacement. Also, many collectors and parts-houses exist to satisfy the need for hard-to-find items, and they usually do it at a price that is dear. If you feel you are not sure about the value of a car in poor condition, it is best to stay away from it and concentrate on solid buys with solid bodies. There are enough of each to satisfy everyone. Just remember to start at a place where you can build your confidence and expertise from the beginning.

III. Chart

Since graphs are visual descriptions in themselves, it is not necessary to go into a detailed examination of them. They are simple, with straightforward numerical values. There is no need to specify that the value of the dollar will not be in two years what it is now, because this is a self-cancelling factor. We live today with the same dollar that existed two, five, ten years ago, and everyone is aware of the price of inflation. Banks do not afford an economic treatise when they offer a 6% interest rate on money saved; nor do stock dividends. At today's rate, the money you earn through interest is eliminated by the time of maturity. Yet we all know that this investing represents an effort to keep some pace with your hard-earned dollars.

While the risk may be higher in dealing with old cars, a confident, knowledgeable collector can do far better than the rate of return offered by routine investments. Profits on the order of 100% and above are quite common. It goes without saying that if you buy a car for $1,000 and sell it a year later for $2,000 you have made less than the 100% profit that shows on paper because of the declining value of the dollar. But you should certainly be ahead of inflation at that rate, or the banks and all the people are in a lot of trouble.

The thing to be cautious about is how much you put into a car before you sell it. Keep track of all costs, such as license, tax, repairs, labor and storage. For you to make a profit, the appreciation of your car must exceed the total cost of all these factors. Don't fear, it almost always does if you know what you buy and refuse to panic. Also in your favor is the fact that if you buy an average car and put it into excellent condition, the value will more than compensate for the cost in doing this. If you look at the charts, you will see that the dotted line drawn between the two solid lines represents the increase in the particular car's value after having done this over a period of two years. In most cases, you can see that the value difference is large enough to afford a hefty investment in the rehabilitation of a car and still make a good profit on it.

The actual projections of future value are based on past rates of accelerated demand and on my own years of intuitive knowledge of fads and trends. It would be unfair to say that all cars increase at some given annual percentage and proceed neatly to graph a series of straight line values. We need only look at the Edsel to see that some cars get "hot" and then cool off, while other potentially valuable cars seem to lie back for years only to burst into the limelight suddenly. The charts will clearly show you the "sleepers" and the fad cars ('55, '56, '57 Chevys, for instance) that are temporarily higher than they should be, as well as the old standards, like the '55, '56, '57 Thunderbird.

Keep in mind that these quirks, or fluctuations, occur mostly with newer cars. It is a shifting that is bound to take place in much the same manner of changes we witness in other aspects of life. A rookie baseball pitcher is not assured of the Hall of Fame on the strength of one or two good years. Time will mellow the peaks and valleys of success with him as it does with automobiles. This is why some older cars are valuable on the strength of age alone. Age, in automobiles, is one positive aspect that everyone respects, and therefore pays for. It is the reason that a 1930 Chevrolet Sedan is worth more than a 1950 Chevrolet Convertible, even though the convertible has more appeal.

The Beginning of the End: 1938-1941

Something I learned as a teacher is that the scientific method, i.e., the specific empirical approach to problem solving, is a wonderful way of developing self-discipline and objective logic, but its practical application is limited to theory development. In a classroom, the teacher is confronted with a complex matrix of real situations, bounding with the very energy of life. There is no time to factor out variables or deduce formulae that will structure the task of teaching. While it helps to be able to organize matters scientifically, the teacher's best aid is charisma. This is a very unscientific word because it is not precise — it cannot be nailed down to an immutable definition. But that's the point! The entire world is dynamic. We best recognize life by observing its changes. To impart knowledge to living people about living things, so that they can go out and work in a living world and grasp the emotions of living relationships, requires primary contact with the spark of life. This is charisma. Yes, charisma is the aura of a person's conscious energy. It is capable of being felt and, hopefully, imparted to others.

The purpose of this prelude is to set the stage for the subject. As it turns out, this book is as much a social commentary as it is a collector's guide to old cars. To understand the nature of man's creations, it is necessary to understand man the creator. If the automobile itself is not alive, it comes from a living source and exists solely to fulfill human needs. Scientific reasoning might explain the automobile as a mechanical device for transporting people and/or goods from one place to another. This is true, but chillingly stoic in approach; for it fails to account for the innumerable personal needs fulfilled by the automobile. The car is a remarkable key to a person's identity, and that identity is a mosaic of emotion and ego which cannot be explained away simplistically.

In coursing through the years covered by this text, I found it most helpful to observe the living aspects that surround the evolution of the automobile. Popular trends and events of great historical significance sweep us through life on a succession of waves, each of which influences our attitude and behavior. These stimuli are responsible for the pulse of any contemporary society. Only by hindsight can we see where one wave has ebbed and another crested. Did we know, in 1951, that the McCarthy paranoia would coerce us into developing a new diplomatic philosophy? Did we notice how that would lead to the cold war? Who noticed the beginnings of détente, or the mini-skirt, for that matter? In retrospect we can say these things influenced us or, in the case of the mini-skirt, that they were fads. What I

14

want to do in this book is look at these fads and moods through the ubiquitous eye of the automobile. I want to illustrate how the flux of America's developing personality is reflected in the cars we have made. Conversely, I want to explore the possibility that the auto industry is the tail that wagged the dog. To do this, I have arranged the contents of "Real Steel" chronologically, in five major sections. These divisions are as arbitrary as the date of that first mini-skirt. The importance is not to pinpoint the calendar so much as to isolate the trends. In this respect, as you will see, there is logic in the choices. Remember, though, it is a "living" logic, and only remotely indebted to empirical substantiation. Relax. Let you mind wander. Loosen up your relfexes. Get in touch with yourself because we're back in 1938 — at the beginning of the end!

Do you feel it? Look around you. There are no computers. The Second World War has not yet spawned them. President Roosevelt's New Deal is tugging us ever so slowly out of the mire of depression. Perhaps you didn't notice it because all eyes are bent on Europe and a man named Hitler. Still, these things are signals, still pictures of a world caught in the act of changing. However somber we were in 1938, or however isolationist, one could not deny the progress of these events. They were, indeed, the beginning of the end; for by 1941, the final year of this scant era, the Depression would be ended, American soldiers would infiltrate many of the world's nations, and the mind of American ingenuity would foster the geometric progression of technology. That's what I mean by waves! Now let's hop back to 1938 and take a closer look at what was going on. The auto industry, I think, will provide some interesting revelations.

Without distinction by make or corporation, certain subtleties are universally apparent in the cars produced between 1938 and 1941. The waning influence of the classic era was giving way to a new identity for the car. Fenders were getting wider, hosting a new location for the headlights. Grilles too were decidedly integrated with the fender area. By 1941, there can be no doubt that the old concept of narrowed, vertical snouts succumbed to a gaping, wide-mouthed, horizontal philosophy.

The American automobile was fast becoming a unified structure. It could no longer be considered a modified carriage with fendered appendages. Channeling the body over the frame rails lowered doors enough to eliminate the necessity of runningboards. The trunk was no longer a boxy, canvas-covered afterthought, as it was in the heyday of the great classics. The concept of unity had seen it incorporated into the pressed steel body structure as a permanent fixture. What was apparently emerging as the shape of things to come never quite had the time to acquire the character of its own finesse. You see, the basic square shape was there by 1941, but the big war aborted efforts to complete the job. On the drawing boards and in various stages of development were plans to complete the new image. These advanced designs were smooth-sided streamliners that more often than not resembled the old Hoover vacuum cleaners. Given time, these expressionless molds would have assumed some sense of meaning; but their fate was unforeseen in 1941.

The transition to more modern body shells between 1938 and 1941 served one other purpose. It sloughed off the marginal, independent manufacturers who could not hope to raise the money necessary for the changeover in dies. Remember this was still the Depression, and times were hard for manufacturers as well as individuals. The death of the independents was an unwitting aid to the solidarity of the big corporations. We will talk about the brief post-war revival of the independents in a later chapter. The vacuum created by their conspicuous rate of attrition in the late 1930's, however, gave carte blanche to the big three to dictate the direction of automotive development. On the other hand, the giants' expanded market provided revenues and tripartite competition that accelerated the rate of this development. It also stabilized the industry by establishing realistic norms, both in production technique and marketing analysis.

We have surveyed the skin of the emerging butterfly; now let us examine the skeleton of its cocoon. Actually, the mechanical state of the art had hit a plateau around this time and history would see its dormancy continue until 1949. Cars were reliable, if unsophisticated, devices prior to World War II. Except for a few in-line overhead engines, the vast majority of cars were powered by a flathead configuration, ranging in design from in-lines to 60″ and 90″ V applications. The impeccably smooth-running V-12 and V-16 powerplants were stubbornly resisting defeat; for they were, it was felt, the apex of engineering achievement. This seems to be confusing engineering with prestige, since their actual efficiency left much to be desired. At any rate, the average car in 1940 proved quite capable of leading a long life. Proportionately speaking, engine power, suspension, and overall size and weight made for a nice package; nothing excessive, just a functional, maintainable commodity. A system of coil springs up front, leaf springs in the rear, and tubular shocks replaced the more antiquated transverse leaf and adjustable shock combination in just about every car except those produced by dyed-in-the-wool Henry Ford. Those nasty (to work on) torque tube drives would somehow survive the war. In the case of some Ramblers they would see the nineteen sixties!

One engineering highlight was the development of the semi-automatic and then the automatic transmission by General Motors between 1938 and 1941. Unable to capitalize on this great step forward before swinging into the production of war machinery, G.M. emerged, a decade later, with a virtual monopoly on the hottest item since firecrackers. Another relatively obscure option to both Cadillac and Packard in 1941 was the air conditioner. Grossly complex and misunderstood, it waited for more affluent times to make a comeback. Nevertheless, things were rather stationary at this point, with annual changes consisting primarily of minor refinements rather than revolutionary advances.

One small occurrence around 1941-42 crept unnoticed into the corporate bag of tricks. It was minor at the time but its ramifications are still being felt, and I fear, misinterpreted. That was the advent of advertising techniques geared to the ultra-consciousness of the collective mind. There was little doubt at this time that there was an impending crisis. As more and more manufacturers retooled for aircraft, tanks, and war machinery, the gist of their automotive slogans reflected this effort. For the first time, instead of being urged to buy a car with ''miracle twin carburetion'' or rubber-cushioned ''floating ride,'' Americans were confronted with choices of nationalistic, even militaristic, nomenclature. Ads for aircraft-inspired names, such as Oldsmobile's 98 Custom Cruiser B-44, and Chrysler's Spitfire engine appeared to challenge a customer's allegiance more than his objectivity. The wheels of war became an adman's best logo by the end of this first era, delaying by proxy the final identity of our new breed of cars. It is only fair to mention that since the identity of the automobile derives its image through the society it serves, there may have been a lack of finality among the citizenry at this time. The confusion caused by the Depression and events in Europe left us strangely withdrawn and catatonic. This lethargy had to change before there could be any expression in our lives, or in our art. Toward the end of 1941, all hell broke loose, and the sleeping giant awoke with a look in his eye, the likes of which had never before been seen. The identity crisis was over.

1938 Packard Sedan

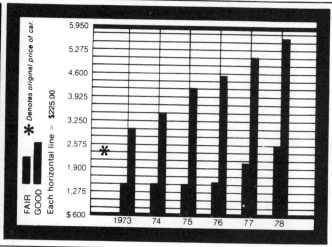

Though 1938 is the era of greatest Packard influence, the car pictured here is not significant in this respect. The huge six-wheeler V-12 roadsters and custom bodied sedans are classic cars well beyond the scope of this book. The average layman is much more apt to come upon a common Packard if he succeeds, at all, in finding one of this vintage. A common Packard for 1938 would be one of the lower series, a straight eight with no sidemounts, and probably in need of a complete restoration.

Still, the car is thoroughly Packard. One look at the eminently recognizable, strong vertical grille should tell you so. Even beyond traditional and heraldic identities, the true nature of the Packard is starkly apparent. It lies in the massive metal and the syncromesh of its mechanics. It lies in the fine fabric and the detailed quality of its assembly. It is craftsmanship at its finest.

The only problem with such quality is that you become the latter day craftsman if the Packard you own is in need of a facelift. The alternative is just to turn the car over and take what you can get for it in its original condition. This act will usually net a profit, but may not be worth the aggravation. To play middleman to a car like a vintage Packard involves time and timing, not to mention the initial cash outlay. While you're awaiting the proper market pulse, that monstrous machine in the backyard is bound to stir some personal interest.

Maybe it will get you for a clutch, some minor reupholstery work, or a set of tires. Whatever the starting point, it's easy to fall in the well if you lean too far. Sometimes it's wise to protect your purse and your sanity by taking out a pencil and paper *in the beginning*, column off the possibilities with their expected expenditures in time and money and, especially, their rate of return. The only thing better than a backyard mechanic is an armchair tycoon. This Packard can make either out of you. Just remember, the choice is yours.

SPECIFICATIONS

Wheelbase	.122″
Tread; Front, Rear	.59″, 60″
Overall Length	.196.5″
Overall Width	.72″
Overall Height	.68″
Weight, Lbs	.3600
Tire Size	.7.00 x 16″

ENGINE

Type	.L-Head, straight 8 cyl.
Bore & Stroke	.3.25″ x 4.25″
Displacement, Cu. In.	.282
Compression Ratio	.6.60 to 1
Horsepower @ RPM	.120 @ 3800
Max. Torque @ RPM	.225 @ 1700
Electrical	.6 Volt, pos. grd.

TRANSMISSION

Type	.3 speed manual
Available	.—

REAR

Type	.Hypoid, semi-floating
Ratio	.4.36 to 1

TUNE UP

Spark Plug Gap	.028″
Point Gap	.017″
Cam Angle, Degrees	.27
Timing	.8° B.T.D.C.
Firing Order	.16258374
Tappet Clearances:	
Intake	.007″
Exhaust	.010″
Compression Pressure, Lbs	.110
Idle Speed, RPM	.400

BRAKES

Type	.Hydraulic, int. exp.
Drum Diameter	.12″

CAPACITIES

Cooling System, Qts	.20
Fuel Tank, Gals	.24.5
Crank Case, Qts	.8
Trans. Pints	.2
Differential, Pts	.6

WHEEL ALIGNMENT

Caster, Degrees	.+2½ pref.
Camber, Degrees	.+⅞ pref.
Toe in, Inches	.0 to 1/16

1939 Buick Sedan

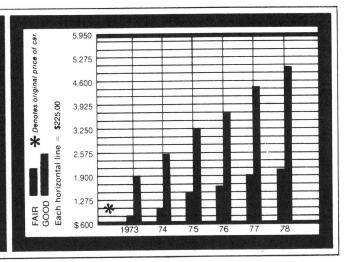

1939 was not a happy year for many people. In Europe, Hitler was making his presence felt, and in America, the great Depression was nearly a decade old — an anniversary no one was celebrating. Those who could find cause for a parade, though, found it almost invariably headed by a Buick. The vacuum created by the middle class drain of the Depression was beginning to be pumped with new life. As the void between Henry's volkswagon and the extravagant classics became filled with middle-priced cars, Buick assumed the role of a respected leader.

Buick prices ranged rather widely for the time, as did its model variations. Prices today will reflect this spectrum. While it would be a consuming task to quantify and qualify a breakdown of this structure, suffice it to say that a Buick sedan without sidemounts is the one most likely to be found, and the one that will be discussed.

Not long ago, these durable cars were comparatively abundant and relatively inexpensive. Somewhere around 1970, car-collecting became serious business. When this happened, a thirty year old car was fair game for fortune hunters; especially a venerable Buick. Needless to say, this open season had the effect of raising prices. But, that's the name of the game. The word is out on 1939 Buicks, even down to the sedans; so, as the man says, "Ya gotta pay the price."

Not exactly a sleeper, this Buick was successful for reasons apparent even in 1939. The thoroughly impressive overhead valve straight eight engine survived until 1953, making it a Buick hallmark. For that matter, its durability is in a select class with Ford's flathead V-8 and, of course, G.M.'s overhead V-8's introduced in 1949. Some models, sporting dual carburetors and loads of torque, were responsible for infiltrating Buick's reputation into the ranks of the contemporary performance cars. Gangsters and politicians alike amply demonstrated their appreciation of this quality.

When seen from another view, the 1939 Buick could be found to possess one of the cleaner front ends for that year. Not too bold and not too cold, the hood-grille area flowed with a lithe dignity befitting a car of its stature. It muted the stodginess of the big sedans as neatly as it accentuated the sportiness of the coupes and convertibles. That stodginess was further balanced by the running boards on the sides. They served more as transitional elements of the car's continuity than as aids for entering passengers. Part of the reason Buick held the number three sales spot so many times was because it actually did build better cars.

SPECIFICATIONS

Wheelbase	126″
Tread; Front, Rear	58.5″, 59.25″
Overall Length	207.5″
Overall Width	72.25″
Overall Height	66.25″
Weight, Lbs	3482
Tire Size	7.00 x 16″

ENGINE

Type	Overhead, in-line 8 cyl.
Bore & Stroke	3.44″ x 4.31″
Displacement, Cu. In.	320.2
Compression Ratio	6.35 to 1
Horsepower @ RPM	141 @ 3600
Max. Torque @ RPM	278 @ 2200
Electrical	6 Volt, neg. grd.

TRANSMISSION

Type	3 speed sliding gear
Available	

REAR

Type	Hypoid, semi-floating
Ratio	3.90 to 1

TUNE UP

Spark Plug Gap	.025″
Point Gap	.015″
Cam Angle, Degrees	31
Timing	6° B.T.D.C.
Firing Order	16258374
Tappet Clearances:	
Intake	.015″
Exhaust	.015″
Compression Pressure, Lbs	130
Idle Speed, RPM	450

BRAKES

Type	Hydraulic, int. exp.
Drum Diameter	12″

CAPACITIES

Cooling System, Qts	17
Fuel Tank, Gals	18
Crank Case, Qts	8
Trans. Pints	2.5
Differential, Pts	3

WHEEL ALIGNMENT

Caster, Degrees	-1¼ to -½
Camber, Degrees	-¼ to +1
Toe in, Inches	0 to 1/16

1939 La Salle Coupe

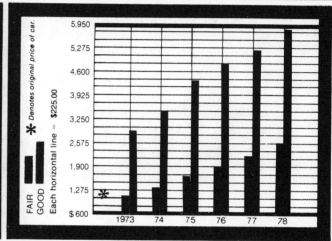

As the La Salle evolved over its short lifetime it gradually became more and more of a Cadillac. This is one of the reasons it was put to rest after 1940. It was a good car in every respect except for the threat it posed to Cadillac sales.

One of the more graceful La Salles is the long, lean 1939 Coupe. Found most often with a stately coat of black paint, its princely appearance will remind anyone of the Cadillac. The between-fender girth looks very wide, an illusion attributable to the sweeping vertical spears which flank the horizontal grille. Bullet-shaped headlite bodies, popularized by G.M., look like they were designed for this car. They catch the arc of the drooping front fenders and push the momentum back along the hoodline. From there, the eye is caught by a rakish roofline, which is accentuated by the oblique angle of the center post. Chasing the gentle slope of the roof, the silhouette slides down a long, classically smooth trunk line — a ride which does not end until it curves neatly under the car, tucking its way out of sight. There is no mistaking the lines of this massive car for anything less than classic.

Mechanical similarities between La Salle and Cadillac are too numerous to mention. Rather than cheapening its image, the La Salle benefits from sharing such regal underpinnings. The strong, silent flathead V-8 had hydraulic lifters so it would remain that way. The tactile obedience of its synchronized transmission provides responsiveness commensurate with the car's looks. It is a complete package of quality.

You can't expect to find one easily. You can't even expect to find an inexpensive one. But, if you ever come across one of these beauties — one that has been forgotten in some miserable place — consider yourself fortunate. Breathe a little life into it and it will attract attention like a magnet attracts iron. Maybe there is some magnetism in this old metal.

SPECIFICATIONS

Wheelbase	126″
Tread; Front, Rear	.58″, 59″
Overall Length	202.5″
Overall Width	.79″
Overall Height	.68″
Weight, Lbs	.3635
Tire Size	.7.00 x 16″

ENGINE

Type	Flathead V-8
Bore & Stroke	3.375″ x 4.50″
Displacement, Cu. In.	.322
Compression Ratio	.6.25 to 1
Horsepower @ RPM	135 @ 3400
Max. Torque @ RPM	234 @ 1800
Electrical	.6 Volt, pos. grd.

TRANSMISSION

Type	.3 speed manual
Available	.—

REAR

Type	Hypoid, semi-floating
Ratio	.3.92 to 1

TUNE UP

Spark Plug Gap	.027″
Point Gap	.015″
Cam Angle, Degrees	.31
Timing	.5° B.T.D.C.
Firing Order	.18736542
Tappet Clearances:	
Intake	Zero, hydraulic
Exhaust	Zero, hydraulic
Compression Pressure, Lbs	.155
Idle Speed, RPM	.375

BRAKES

Type	Hydraulic, int. exp.
Drum Diameter	.12″

CAPACITIES

Cooling System, Qts	.24.5
Fuel Tank, Gals	.23
Crank Case, Qts	.7
Trans. Pints	.2.5
Differential, Pts	.5

WHEEL ALIGNMENT

Caster, Degrees	−¼ to −1¼
Camber, Degrees	−¼ to +¾
Toe in, Inches	.¹/₃₂ to ³/₃₂

1939 Mercury Coupe

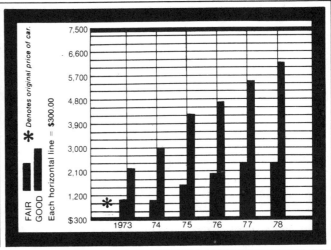

By the late 1930's, Ford was feeling the sting of the Chrysler and G.M. price spread. The decision to extend the distribution of its own prices was consummated in the birth of the Mercury. In Greek mythology this messenger of the gods was known for his swift dispatch of duty. His metallic counterpart became a courier of another kind, delivering for Ford Motor Company the much needed profit of a successful middle-class car.

From its inception, there was little doubt that the Mercury was a lightly disguised Ford. Since Dodge-Plymouth and Chevrolet-Pontiac were also cosmetically differentiated cousins, the relationship didn't hurt any. In fact, the extensive Ford model lineup gave Mercury a sure-footed start in the race for the mid-priced market.

The biggest difference between Mercury and the other cars, Ford included, was to be found in the coupe. Mercury's sharply defined centerpost was highlighted by stainless molding that brightened the borders of the side windows. The visual effect was very similar to the hardtop coupes that would not appear for another ten years. By dropping the sheet-metal slightly into the radius of the rear wheel cutouts, Mercury kept the focal point above the beltline.

A slightly stronger version of Ford's flathead V-8 provided Mercury with all the guts and charm it needed, clear up 'til 1954. The longevity of its basic

mechanical structure provides a relief to the parts dilemma that Mercury also shares with Ford. The problem with the '39 Mercury Coupe is in finding a car to rebuild more than the parts to rebuild with. As usual, scarcity is a factor of value, as is the first year of a car's production. The gods looked favorably upon Mercury: a blessing made mortal by the popularity of the car that bears his name.

SPECIFICATIONS

Wheelbase ....116"
Tread; Front, Rear ....55.75", 58.25"
Overall Length ....195.9"
Overall Width ....61.9"
Overall Height ....67.3"
Weight, Lbs 3000
Tire Size ....6.00 x 16"

ENGINE

Type ....Flathead V-8
Bore & Stroke ....3.1875" x 3.75"
Displacement, Cu. In. 239
Compression Ratio ....6.15 to 1
Horsepower @ RPM ....95 @ 3800
Max. Torque @ RPM ....170 @ 2100
Electrical ....6 Volt, pos. grd.

TRANSMISSION

Type ....3 speed manual
Available ....2 speed rear

REAR

Type ....Spiral bevel ¾ floating
Ratio ....3.54 to 1

TUNE UP

Spark Plug Gap ....025"
Point Gap ....015"
Cam Angle, Degrees 36
Timing ....4° B.T.D.C.
Firing Order 15486372
Tappet Clearances:
    Intake ....012"
    Exhaust ....014"
Compression Pressure,
Lbs 112
Idle Speed, RPM 425

BRAKES

Type ....Hydraulic, int. exp.
Drum Diameter ....12"

CAPACITIES

Cooling System, Qts 22
Fuel Tank, Gals 15
Crank Case, Qts 5
Trans. Pints 2.5
Differential, Pts 2.5

WHEEL ALIGNMENT

Caster, Degrees ....+4½ to +9
Camber, Degrees ....+¼ to +1
Toe in, Inches 1/16

21

1940 Buick Coupe

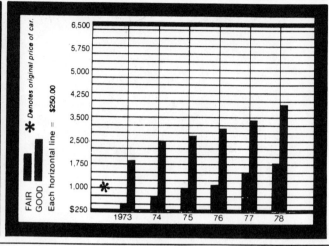

In 1940, the Buick name was a solid indication of motoring achievement. It was not the greatest of cars, but it was well above the average. It was a good dollar bargain. For a few dollars more, the person who bought a Buick got more than just a fancied-up, low-priced machine. You don't earn a prestigious reputation that way, as De Soto found out in 1960.

The Buick approach in 1940 was to build a sound car of superior quality and reliability. While it is true that some components were shared with other G.M. products, in the final analysis the Buick was more of a thoroughbred than a mongrel. It had its own engine and a good overhead design that pleased, rather than appeased, its engineers and its customers. It had a distinctive look about it too, because the stylists were able to maintain a sense of symmetry. They knew what the Buick was. Their pride in the product was a conceptual thing. The Buick identity was not composed of the bits and pieces that differentiate cars. It was not a retranslation of borrowed themes. When you're good — and confident that you're good — you don't look elsewhere for affirmation; you are the leader.

Things have not always been that way for Buick. There have been good years and bad years. Mickey Mantle had good years and bad years too. This does not mean that the 1940 Buick was the Mickey Mantle of automobiles, but it *was* an all-star.

Whether you are collecting antiques or dealing in nostalgia, the cushion of a good name will always insulate the value of the item. You may have to pay more for the padding, but the dividends will warrant it.

A 1940 Buick Coupe strikes a happy medium. It is not as resplendent as the big Limited and not as inspiring as the convertibles. The graceful roof line and sloping trunk free the silhouette from the rigidity imposed by the interior demands of two- and four-door sedans. The coupe has a savvy of its own. Catch it if you can!

SPECIFICATIONS

Wheelbase	121"
Tread; Front, Rear	58.25", 59.25"
Overall Length	209"
Overall Width	74.365"
Overall Height	66"
Weight, Lbs	3735
Tire Size	7.00 x 16"

ENGINE

Type	Overhead in-line 8 cyl.
Bore & Stroke	3.0938" x 4.125"
Displacement, Cu. In.	248
Compression Ratio	6.10 to 1
Horsepower @ RPM	107 @ 3400
Max. Torque @ RPM	269 @ 2000
Electrical	6 Volt, neg. grd.

TRANSMISSION

Type	3 speed manual
Available	—

REAR

Type	Hypoid, semi-floating
Ratio	3.90 to 1

TUNE UP

Spark Plug Gap	.025"
Point Gap	.015"
Cam Angle, Degrees	31
Timing	6° B.T.D.C.
Firing Order	16258374
Tappet Clearances:	
Intake	.015"
Exhaust	.015"
Compression Pressure, Lbs	130
Idle Speed, RPM	450

BRAKES

Type	Hydraulic, int. exp.
Drum Diameter	12"

CAPACITIES

Cooling System, Qts	13.25"
Fuel Tank, Gals	17
Crank Case, Qts	6
Trans. Pints	13.75
Differential, Pts	3

WHEEL ALIGNMENT

Caster, Degrees	0 to +¾
Camber, Degrees	-¼ to +1
Toe in, Inches	0 to 1/16

1940 Chevrolet Coupe

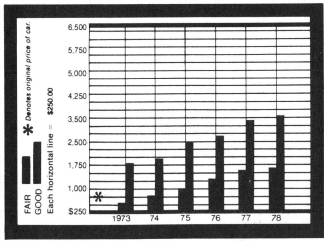

Largely due to the zip and intrigue of the Ford flathead V-8, the early days of hot-rodding left Chevrolet neglected. Because of the persistent efforts of rodders to improve the 1940 Ford Coupe, its public image never faded. Hence, when the time was right to collect common coupes of this vintage, the Fords went first. When, by the mid-fifties, the overhead engines had proven their superiority, Chevrolets began to interest a few people. Not so much because they had an overhead engine, albeit a six, but because the reason for Ford's superior demand was no longer apparent. Flathead loyalty turned to stubbornness in a short while, and finally became nostalgia. Ironically, the current price of nostalgia is higher than the price of hot rods! A look at the Chevy on its own merit reveals nothing to indicate that it would be less popular than the Ford, were it not for the history of the engines.

The rounded features of the 1940 Chevrolet Coupe are quite pleasing, especially from the front. Evolution had just about placed the headlights flush in the fenders, allowing them to meet the hood at a higher angle. This created the illusion of greater width. By rounding the hood peak and accenting the widened grille cavity with a horizontal pattern, Chevrolet exemplified the philosophy of the forties. From 1941 to 1948, hardly a car in America would deviate from this theme.

The curvature of the fenders continued this gracefulness on to the side view of the car where an angled centerpost further projected an air of lightness. 1940 was the last year for running boards. They were no longer necessary. In fact, they impeded the widening of the car's body at a time when it was the logical pursuit of style.

The rear deck gives final confirmation to Chevy's rounded lines. By gently rolling it under at the bottom edge to conform to the curvature of the rear fenders, the stylists succeeded in eliminating all harsh angles and focal points from the design. Inside, even the dash was clean and balanced, in keeping with the conservative simplicity of the interior.

Except for a fickle vacuum shift setup and knee action shocks that failed to live up to expectations, the 1940 Chevy Coupe had no weaknesses. Unfortunately, it also had no specific uniqueness that could identify its character or generate the excitement of individuality. As I said, Ford had that.

SPECIFICATIONS

Wheelbase . . . . .113"
Tread; Front, Rear . . . . .57^{17}/$_{32}$", 59"
Overall Length . . . . .192.5"
Overall Width . . . . .72"
Overall Height . . . . .70"
Weight, Lbs 2980
Tire Size . . . . .6.00 x 16"

ENGINE

Type . . . . .Overhead in-line 6
Bore & Stroke . . . . .3.50" x 3.75"
Displacement, Cu. In. .216.5
Compression Ratio . . . . .6.25 to 1
Horsepower @ RPM . . . . .85 @ 3200
Max. Torque @ RPM . . . . .170 @ 900
Electrical . . . . .6 Volt, neg. grd.

TRANSMISSION

Type . . . . .3 speed manual
Available . . . .—

REAR

Type . . . . .Hypoid, semi-floating
Ratio . . . . .4.11 to 1

TUNE UP

Spark Plug Gap . . . . .040"
Point Gap . . . . .020"
Cam Angle, Degrees 35
Timing . . . . .Steel ball in flywheel
Firing Order 153624
Tappet Clearances:
    Intake . . . . .006"
    Exhaust . . . . .013"
Compression Pressure,
  Lbs 135
Idle Speed, RPM 350

BRAKES

Type . . . . .Hydraulic, int. exp.
Drum Diameter . . . . .11"

CAPACITIES

Cooling System, Qts 14
Fuel Tank, Gals 16
Crank Case, Qts 5
Trans. Pints 1.5
Differential, Pts 3.5

WHEEL ALIGNMENT

Caster, Degrees . . . .+1¾ to +2¾
Camber, Degrees . . . .—½ to +1½
Toe in, Inches . . . .^{5}/$_{64}$ to ⅛

1940 Ford Coupe

Note: 1939 Mercury and 1940 Ford Coupes have almost identical bodies. This explains our use of the same photo for both cars.

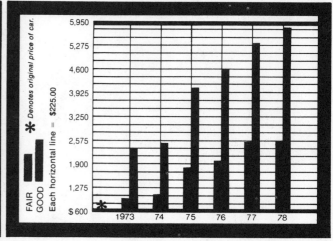

* Denotes original price of car.

Each horizontal line = $225.00

FAIR GOOD

$600 1,275 1,900 2,575 3,250 3,925 4,600 5,275 5,950

1973 74 75 76 77 78

What a story! From hot rod to custom car to nostalgic favorite — the 1940 Ford Coupe has enjoyed a complete and fulfilled life, seldom approached in the annals of the automobile. Now, in the autumn of its influence, the venerable Ford Coupe is a prized memorial to the cumulative events of the past. The spark that ignited this rambling love affair was appropriately the heart of the car: its engine. Over the years, the flathead romance became so faceted that it is difficult, even in retrospect, to isolate its beginnings. Words cannot describe the spirit of this type of magnetism, anyway. Suffice it to say the feeling was the same in 1955 when the Chevy V-8 finally replaced the flathead as the inspiration of a new generation.

Like its protegé, the Ford Coupe has been all things to all people. Parts and accessories to fit it are being remanufactured to supply the never-ending demand. They're a lot more expensive now, as are "new old stock"* pieces and the remaining parts-cars. This is part of the reason for escalating prices of restored cars. The mania for perfection can be carried to extremes with available items, such as Ford script tires and battery. Early speed equipment for the flathead is also still around, presenting an increasingly tantalizing option to the refurbishers.

Thirty-five years of hunting for a '40 Ford Coupe with an unwary owner have amply demonstrated the slim chance of finding one. It's not one of those cars you pick up and tinker with for a few weeks and then sell for a quick buck. It's more of a high-priced memento to be cherished and displayed selectively.

At the risk of blasphemy, it should be pointed out that, objectively, the 1940 Ford was at a lesser state of refinement than its competition, both physically and mechanically. Transverse leaf springs front and rear were already a Ford anachronism. In fact, the whole rear assembly, keyed axles included, had been otherwise improved by 1940. The teardrop headlights of the cleaner looking '39 Coupe were replaced with drooping chrome bezels for 1940. There is no doubt about the subjective attraction here, but objectively this feature, plus the sharp contrast of the grille, was less in keeping with the trend toward wider flatter fronts with horizontal prominence. Neither did any Ford ever see a slanted door pillar, so common at the time.

Henry Ford has been called a conservative man and a stubborn man. He did what he thought was instinctively right. Is it any wonder his cars inherited this character?

*"New old stock" refers to recently remanufactured parts that are the exact duplicate of certain scarce original items.

SPECIFICATIONS

Wheelbase	112″
Tread; Front, Rear	55.75″, 58.25″
Overall Length	188.625″
Overall Width	69.1″
Overall Height	67.5″
Weight, Lbs	2721
Tire Size	6.00 x 16″

ENGINE

Type	Flathead V-8
Bore & Stroke	3.0625″ x 3.75″
Displacement, Cu. In.	221
Compression Ratio	6.15 to 1
Horsepower @ RPM	85 @ 3800
Max. Torque @ RPM	155 @ 2200
Electrical	6 Volt, pos. grd.

TRANSMISSION

Type	3 speed manual
Available	2 speed rear

REAR

Type	¾ floating
Ratio	3.78 to 1

TUNE UP

Spark Plug Gap	.025″
Point Gap	.015″
Cam Angle, Degrees	36
Timing	4° B.T.D.C.
Firing Order	15486372
Tappet Clearances:	
Intake	.012″
Exhaust	.014″
Compression Pressure, Lbs	140
Idle Speed, RPM	425

BRAKES

Type	Hydraulic, int. exp.
Drum Diameter	12″

CAPACITIES

Cooling System, Qts	22
Fuel Tank, Gals	15
Crank Case, Qts	5
Trans. Pints	2.75
Differential, Pts	2.5

WHEEL ALIGNMENT

Caster, Degrees	+6¾ pref.
Camber, Degrees	+⅝ pref.
Toe in, Inches	1/16 pref.

1940 Lincoln Zephyr Sedan

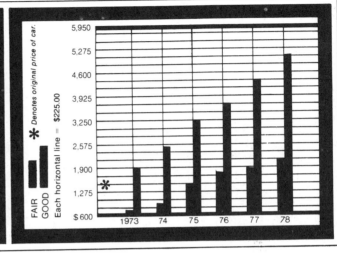

When it arrived in November of 1935, the Zephyr name was already woven into the fabric of history. With the Briggs Body Company building for both Ford and Chrysler at the same time, it was bound to fall into disfavor with someone. That someone turned out to be Henry Ford. To recover some amicability, Briggs proposed a medium-priced Lincoln and tried to sell the idea through Edsel Ford. It worked, but not before undergoing a few design changes. The original concept was for a rear-engined car, using Ford's existing V-8. The prototype for this car was built in 1934 and looks something like an overgrown four-door Volkswagen. The resemblance may be more than coincidence, since Ferdinand Porsche, designer of the VW, saw the car.

As the project moved along, public favor learned toward a front engine placement. The number of cylinders during the Depression years somehow became proportional to the amount of status. The simplest thing to do, since this was a lower priced Lincoln, was to rework the Ford V-8 to take four more cylinders in a V-12 fashion. The styling was cleaned up and a result was the introduction of the Lincoln Zephyr V-12!

It was a honey of a car. In fact, it laid the groundwork for the Lincoln Continental in 1940. Around that same year, the Zephyr was refined to a state of elegant perfection. It doesn't show so much on the sedans, but skirted

fenders and push-button doors did a lot to enhance the coupe and convertible models. Ford's familiar transverse leafspring arrangement reached a point of sophistication in the Zephyr that provided excellent handling. A Columbia two-speed rear could pitch in four more miles per gallon at 60 m.p.h. Quite a combination!

These are only a few of the reasons for the Zephyr's outstanding present value. Many four-door sedans are still lurking in strange hideaways, waiting to show you more good reasons. Keep your eyes peeled. There's gold in those hills!

SPECIFICATIONS

Wheelbase	.125"
Tread; Front, Rear	.55.5", 60.25"
Overall Length	.209.8"
Overall Width	.74"
Overall Height	.69.5"
Weight, Lbs	.3565
Tire Size	.7.00 x 16"

ENGINE

Type	.Flathead V-12
Bore & Stroke	.2.875" x 3.75"
Displacement, Cu. In.	.292
Compression Ratio	.7.20 to 1
Horsepower @ RPM	.120 @ 3500
Max. Torque @ RPM	.186 @ 2000
Electrical	.6 Volt, pos. grd.

TRANSMISSION

Type	.3 speed manual
Available	.2 speed rear

REAR

Type	.Hypoid, spiral bevel gears
Ratio	.4.44 to 1

TUNE UP

Spark Plug Gap	.028"
Point Gap	.015"
Cam Angle, Degrees	.36
Timing	.2° B.T.D.C.
Firing Order	.149852, 11, 10, 3, 6, 7, 12
Tappet Clearances:	
Intake	.Zero, hydraulic
Exhaust	.Zero, hydraulic
Compression Pressure,	
Lbs	.110
Idle Speed, RPM	.450

BRAKES

Type	.Hydraulic, int. exp.
Drum Diameter	.12"

CAPACITIES

Cooling System, Qts	.27
Fuel Tank, Gals	.19.5
Crank Case, Qts	.5
Trans. Pints	.2.75
Differential, Pts	.4

WHEEL ALIGNMENT

Caster, Degrees	.+3 to +5
Camber, Degrees	.+¼ to +¾
Toe in, Inches	.¹/₁₆

1941 Cadillac Sedan

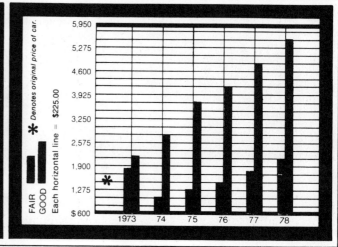

* Denotes original price of car.

Each horizontal line = $225.00

FAIR GOOD

5,950
5,275
4,600
3,925
3,250
2,575
1,900
1,275
$600

1973 74 75 76 77 78

In America, the evolutionary development of mass-produced items has led to the science of simplified components. The automobile of the future may well be a segmented structure consisting of replaceable front, middle and rear units. The amalgamated car will swap individuality for functionalism, relying on its name alone for status.

As this occurs, older cars are sure to be appreciated for the implication of their solitary artistic endeavor. For better or for worse, they will speak only for themselves. One potential curio is the 1941 Cadillac Sedan. Rather prolific for a Cadillac, it will at least survive for this randezvous with destiny.

Maybe it has already arrived. For, in truth, it is not the most elegant Cadillac. Nor is there any particular aspect about it that is innovative beyond the norm. It is average, even in appearance. Still, it has collector value greater than its name and age suggest. It must be that it possesses some solitary artistic meaning. And it does! Unlike the 1940 Cadillac La Salle in appearance, the stillborn 1941 never returned in any similar form after World War II. Pearl Harbor, of course, abbreviated 1942 production, effectively insuring the autonomy of the 1941 Cadillac.

There it is. A car that stands alone, on its own merit. Its separatism is not very endearing. There is very little warmth in its formal, conservative lines. It

lacks the magnetism that draws interest beyond objectivity. To the genteel who owned these Cadillacs in 1941, they fulfilled the basic requirements of status and transportation. Style was of secondary importance because, regardless of how it looked, the car would still have assumed the role of a Cadillac. If you can excuse the insensitivity, it will dutifully repeat this efficiency of purpose in the role of a collector's car.

SPECIFICATIONS

Wheelbase	126"
Tread; Front, Rear	59", 63"
Overall Length	216"
Overall Width	78.3"
Overall Height	68.5"
Weight, Lbs	4115
Tire Size	7.00 x 15"

ENGINE

Type	L-Head V-8
Bore & Stroke	3.50" x 4.50"
Displacement, Cu. In.	346
Compression Ratio	7.25 to 1
Horsepower @ RPM	150 @ 3400
Max. Torque @ RPM	283 @ 1700
Electrical	6 Volt, pos. grd.

TRANSMISSION

Type	3 speed manual
Available	Automatic

REAR

Type	Hypoid, semi-floating
Ratio	3.77 to 1

TUNE UP

Spark Plug Gap	.025"
Point Gap	.015"
Cam Angle, Degrees	31
Timing	5° B.T.D.C.
Firing Order	18736542
Tappet Clearances:	
Intake	Zero, hydraulic
Exhaust	Zero, hydraulic
Compression Pressure,	
Lbs	182
Idle Speed, RPM	375

BRAKES

Type	Hydraulic, int. exp.
Drum Diameter	12"

CAPACITIES

Cooling System, Qts	25
Fuel Tank, Gals	20
Crank Case, Qts	7
Trans. Pints	2.5
Differential, Pts	5

WHEEL ALIGNMENT

Caster, Degrees	−1¾ to −2¾
Camber, Degrees	−³⁄₈ to +³⁄₈
Toe in, Inches	¹/₃₂ to ³/₃₂

1941 Plymouth Coupe

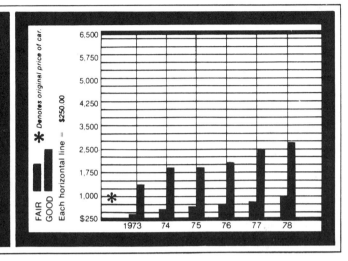

By 1941, the golden age of automobiles had very little glitter left. Cars were a matter of economics. The corporations were powerful and organized. So what if they forced out the likes of Pierce and Graham and Duesenberg? The giants' technology better consolidated and improved the makings of the machine.

Chrysler Corporation foresaw the public need better than its competition when it introduced the Plymouth Business Coupe in 1941. It had the tube shocks, coil, and leaf spring arrangement that would become the industry norm until the late fifties. It had good brakes, a smooth-shifting transmission with excellent ratios, and a reliable engine that would propel Chrysler's six-cylinder cars until 1958. The steering didn't bind or wear quickly, as with the competition, and the engine didn't overheat easily. All these were benefits of allowing a large corporation to pool its resources to build a better product.

It doesn't always work that well, but it worked then. The style of the 1941 Plymouth turned out the same. It was sound and simple. Effectively conservative might be the word for it. In fact, conservative might be the word for the entire car. But that means average. Well-done average, but still mediocre.

It's only because they're so old now that these groups are noticeable. The fact that they are around to be noticed confirms the quality of the 1941 Plymouth. This does not, however, make it as valuable as its contemporary Ford or Chevrolet offerings. In other words, buy it if you like it. Use it and you'll never enjoy a car more for the money. This is not a car to store as an investment. It would return a profit; but unless you find an exceptionally clean coupe, you're as well off getting some use out of it. Take it shopping for large objects, or camping. It's made for that. Besides, the trunk is large enough to hold a motorcycle!

SPECIFICATIONS

Wheelbase	117"
Tread; Front, Rear	57", 60"
Overall Length	195"
Overall Width	73.5"
Overall Height	68.375"
Weight, Lbs	2889
Tire Size	6.00 x 16"

ENGINE

Type	L-Head, 6 cyl.
Bore & Stroke	3.125" x 4.375"
Displacement, Cu. In.	201.3
Compression Ratio	6.70 to 1
Horsepower @ RPM	87 @ 3800
Max. Torque @ RPM	160 @ 1200
Electrical	6 Volt, pos. grd.

TRANSMISSION

Type	3 speed manual
Available	powermatic

REAR

Type	Hypoid, semi-floating
Ratio	4.10 to 1

TUNE UP

Spark Plug Gap	.025"
Point Gap	.020"
Cam Angle, Degrees	38
Timing	T.D.C.
Firing Order	153624
Tappet Clearances:	
Intake	.008"
Exhaust	.010
Compression Pressure, Lbs	114
Idle Speed, RPM	400-500

BRAKES

Type	Hydraulic, int. exp.
Drum Diameter	10"

CAPACITIES

Cooling System, Qts	14
Fuel Tank, Gals	17
Crank Case, Qts	5
Trans. Pints	2.75
Differential, Pts	3.25

WHEEL ALIGNMENT

Caster, Degrees	−1 to +1
Camber, Degrees	0 to +¾
Toe in, Inches	0 to ⅛

Getting It Together: 1946·1948

For the latter half of 1942 and all of 1943-45, the auto manufacturers deployed their talents and resources wholeheartedly to the war effort. No civilian cars were produced during this time. By the time the job was done overseas, Europe had been devastated. America emerged unscathed and uncontested as the most powerful country on earth. If that doesn't put a little expression in one's face, nothing will! We had a new president and a whole lot of work to do. Besides shifting our own economy from guns to butter, we had to feed and rebuild half the world. But big countries move like snakes. It takes time for the motion to reach the point of movement.

1946-48 was a transitional period. It represents the time lag between just producing and producing something new. So, for these years the large corporations contented themselves with dusting off the old pre-war dies and slapping on some chrome to celebrate the return of its availability. Meanwhile, something strange was happening with the remaining independents. They were rushing to produce the first all-new cars in an effort to regain some sales strength. Were these the faceless prototypes of our past? Unfortunately, they were, but this was not readily apparent until the big boom of 1949 posed the threatening alternative of modern design.

We are getting ahead of our story a little. It is only necessary to know the origins of the first post-war cars. It is a tribute to the independents that they could produce a car — any car — while in the recession that gripped the country. The war had strenghtened the remaining small manufacturers by providing them full use of their manufacturing capabilities. This and the fact that smaller wheels get turning faster than big ones gave the shot in the arm needed to put their new cars on the market.

The real booty gained from the war came in the form of an abstract quality of cohesion. True, the unifying force of nationalism did much for the people, but in terms of industry, there seemed to be an effusion of goal-oriented morale. The disciplined, military pursuit of an objective became the basis of high style business tactics. The confidence was there, the energy was there, and the method was there to achieve the ultimate goal. It was billed as the American Dream. We set forth to assemble it with revitalized energy. From everywhere, the resources of wartime technology were pooled to assist in the creation of the American Dream Machine. Gradually, the products and by-products reached our homes. When they did, they were in the form of televisions and transistors as well as the automobile. To properly secure their demand, the power of propaganda was put to peacetime use. The cat was in the bag. Let's look at what he saw.

As mentioned, the styling trends prevalent among automobiles were an extension of pre-war philosophy. The emphasis was definitely toward flat, horizontal front ends. Even Packard, when it introduced its post-war models, opted for a stylistic reminder of its strong macho vertical grille and set it against a diluting background of horizontal linearity. It made little matter, for Packard groveled in antiquity just long enough to lose pace with the rapidly advancing industry. A few years later, when the company jumped back on the track, it overshot things a bit and fell off the deep end.

The auto industry was giving us that squared-off package again and still did not know what to call it. Only this time they weren't so bent on giving it a name as a home. While the independents labored with orphan dreamcars of a bygone era, the wise men (who mostly resided at G.M.) knew that it was a whole new ball game and were busily shaping the cars of tomorrow. Mechanical doldrums prevailed in this period, at least as far as the public was concerned. Things were feverish at the drawing boards but the fruits of those labors would not be born until 1949. Hydramatic was still available but didn't make a big splash because it was sluggish off the line and as yet a rather complex novelty. Even though changes were on the way, the status quo of the automobile was too conservative. Somebody had to do something about it.

Enter the heroes. The soldiers who returned in 1945 were not the same boys who left in 1941. They were alert, alive and aware. The sheer power of their numbers was one thing; but the undissipated energy of their unrest due to the hassles of reentering society needed some release. For many, that fit of pique manifested itself in the form of a chopped-down, hopped-up model A. For a host of others it was the 1940 Ford Coupe, or a 1946 Chevy Convertible, or anything they could get their hands on. These hands were eager to work and these souls were yearning to be noticed. Both drives were satisfied by the hot rod and the custom car. This was a youthful portent of power and peacockery that would only die when Detroit, a good while later, out-chopped and out-hopped the backyard mechanic. The hot rod movement also spawned the likes of Marlon Brando and James Dean, for it was the brashness of an outrageous generation caught in the pinch of somewhere going and somewhere been that gave us these heroes and all their new-fangled keepsakes. There was good reason for their irreverence of tradition. The past had never given this group of young people much to cherish. Their lives were spent amid depression and war. They sensed something different in their future, but were literally "jittery" over its arrival. Here they were, the youthful inheritors of world power and prestige, sitting on an atomic time bomb, knowing something's gonna happen! The accompanying rage to live sold so many convertibles in those post-war years that it inspired the creation of the hardtop!

In the three immediate post-war years, there was a shuffle of activity while everyone waited for signs of the new dawn. Stalin's acquisition of the atom bomb during this time was a pressure we didn't need. Yet, full-scale paranoia didn't set in at this point. We all know that fear originates internally. We had a strong, perhaps aggressive, foreign policy under President Truman. The Marshall Plan laid the groundwork for the Americanization of Europe, as well as the boundary for the toleration of Communism. The Berlin Airlift was a victory of positive thinking over equivocal fear. In reality, the Russians were playing Devil's advocate for us then, forcing our competitiveness.

While all this was happening, the increasingly cosmopolitan American was thinking of his own dreams. A trickle of foreign names haunted the minds of a few curious individuals. Once in a great while the whispers were confirmed by the sight of one. What were they? Where did they come from? They were the foreign cars and they came from the need to have something exotic and flashy. The names were spelled in different ways, but they all spelled something new in the wind. Could this be what they were waiting for? Hold your hats. We're in for a ride.

1947 Cadillac Convertible

CONVERTIBLE CLUB COUPE

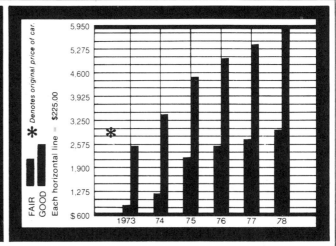

It's an older Cadillac and it's a convertible, so it's automatically worth a lot of money. Even in poor condition a 1947 Cadillac Convertible is worth investigating. That's how strong the present demand is for this car. Like a vintage wine, this possessor of a pround and elegant heritage has come of age.

This is a long, low looking car that resembles no other convertibles of the time. The long sweeping fenderlines that serve its proportions so well distinguish it from the contemporary, billowy convertible pattern. If it were a cloud, it would be a stratus cloud in a sky filled with puffy marshmallows. The narrow pointed nose takes full advantage of the car's great length to extend the illusion of its rakishness. The hoodline seems longer than it actually is because of the extension of the pontoon fenders well into the area of the doors. The added length of the rear fenders, both fore and aft of the wheels, is equally pleasing to the eye. Fender skirts prevent any interruption of continuity, and the clever positioning of long, low spears of chrome dramatically highlights the car's silhouette. When viewed from the front, the wide rectangular pattern of the grille is set low enough to convey the image of width while lending contrasting emphasis to the strong, high hoodline.

Underneath that classic nose lies a flathead V-8 engine still unrivaled for its smoothness and delivery of power. Hydramatic was available on the 1947

Cadillacs, providing carefree driving and an unnecessary edge over the competition. For those who still preferred, the manual shift transmission was available. Either way, the result was typical of the high degree of reliability built into this Cadillac.

In this last year before fishtail fins, the Cadillac strategy was to refine the elements of the automobile to a point of conservative perfection. Having accomplished this goal, the body by Fisher that adorned the 1947 Cadillac was left with no other choice but to pursue the more radical ideas of the future. Thus, the testimony of its last great decade of refinement is reflected in current prices of the 1947 Cadillac Convertible.

SPECIFICATIONS

Wheelbase . . . . .129"
Tread; Front, Rear . . . . .59", 63"
Overall Length . . . . .219"
Overall Width . . . . .81"
Overall Height . . . . .67"
Weight, Lbs 4450
Tire Size . . . . .7.00 x 15"

ENGINE

Type . . . . .L-Head V-8
Bore & Stroke . . . . .3.50" x 4.50"
Displacement, Cu. In. 346
Compression Ratio . . . . .7.25 to 1
Horsepower @ RPM . . . . .150 @ 3400
Max. Torque @ RPM . . . . .274 @ 1600
Electrical . . . . .6 Volt, neg. grd.

TRANSMISSION

Type . . . . .3 speed manual
Available . . . . .Automatic

REAR

Type . . . . .Hypoid, semi-floating
Ratio . . . . .3.77 to 1

TUNE UP

Spark Plug Gap .028"
Point Gap . . . . .015"
Cam Angle, Degrees 31
Timing .I.G.A. or I.G.N.
Firing Order 18736542
Tappet Clearances:
    Intake . . . . .Zero, hydraulic
    Exhaust . . . . .Zero, hydraulic
Compression Pressure,
Lbs 182
Idle Speed, RPM 375

BRAKES

Type . . . . .Hydraulic, int. exp.
Drum Diameter . . . . .12"

CAPACITIES

Cooling System, Qts 22
Fuel Tank, Gals 20
Crank Case, Qts 7
Trans. Pints 2.5
Differential, Pts 5

WHEEL ALIGNMENT

Caster, Degrees . . . .−1¾ to −2¾
Camber, Degrees . . . .−⅜ to +⅜
Toe in, Inches . . . . .¹/₃₂ to ³/₃₂

1947 Mercury Convertible

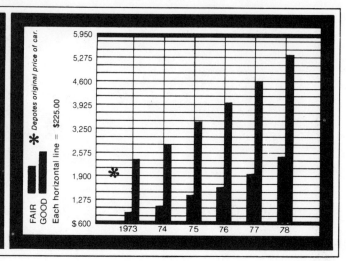

The prices of old convertibles have skyrocketed in the last two years. The typical 1946-48 Ford-Mercury Convertible in respectable condition brings three to four thousand dollars. That puts it out of the typical class right away. It also tells you that the word is out on these cars and the likelihood of finding a bargain convert is rather poor. If you do locate one, chances are it will need a complete restoration, which will cost about the same as you could get for the car when it's done. Especially for Mercury, good parts are hard to come by from any other than an expensive "new old stock" source. Upholstery, which goes almost without question in a ragtop, is another expensive proposition. Don't expect your average Rayco dealer to be of much assistance. A good upholsterer, one who can do the job with the correct material and the correct pattern in a reasonable amount of time and for a reasonable amount of money, is very hard to come by. If you find one, your good fortune is second only to the person who can do the job himself.

On the other hand, everybody seems to know of a good painter. The only caution here is that there is no substitute for good preparation. And there is still nothing that does more for a car than a good coat of paint.

The Mercury Convertible pictured above is worthy of restoration. It is basically a Ford with more chrome, but 1948 was the last year either car looked like this. From then on, it was strictly modern times. As times get more modern the prices of pre-1949 convertibles will soar even higher, securing what may be high initial investment. Tons of everything one could need to replenish this car with are on hand. Everything from literature to parts to people is at your disposal. It always seems that the people who have cars like this are the most earnest with the hobby, lending help and advice at every opportunity. If you want a rare prize, an attention-grabbing hunk of real steel, find an old ragtop. If you want to practice a little one-upmanship, make it a Mercury instead of a Ford. You'll be the envy of a very large crowd.

SPECIFICATIONS

Wheelbase	118"
Tread; Front, Rear	58", 60"
Overall Length	202"
Overall Width	74"
Overall Height	69"
Weight, Lbs	3298
Tire Size	6.50 x 15"

ENGINE

Type	Flathead V-8
Bore & Stroke	3.1875" x 3.75"
Displacement, Cu. In.	239.4
Compression Ratio	6.75 to 1
Horsepower @ RPM	100 @ 3800
Max. Torque @ RPM	180 @ 2000
Electrical	6 Volt, pos. grd.

TRANSMISSION

Type	3 speed manual
Available	2 speed rear

REAR

Type	Hypoid, ¾ floating
Ratio	3.54 to 1

TUNE UP

Spark Plug Gap	.030"
Point Gap	.015"
Cam Angle, Degrees	36
Timing	4° B.T.D.C.
Firing Order	15486372
Tappet Clearances:	
Intake	.011"
Exhaust	.013"
Compression Pressure, Lbs	160
Idle Speed, RPM	425

BRAKES

Type	Hydraulic, int. exp.
Drum Diameter	12"

CAPACITIES

Cooling System, Qts	22
Fuel Tank, Gals	17
Crank Case, Qts	5
Trans. Pints	2.75
Differential, Pts	2.5

WHEEL ALIGNMENT

Caster, Degrees	+4½ to +9
Camber, Degrees	+¼ to +1
Toe in, Inches	1/16

1947 Oldsmobile Sedan

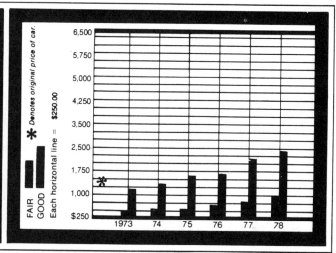

If you've been reading the book straight through, you should have the idea by now that cars built prior to 1949 are easily distinguishable by their high hoods and pronounced fenders. This fact alone does not render them valuable, but it is the sign of a good start. You might also be aware by now that sedans, especially four-door sedans, are basically designed to transport four to six people in comfort more than style. It is a perfectly arguable point that this is the function of the automobile in general.

To the collector, however, style means more than comfort. Seldom will a top-notch collector's car be used for toting people from one place to another unless the places are car shows. The collector's roving eye is always cast toward the aesthetic or the flashy or the rare and different car. Sedans can wait years longer than coupes or convertibles to be appreciated, and then at a fraction of their price. It's a game of supply and demand. Since the supply usually runs a bit ahead of the demand on the average four-door sedan, it is the kind of car that is easy to find and hard to sell. Superb condition will sell the ugliest car in the world, so that's not what we're talking about. What we have in mind is more of an average sedan in average condition.

The 1948 Oldsmobile is really a nice looking car. An extremely smooth-looking grille highlights the front end. The slightly bulbous taper of the headlights helps to elicit the car's character. Underneath the long, high hood there is either a six- or an eight-cylinder engine of the in-line variety. Both provide peppy performance when properly tuned. Either can be found with the Hydramatic transmission or the stick setup. There is no real difference in value either way. Inside is where the sedan comes to life. A clean interior means a lot in a sedan, as you may well imagine. Driver's seat, arm rests and front door panels usually show the earliest signs of wear. If your car does not, you've got a sedan worth having. A day with a bucket and lots of rags should net a tidy profit.

SPECIFICATIONS

Wheelbase	.125″
Tread; Front, Rear	.58″, 62″
Overall Length	.213″
Overall Width	.76″
Overall Height	.65″
Weight, Lbs	.3638
Tire Size	.6.50 x 16″

ENGINE

Type	.L-Head, straight 8 cyl.
Bore & Stroke	.3.25″ x 3.875″
Displacement, Cu. In.	.257.1
Compression Ratio	.6.50 to 1
Horsepower @ RPM	.110 @ 3600
Max. Torque @ RPM	.210 @ 2000
Electrical	.6 Volt, neg. grd.

TRANSMISSION

Type	.3 speed manual
Available	.Automatic

REAR

Type	.Hypoid, semi-floating
Ratio	.4.30 to 1

TUNE UP

Spark Plug Gap	..030″
Point Gap	..015″
Cam Angle, Degrees	.31
Timing	.2° B.T.D.C.
Firing Order	.16258374
Tappet Clearances:	
Intake	..008″
Exhaust	..011″
Compression Pressure, Lbs	.115
Idle Speed, RPM	.425

BRAKES

Type	.Hydraulic, int. exp.
Drum Diameter	.11″

CAPACITIES

Cooling System, Qts	.21.5
Fuel Tank, Gals	.19
Crank Case, Qts	.6
Trans. Pints	.2
Differential, Pts	.3.75

WHEEL ALIGNMENT

Caster, Degrees	.0 to −¾
Camber, Degrees	.−¼ to −¾
Toe in, Inches	.¹/₁₆ to ¹/₈

1948 Chevrolet Convertible

The Fleetmaster Club Coupe

EXTRA FEATURES: Sliding rear-quarter windows. Full-width rear seat. In rear compartment—two assist straps, coat hooks, ash receivers, parcel shelf.

The Fleetmaster Cabriolet

EXTRA FEATURES: Automatic folding top. Bright-finished metal moldings framing windshield and windows. Lowering door windows, swiveling rear-quarter windows. Safety plate glass throughout. Three-passenger adjustable front seat, divided back. Full-width rear seat. Genuine leather and Bedford cord seat covering. Front seat arm rests. Fabric top boot.

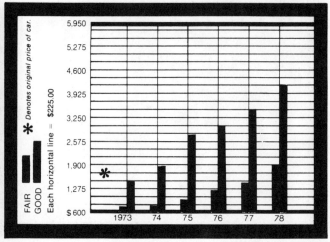

Even though the long sweeping front fenders of the Aerosedan grace the convertible, the boxier roof and rear of this model are not so flattered by such local streamlining. In fact, the fenders seem to make the hood line appear too high in this application, throwing off an otherwise well balanced design. With the horizontal grille pattern that was so prevalent in the late forties, this Chevy joined the glitter parade, though not distastefully.

What makes this car valuable is that it is a convertible and representative of the last of the pre-war body styles: the ones that had the distinct fenders all the way around, enclosing in typical good proportion the high hood and body section. So, even if the front fenders are a little low in relation to the hood line, the car closed out an era that will never return.

In recent years, the prices of these convertibles have gone sky high. Even one in need of a total restoration is worth having. It's next to impossible to lose money on a pre-1949 convertible of any make! In 1948, Chevrolet offered a few bright colors on these cars that can make them real eye-catchers if you are restoring one. A good choice of color will sell a car as quickly as any other effort you put into it.

And if you are putting your effort into a Chevy of this vintage, you will be pleased to know that virtually any part can be had cheaply and quickly. Parts abound but parts cars are the best approach. That way, you can usually sell what's left and get most of your original cash back.

Mechanically, these Chevys are hard to beat. They're almost indestructible. By 1948, Chevy had already been using the overhead six-cylinder engine for eleven years. The torque tube drive presents complications when a clutch job is due, but nothing a little labor of love cannot overcome. Yes, if you want economy and reliability in a pretty package, get a Chevy Convertible.

In many respects, it's better than a new car. The interior certainly is more impressive than newer cars'. That's the way they built them in 1948, though. No one foresaw the excessive use of synthetics then. It was a real world and the Chevy Convertible is a vivid reminder of the way we were.

SPECIFICATIONS

Wheelbase . . . . .116"
Tread; Front, Rear . . . . .57⅝", 60"
Overall Length .197¾"
Overall Width . . . . .72¾"
Overall Height . . . . .69⅜"
Weight, Lbs 2134
Tire Size . . . . .6.00 x 16"

ENGINE

Type .Overhead in-line 6
Bore & Stroke . . . . .3.50" x 3.75"
Displacement, Cu. In. 216.1
Compression Ratio . . . . .6.50 to 1
Horsepower @ RPM . . . . .90 @ 3300
Max. Torque @ RPM . . . . .174 @ 2000
Electrical . . . . .6 Volt, neg. grd.

TRANSMISSION

Type . . . . .3 speed manual
Available . . . .—

REAR

Type . . . . .Hypoid, semi-floating
Ratio . . . . .4.11 to 1

TUNE UP

Spark Plug Gap . . . . .040"
Point Gap . . . . .018"
Cam Angle, Degrees 38
Timing . . . . .Steel ball in flywheel
Firing Order 153624
Tappet Clearances:
    Intake . . . . .006"
    Exhaust . . . . .013"
Compression Pressure,
Lbs 110
Idle Speed, RPM 350

BRAKES

Type .Hydraulic, int. exp.
Drum Diameter . . . . .11"

CAPACITIES

Cooling System, Qts 15
Fuel Tank, Gals 16
Crank Case, Qts 5
Trans. Pints 1.5
Differential, Pts 3.5

WHEEL ALIGNMENT

Caster, Degrees . . . . .0 pref.
Camber, Degrees . . . .−¼ pref.
Toe in, Inches . . . . .¹/₃₂ pref.

34

1948 Chrysler Town & Country

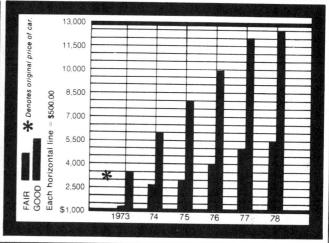

1. Wood and convertible
2. 1948 again

This car really doesn't belong in this book. It's come to the point where you can't find them, can't afford them, and don't even see them any more. This is no great surprise when you realize that the 1948 Town & Country combines all the most desirable elements of a collectible car. The car has real wood, a convertible top, pre-1949 styling,* limited production, good looks and a good name. What more could you ask for? $8,000 might be the answer to that question . . . which brings us back to why the car does not belong in this book.

If you ever saw one, though, you couldn't not mention it when mentioning fine cars. As a Chrysler, the Town & Country enjoyed a sophisticated level of refinement throughout. This is not to be confused with achievement, which, engineering-wise, had been on the wane for the better part of the decade. In this case, it seems to work in Chrysler's favor. There's something about the old L-head straight eight that captures the elegance of the Town & Country fixation. It is the taming of the beast of nuts and bolts. It represents the epitomé of classical simplicity. Looking at this car is like reviewing the highlights of the last great decade of automobiles before computer-age technology took over.

Even the grille treatment deploys an oft-repeated pattern of success.

Using the typical cross-hatch theme, Chrysler chose to make the bars thin and fine, barely oblong in pattern, and highlighted every so often by a slightly wider bar. If you look at the newer cars (the Monte Carlo is a fine comparison), you can see the same evolution take place in the grille as both body series matured from 1970 to 1975.

Inside the story is the same. There was some brightness but always in an understated decor. The dash is reserved, yet potent in the way it continues to characterize the richness of the car. Same for the seats. If you've ever sat in one of these leather chairs and felt the presence of canvas and chrome overhead, wood on the outside of you, and gracefully tapered fenders accentuating the classic long hoodline, you probably wouldn't give up the seat for less than $8,000 either.

*After 1948 most cars were of sufficiently modern design that we can easily recognize the preceeding years as a group, giving them identity and value.

SPECIFICATIONS

Wheelbase	127.5"
Tread; Front, Rear	58", 62"
Overall Length	214.5"
Overall Width	77.75"
Overall Height	68"
Weight, Lbs	4332
Tire Size	7.00 x 15"

ENGINE

Type	L-Head, in-line 8 cyl.
Bore & Stroke	3.25" x 4.875"
Displacement, Cu. In.	323.5
Compression Ratio	6.70 to 1
Horsepower @ RPM	135 @ 3400
Max. Torque @ RPM	270 @ 1600
Electrical	6 Volt, pos. grd.

TRANSMISSION

Type	3 speed manual
Available	Fluid drive

REAR

Type	Hypoid, semi-floating
Ratio	3.91 to 1

TUNE UP

Spark Plug Gap	.025"
Point Gap	.017"
Cam Angle, Degrees	27
Timing	2° A.T.D.C.
Firing Order	16258374
Tappet Clearances:	
Intake	.008"
Exhaust	.010"
Compression Pressure, Lbs	165
Idle Speed, RPM	425

BRAKES

Type	Hydraulic, int. exp.
Drum Diameter	12"

CAPACITIES

Cooling System, Qts	26
Fuel Tank, Gals	20
Crank Case, Qts	6
Trans. Pints	2.75
Differential, Pts	3.25

WHEEL ALIGNMENT

Caster, Degrees	−1 to +1
Camber, Degrees	0 to +¾
Toe in, Inches	0 to 1/16

1948 Chrysler Windsor 4-Door Sedan

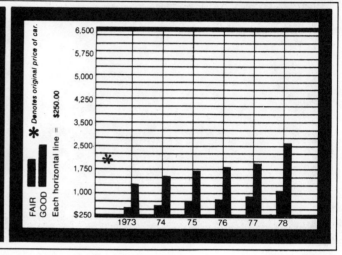

If we could get outside it all, that is, far enough above the earth to get an astronaut's view, I think we would be surprised at what we would see. In the developed nations, at least, cars would dominate the landscape. The network of roads and the proliferation of attendant facilities might even deceive an alien into believing that the automobile is the dominant life form and man is there merely to service it. While this situation is hypothetical, it presupposes the question of which specimens the spacemen would take with them to fill their zoos.

One car that would surely not be on the first flight home would be the 1948 Chrysler Windsor Sedan. It would not be so much overlooked for its scarceness as for its unassuming nature. You see, some cars have appeal from the moment they're made. They are the fortunate ones. Some people are that way too; born to take the world by the tail. Other cars, like other people, come on more slowly. They become stars through effort and endurance. This is more the life style of the Chrysler Windsor.

The Windsor is a car about to blossom. It has put in its time and proven its service. All that remains is for someone to give it the breath of life. That someone is not likely to be spaceman, but it could be you! After all, cars are extensions of our personalities. The beauty, therefore, comes from within. If you feel it, the energies of your toil will be harbored

in the car you rebuild. That car will be a prism, radiating the labor of your love. In this Chrysler such radiance is in the form of class. The Windsor is a large car with no abrupt lines; one given to conservative luxury. To revive the low-key approach to status is to beat the game of class distinction in old cars. A well-done Chrysler of this vintage commands veneration. It makes you wonder why it never occurred to you that such an unobtrusive car could be so stunning.

If you see it this way, there is both good news and bad news awaiting you. The good news is that these cars are relatively common and inexpensive in average condition. The bad news is that once you perk it up a bit, you're liable to catch the fancy of some very strange looking creatures. Wouldn't Mr. Von Daniken be surprised to learn that the real chariot of the gods is the 1948 Chrysler Windsor? Wouldn't you?

SPECIFICATIONS

Wheelbase	127.5"
Tread; Front, Rear	57.8125", 61.5625"
Overall Length	214.25"
Overall Width	77.75"
Overall Height	68"
Weight, Lbs	3972
Tire Size	6.50 x 15"

ENGINE

Type	L-Head, in line 8
Bore & Stroke	3.25" x 4.875"
Displacement, Cu. In.	323.5
Compression Ratio	6.70 to 1
Horsepower @ RPM	135 @ 3400
Max. Torque @ RPM	270 @ 1600
Electrical	6 Volt, pos. grd.

TRANSMISSION

Type	3 speed manual
Available	semi-automatic

REAR

Type	Hypoid, semi-floating
Ratio	3.91 to 1

TUNE UP

Spark Plug Gap	.025"
Point Gap	.017"
Cam Angle, Degrees	27
Timing	2° A.T.D.C.
Firing Order	16258374
Tappet Clearances:	
Intake	.008"
Exhaust	.010"
Compression Pressure,	
Lbs	165
Idle Speed, RPM	425

BRAKES

Type	Hydraulic, int. exp.
Drum Diameter	12"

CAPACITIES

Cooling System, Qts	26
Fuel Tank, Gals	20
Crank Case, Qts	6
Trans. Pints	2.75
Differential, Pts	3.25

WHEEL ALIGNMENT

Caster, Degrees	−1 to +1
Camber, Degrees	.0 to +¾
Toe in, Inches	.0 to 1/16

1948 Continental Cabriolet

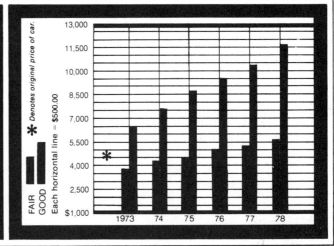

If you study the picture of this car, its success is apparent. Granted, the grille is massive and somewhat detached from the overall continuity of line; but still the overwhelming feeling that hits you when you look at this car is that it is, well, a classic. From its inception in 1940, the Continental was so intrinsically refined in its statement of classical elegance that it is barely defaulted by any abundance of chrome or gadgetry.

It was, in 1948, the only American car with a V-12 engine, a direct carryover from the classic era of the thirties. It captured that feeling, too, with its hushed rear seat. The roofline had no rear windows, so the convertible top hid the passengers in sumptuous leather, far from the cruel world outside. Up front, the driver peered through a flat, one-piece windshield and over a long hood, also highly reminiscent of the great marques.

Yet there was an air of the future in this timeless car. The push-button doors and fully skirted rear fenders were as slick as could be. The spare tire mounted as such in the rear, and enveloped by the fender lines, inspired such a trend that even today a rear-mounted spare is called a "continental kit."

All of these marks of distinction only serve to render a complete picture of a classic. That is what it takes. That is how it should blend together. That is why these cars have always been desirable and valuable. There was, however, a period of disrespect for the

Continental in the early fifties, when many a tired flathead V-12 was replaced with a more capable Olds or Cadillac overhead V-8. Sometimes this updating included an automatic transmission, and almost always it extended the car's life many fold. In fact, many Continentals still have these G.M. drivetrains and manage to maintain a goodly portion of their potential value.

If you come across one like this it wouldn't hurt to leave it that way, because these cars will have their day, just as the original hot rods have returned to the limelight. But for the purist there can be no other way than to restore to perfection. The V-12 was part of the original mystique of the Continental and its legend has far outweighed its faults.

SPECIFICATIONS

Wheelbase	.125"
Tread; Front, Rear	.59", 61"
Overall Length	.218"
Overall Width	.78"
Overall Height	.67"
Weight, Lbs	.4015
Tire Size	.7.00 x 15"

ENGINE

Type	.Flathead 75° V-12
Bore & Stroke	.2.875" x 3.75"
Displacement, Cu. In.	.292
Compression Ratio	.7.20 to 1
Horsepower @ RPM	.125 @ 3600
Max. Torque @ RPM	.214 @ 1600
Electrical	.6 Volt, pos. grd.

TRANSMISSION

Type	.3 speed manual
Available	.overdrive

REAR

Type	.¾ floating
Ratio	.4.22 to 1

TUNE UP

Spark Plug Gap	.025"
Point Gap	.015"
Cam Angle, Degrees	.36
Timing	.2° B.T.D.C.
Firing Order	.149852, 11, 10, 3, 6, 7, 12
Tappet Clearances:	
Intake	.Zero, hydraulic
Exhaust	.Zero, hydraulic
Compression Pressure,	
Lbs	.105-125
Idle Speed, RPM	.500

BRAKES

Type	.Hydraulic, int. exp.
Drum Diameter	.12"

CAPACITIES

Cooling System, Qts	.27
Fuel Tank, Gals	.19.5
Crank Case, Qts	.5
Trans. Pints	.2.75
Differential, Pts	.4

WHEEL ALIGNMENT

Caster, Degrees	.+4
Camber, Degrees	.0 to +1
Toe in, Inches	.0 to 1/16

1948 Dodge Coupe

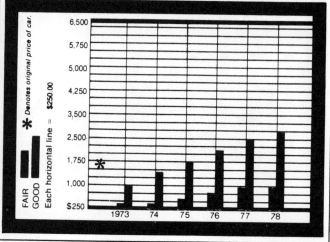

There comes a time in the life of every car when it passes through adolescence and into maturity. In adolescence, the car is an uncommon sight, but not a shocking surprise. It will turn up now and then to bring a smile, or the turn of a head from an appreciative passerby. It has worth, but not enough to keep it from occasional service. Finally, it is not in perfect shape, but not in the poorest of shape. It may need some attention, but the parts and the labor are reasonably available.

On the other hand, when it crosses that invisible barrier to maturity, a car becomes suddenly more fragile. It is given better attention at a greater expense, but it is seldom used in less than ideal situations. The crowd reaction becomes expected. Often the owner feels cheated if his car does not receive proper homage. Chances are, he is a new owner and he paid rather dearly for the car. Inwardly, he probably bought it for its uniqueness, knowing this would cause it to attract much wanted attention. In fact, no one will pamper it more than he. Call it an alter ego, or an escape mechanism, or even a rewarding pursuit of interest; everyone knows there is a fine line that separates hobby from obsession.

Anyway, the car comes out ahead! Its value as a matured car has literally jumped to a whole new level, from which point it will show a normal, steady rate of increase. There is no magic moment when all of this happens. Like a person, the car comes of age when its time comes.

Presently, there seems to be a general trend among coupes of almost any 1946-48 Chrysler Corporation variety toward maturity. They are all quite similar. The Dodge five-passenger coupe typifies this crowd. Flat in the front, long in the rear and high at the beltline, with gently tapering front fenders, could as well describe a Chrysler or De Soto coupe of this period. It would not be wrong to include even Plymouth coupes with an L-head six-cylinder engine mated to either a standard manual transmission or a version of the popular semi-automatic transmission. In looks and feel, all these cars are similar. Prices will vary from model to model. De Sotos, being no longer extant, and the business coupes, having no rear seat, present two factors that can influence the final figure. Whatever the exact numbers are found to be, they will all be in the same ballpark. And for all of them, it's a whole new ball game.

SPECIFICATIONS

Wheelbase	120"
Tread; Front, Rear	57", 60"
Overall Length	205"
Overall Width	76"
Overall Height	67.5"
Weight, Lbs	3256
Tire Size	6.00 x 16"

ENGINE

Type	L-Head In-line 6 cyl.
Bore & Stroke	3.25" x 4.625"
Displacement, Cu. In.	230.2
Compression Ratio	6.70 to 1
Horsepower @ RPM	102 @ 3600
Max. Torque @ RPM	184 @ 1200
Electrical	6 Volt, pos grd.

TRANSMISSION

Type	3 speed manual
Available	semi-automatic

REAR

Type	Hypoid, semi-floating
Ratio	3.90 to 1

TUNE UP

Spark Plug Gap	.025"
Point Gap	.020"
Cam Angle, Degrees	38
Timing	2° A.T.D.C.
Firing Order	153624
Tappet Clearances:	
Intake	.008"
Exhaust	.010"
Compression Pressure, Lbs	160
Idle Speed, RPM	450

BRAKES

Type	Hydraulic, int. exp.
Drum Diameter	11"

CAPACITIES

Cooling System, Qts	15
Fuel Tank, Gals	17
Crank Case, Qts	5
Trans. Pints	2.75
Differential, Pts	3.25

WHEEL ALIGNMENT

Caster, Degrees	−1 to +1
Camber, Degrees	0 to +¾
Toe in, Inches	0 to ¹/₁₆

1948 Ford Coupe

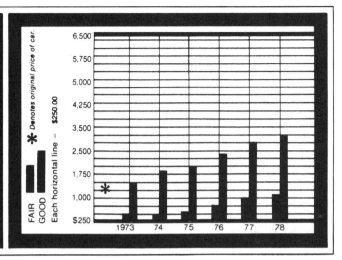

The 1948 Ford Coupe used to be a good car to knock around in. Nobody ever took it seriously. It was a neat car to have then, because it was cheap and it was a good looker. Those who tried of its flathead engine (or inherited it that way) discovered the joy of new-found power and status in the omnipresent Olds overhead conversion. Shortly thereafter, most of them discovered the heartbreak and fatigue of replacing a drivetrain too weak to sustain such abuse. If nothing else, these Ford Coupes provided an inexhaustible aptitude test for a fledgling mechanic. Many successful young men grew up on a steady regimen of such coupes. It was a lot cheaper than what it costs the kids today to build up a '55-57 Chevy.

To the chagrin of many, the '48 Ford Coupe can no longer play the role of the adolescent's erector set. Neither do the junkyards abound in cheap parts for it. Nor, for that matter, does the car itself abound! Suddenly it's getting too old for all that. Dare I say the same for the kids that grew up with them? Only if, in fairness, I admit that the Ford is entitled to the same reward of success brought about by time and effort.

Actually, this is all that happened. People and cars both mature, passing, as they do, through various stages of life. They don't exactly parallel each other; though it would be nice if they did. Unfortunately, man does not treat his own kind with an equal respect for seniority. Too often,

man observes his world from an immutable vantage point, failing to notice as things go by, that he, too, is dynamic.

If we see something move or change, we recognize that as a sign of life. The Ford Coupe is merely demonstrating its vitality as it follows the calendar into a new and different phase of its life cycle. There is no doubt that it will become, as did the older Model A, restored in the pride and dignity befitting the passive participation it played in our lives. It is axiomatic that, as it fills this new role, the 1948 Ford Coupe will revalue upward, bearing in a way, the interest of its investment in the American Dream.

SPECIFICATIONS

Wheelbase	114"
Tread; Front, Rear	58", 60"
Overall Length	198"
Overall Width	73"
Overall Height	66"
Weight, Lbs	3040
Tire Size	6.00 x 16"

ENGINE

Type	Flathead V-8
Bore & Stroke	3.187" x 3.75"
Displacement, Cu. In.	239
Compression Ratio	6.75 to 1
Horsepower @ RPM	100 @ 3800
Max. Torque @ RPM	180 @ 2000
Electrical	6 Volt, pos. grd.

TRANSMISSION

Type	3 speed manual
Available	2 speed rear

REAR

Type	¾ floating
Ratio	3.54 to 1

TUNE UP

Spark Plug Gap	.025"
Point Gap	.015"
Cam Angle, Degrees	36
Timing	4° B.T.D.C.
Firing Order	15486372
Tappet Clearances:	
Intake	.011"
Exhaust	.015"
Compression Pressure, Lbs	160
Idle Speed, RPM	425

BRAKES

Type	Hydraulic, int. exp.
Drum Diameter	12"

CAPACITIES

Cooling System, Qts	22
Fuel Tank, Gals	17
Crank Case, Qts	5
Trans. Pints	2.75
Differential, Pts	2.5

WHEEL ALIGNMENT

Caster, Degrees	+4½
Camber, Degrees	−¼ to −1
Toe in, Inches	.0 to 1/16

1948 Ford Sedan

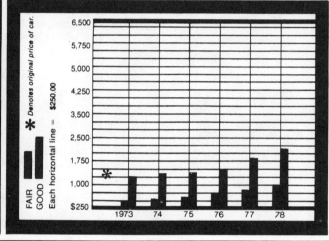

This sedan is typical of Ford and Mercury cars of 1941 through 1948. Mercurys, of course, are worth a little more. They never set the world on fire, but they did pretty well cover it at one time. For this reason, these cars deserve mention. Anything short of a super clean one is going to have to wait awhile to appreciate to a profitable extent. If you prefer to hasten this process by amateur restoration, be reminded that the supply of old Ford parts is limited and nearly priceless. One a piecemeal basis, refurbishing one of these sedans would be a losing proposition.

A lot of old sedans are sleepers. They sit around awhile and gather dirt and dry rot. They don't look good at first glance, but a trained eye can tell the difference a good cleaning-up will make. A good day's scrubbing is usually worth a couple of hundred dollars on cars like these. If you pay the going price for one that's already been prepped, be prepared to enjoy it or sit on it. But don't worry; it will never be worth less. The conversation you encounter on your first outing should be an indication of the people part of old cars — the part that doesn't ever show up in terms of dollars.

And people will talk to you, because the 1948 Ford Sedan is a nice car. It has a very clean front end and a pleasing slope to its roofline. It is neither gaudy nor spartan. It is a Ford and it has a flathead engine, perhaps even a V-8. If this is not enough to prove its worth, its age and pre-1949

appearance, with bulging fenders and high hood and rooflines, should be convincing arguments. Many are already convinced of the imminent demand for sedans. They know they appreciate in value. It just takes a little longer. The waiting period is about over for the 1948 Ford Sedans.

One final thought: If you have enough patience, you can make your money several times over by parting-out an old Ford or Mercury sedan. Take it down to the smallest bolt — there's always a nut to fit it.

SPECIFICATIONS

Wheelbase	.114"
Tread; Front, Rear	.58", 60"
Overall Length	.198"
Overall Width	.73"
Overall Height	.66"
Weight, Lbs	.3213
Tire Size	.6.00 x 16"

ENGINE

Type	In-line 6 cyl.
Bore & Stroke	.3.30" x 4.40"
Displacement, Cu. In.	.226
Compression Ratio	.6.80 to 1
Horsepower @ RPM	.95 @ 3300
Max. Torque @ RPM	.180 @ 1200
Electrical	.6 Volt, pos. grd.

TRANSMISSION

Type	.3 speed manual
Available	.2 speed rear

REAR

Type	.¾ floating
Ratio	.3.78 to 1

TUNE UP

Spark Plug Gap	.030"
Point Gap	.016"
Cam Angle, Degrees	.36
Timing	.1° B.T.D.C.
Firing Order	.153624
Tappet Clearances:	
Intake	.014"
Exhaust	.014"
Compression Pressure,	
Lbs	.105-125
Idle Speed, RPM	.450

BRAKES

Type	.Hydraulic, int. exp.
Drum Diameter	.12"

CAPACITIES

Cooling System, Qts	.17
Fuel Tank, Gals	.17
Crank Case, Qts	.5
Trans. Pints	.2.75
Differential, Pts	.2.5

WHEEL ALIGNMENT

Caster, Degrees	.+6¾ pref.
Camber, Degrees	.+⅝ pref.
Toe in, Inches	.1/16 pref.

1948 Ford Wooden Station Wagon

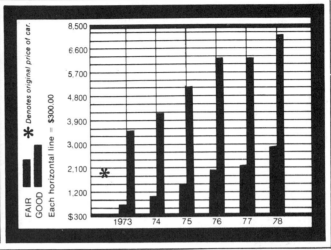

* Denotes original price of car.

Each horizontal line = $300.00

FAIR GOOD

8,500 / 6,600 / 5,700 / 4,800 / 3,900 / 3,000 / 2,100 / 1,200 / $300

1973 74 75 76 77 78

Just one look will make the value of this car apparent. The full wooden body* and the last of the masculine, bulging fenders combine with the throaty nostalgic rapture of the famous flathead V-8 to create one of the most desired collector's cars. Heads turn from blocks away to catch a glimpse of even a tattered specimen; and, prices reflect this admiration.

In 1948, Henry Ford was still clinging to a twenty year old chassis design with transverse springs and torque-tube drive. In fact, Ford would not introduce its new post-war body until 1949, but the quality and craftsmanship of the 1948 Woody may never be seen again. This was to be the final all wood-bodied wagon made in America. Its value is indicative of any all-wooden wagon; the impact of real materials and quality craftsmanship is stunningly responsible.

Even the roof was made of wooden slats covered with canvas. The only metal pieces to be found in this body are in the door latches and window mechanism! You can sit on the high leather seats and be enveloped by perfection in wood. You can breathe it! It's exhilarating like no other car. A ride in a Woody will steal your heart forever.

The 1948 Ford Wagon is nearly identical to the 1946, 1947 Ford and Mercury offerings in both appearance and value. These cars can still be found, but weathered wood and

spiraling demand have numbered the ranks.

If you can find one, virtually every part is available for it; but some, such as rear fenders, can be hard to come by because they are not interchangeable with the sedan's. As it may take a while to find some wooden parts, it is wise to locate a good carpenter. The truth is, though, that many wooden pieces are flat and easy to reproduce and replace, even for the novice. Of course, it is always helpful to buy a parts-car for those little pieces, or, perhaps, a Columbia 2-speed rear.

It seems the old Ford Woody has graduated from its California surf buggy status to one of more respect. Maybe we are too old and wise to be beach boys now, or maybe this is that type of car that is a winner in any role. At any rate, the price of such knowledge is very high today and is not likely to decline as long as Detroit continues to sacrifice the craftsmanship and synthetisize the character of the automobile.

*Ford owned his own forest reserves and his carpenters built the bodies; other manufacturers purchased their wood bodies from outside companies.

SPECIFICATIONS

Wheelbase	114"
Tread; Front, Rear	58", 60"
Overall Length	198"
Overall Width	74"
Overall Height	70"
Weight, Lbs	3490
Tire Size	6.00 x 16"

ENGINE

Type	Flathead 90° V-8
Bore & Stroke	3.187" x 3.75"
Displacement, Cu. In.	239
Compression Ratio	6.75 to 1
Horsepower @ RPM	100 @ 3800
Max. Torque @ RPM	180 @ 2000
Electrical	6 Volt, pos. grd.

TRANSMISSION

Type	3 speed manual
Available	2 speed rear

REAR

Type	Hypoid, spiral bevel gears
Ratio	3.54 to 1
	Available with Columbia overdrive

TUNE UP

Spark Plug Gap	.025"
Point Gap	.014" - .016"
Cam Angle, Degrees	36
Timing	4° B.T.D.C.
Firing Order	15486372
Tappet Clearances:	
Intake	.011 to .015"
Exhaust	.015"
Compression Pressure,	
Lbs	105-125
Idle Speed, RPM	400-500

BRAKES

Type	Hydraulic, int. exp.
Drum Diameter	12"

CAPACITIES

Cooling System, Qts	22
Fuel Tank, Gals	17
Crank Case, Qts	5
Trans. Pints	2¾
Differential, Pts	2½

WHEEL ALIGNMENT

Caster, Degrees	+6¾
Camber, Degrees	+⅝
Toe in, Inches	1/16

1948 Packard Super 8 Sedan

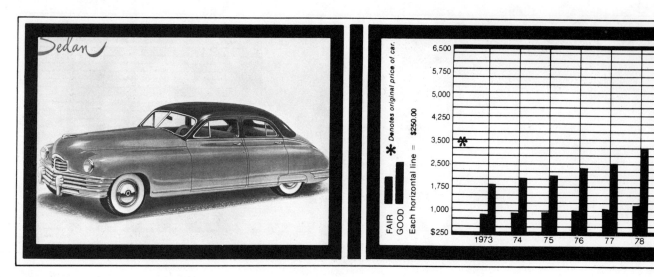

Packards are such heavyweight cars that it is necessary to differentiate models, even within the parameters of the four-door sedan, in order to affix accurate values. The plentiful 1948-49 sedans add importance to the condition factor, as well. It gets confusing before you begin shopping. Many people actually specialize in Packards, spending years developing a discerning eye. The same is true of other valuable cars; the price of such specialization results in weakness in other areas.

A person who cultivates a good intuitive approach toward cars can play ball in anybody's park without being embarrassed. An insurance estimator does basically this. He can look at a car, objectively survey its damage and estimate the repair cost. The complexities of model and series designation are less overpowering when you are armed with a little perspective and objectivity. Remember, nobody can set a price on beauty better than its beholder. If you're out looking, you always have that advantage. Just be sure to see what you're looking at. Many a wide-eyed car nut has been temporarily blinded by the sight of a car he loves, only to buy it and find it at the point of diminishing return.

Fortunately, most '48-49 Packards that have lasted this long are in pretty good shape. They are not prone to early cancer. Packard's reputation for quality extends to the use of chrome instead of stainless on some trim

pieces. If neglected, they will rust. Diligence is the best solution to this problem.

The unbroken smoothness of line on these Packards requires a very straight body to maintain its appeal, much like the 1960 Cadillac. Underneath that smooth body, there is nothing too difficult to fix or too hard to find. Multiple mechanical problems spell caution. If profit is the motive, any combination of minor ills can spell diaster. Unless you are a Packard buff, the best thing to do is let the car find *you*. If you are a Packard nut, you know where to find the right car and you know how to remedy any ills.

SPECIFICATIONS

Wheelbase	.120″
Tread; Front, Rear	.60″, 61″
Overall Length	.205″
Overall Width	.77″
Overall Height	.64″
Weight, Lbs	.3855
Tire Size	.7.60 x 15″

ENGINE

Type	.L-Head, in-line 8 cyl.
Bore & Stroke	.3.50″ x 4.25″
Displacement, Cu. In.	.327
Compression Ratio	.7.00 to 1
Horsepower @ RPM	.145 @ 3600
Max. Torque @ RPM	.266 @ 2000
Electrical	.6 Volt, pos. grd.

TRANSMISSION

Type	.3 speed manual
Available	.overdrive

REAR

Type	.Hypoid, semi-floating
Ratio	.3.90 to 1

TUNE UP

Spark Plug Gap	.028″
Point Gap	.017″
Cam Angle, Degrees	.27
Timing	.6° B.T.D.C.
Firing Order	.16258374
Tappet Clearances:	
Intake	.007″
Exhaust	.010″
Compression Pressure,	
Lbs	.110
Idle Speed, RPM	.400-450

BRAKES

Type	.Hydraulic, int. exp.
Drum Diameter	.12″

CAPACITIES

Cooling System, Qts	.19
Fuel Tank, Gals	.20
Crank Case, Qts	.7
Trans. Pints	.2
Differential, Pts	.4

WHEEL ALIGNMENT

Caster, Degrees	.+1½ to +2½
Camber, Degrees	.−¼ to +¾
Toe in, Inches	.0

42

1948 Pontiac Torpedo Coupe

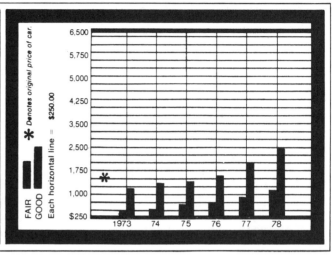

The 1948 Torpedo Coupe is an average example of a body style introduced in 1942 on a series-wide basis by General Motors. This specific body shell was shared with Chevrolet and Oldsmobile while the larger series Buick and Cadillac offered a similar fastback design. 1948 was the last year for this style; its difference with all subsequent cars is readily discernible. Herein lies its value.

This coupe represents the epitome of pre-war G.M. styling. The extended sweep of the front fenders and the rakish angle of the center post lend a look of motion. Yet, the overall impression of size and proportion labels it immediately as an evolutionary refinement of pre-war design philosophy. By the following year, the industry had universally launched the modern age of automobiles, both in design and engineering technology. In fact, the independents had already unveiled portents of the post-war styling revolution.

But I did say the Pontiac Torpedo was an average example of the state of the art. This was so even in 1948 when the car was known as the staid but reliable transportation of the school marm. It is a fact that the inline flathead six- or eight-cylinder engine was no barnstormer, but, in all fairness, neither was the competition. Still, the overall appeal of this car has much to do with the fact that it was in every way consistent with its refined but understated appearance, save perhaps a splashy non-integrated grille motif.

Nevertheless, a properly optioned Torpedo can be very eye-catching. For some unknown reason, windshield sun visors found their way onto many of these Pontiacs, thus necessitating another Pontiac hallmark, the dash-mounted traffic light reflector.

Throw on a rear windshield wiper and a spotlight or two, and who could deny that this anonymous old Pontiac has become downright spiffy? Well, maybe anonymous is a harsh word for a car that was as identifiable by its "Silver Streak" as Buick was by its famous portholes. But spiffy is nostalgic — and that means money.

It's worth noting, too, that while these Torpedo Coupes didn't creater riots at the dealers' showrooms, they did successfully achieve that ever-elusive balance of proportion. This symmetry inspired the fastback revival of the middle sixties. Unfortunately, by this time, cars were too long and too low to create the desired effect. Ironically, the resultant disproportionate uniqueness of such cars as the Rambler Marlin and Dodge Charger has prompted them to be desirable.

SPECIFICATIONS

Wheelbase	.119"
Tread; Front, Rear	.58", 62"
Overall Length	.205"
Overall Width	.76"
Overall Height	.66"
Weight, Lbs	.3415
Tire Size	.6.00 x 16"

ENGINE

Type	L-Head, in-line 8 cyl.
Bore & Stroke	.3.25" x 3.75"
Displacement, Cu. In.	.248.9
Compression Ratio	.6.50 to 1
Horsepower @ RPM	.107 @ 3700
Max. Torque @ RPM	.192 @ 2100
Electrical	.6 Volt, neg. grd.

TRANSMISSION

Type	.3 speed manual
Available	.Automatic

REAR

Type	.Hypoid, semi-floating
Ratio	.4.10 to 1

TUNE UP

Spark Plug Gap	.025"
Point Gap	.015"
Cam Angle, Degrees	.31
Timing	.4° B.T.D.C.
Firing Order	.16258374
Tappet Clearances:	
Intake	.012"
Exhaust	.012"
Compression Pressure, Lbs	.158
Idle Speed, RPM	.375

BRAKES

Type	.Hydraulic, int. exp.
Drum Diameter	.11"

CAPACITIES

Cooling System, Qts	.19.5
Fuel Tank, Gals	.12
Crank Case, Qts	.5
Trans. Pints	.1.75
Differential, Pts	.3.25

WHEEL ALIGNMENT

Caster, Degrees	−¾ to −1
Camber, Degrees	.0
Toe in, Inches	.0 to ¹/₁₆

1948 Studebaker Starlite Coupe

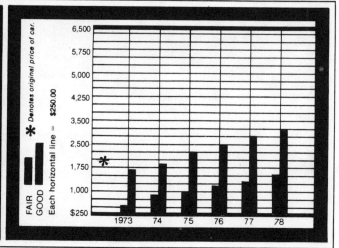

Studebaker rebounded after World War II with a lust for modern art that put the automobile empire on the defensive. The first manufacturer to produce a modern post-war design left no doubt as to its intentions. More than just an evolution of the forties, the Starlite Coupe set the stage for the revolution of the fifties.

The sweeping wraparound rear window that slithered halfway 'round the car was definitely the focal point of this all new Studebaker. Its forward rake suggested movement that seemed to dispute Newton's Third Law. The angle of the center post was reenacted in the contour of the rear fenders. From there, the light, low lines flowed down and back to meet the graceful taper of the trunk. While not as popular as the 1953 Studebakers he designed, Raymond Loewy showed in these coupes early indications of his talent for cultivating ethereal images. For this reason alone, these cars are undervalued.

Part of the reason Starlite Coupes are still comparatively inexpensive is that they were offered for so many years that they became common in the wake of other post-war designs. In fact, the aircraft-inspired, bullet-nosed grille that found its way onto some of these Studebakers became the exception, rather than the rule, of post-war design. The strength of producing a vast number of cars, whatever their design, gives the major manufacturer an overwhelming edge in dictating public taste. More than once the cart

has gone before the horse simply because the majority put it there. 1950 left Studebaker playing the part of the devil's advocate — speaking for an opposing, even unwanted, point of view. It would be another three years before the magic of Mr. Loewy would vindicate this worthy automobile.

SPECIFICATIONS

Wheelbase	112"
Tread; Front, Rear	56", 54"
Overall Length	193"
Overall Width	70"
Overall Height	61"
Weight, Lbs	2735
Tire Size	5.30 x 15"

ENGINE

Type	L-Head, in-line 6 cyl.
Bore & Stroke	3.00" x 4.00"
Displacement, Cu. In.	169.6
Compression Ratio	6.50 to 1
Horsepower @ RPM	80 @ 4000
Max. Torque @ RPM	176 @ 1600
Electrical	6 Volt, pos. grd.

TRANSMISSION

Type	3 speed manual
Available	overdrive

REAR

Type	Hypoid, semi-floating
Ratio	4.10 to 1

TUNE UP

Spark Plug Gap	.025"
Point Gap	.020"
Cam Angle, Degrees	35
Timing	2° B.T.D.C.
Firing Order	153624
Tappet Clearances:	
Intake	.016"
Exhaust	.016"
Compression Pressure, Lbs	105
Idle Speed, RPM	500

BRAKES

Type	Hydraulic, int. exp.
Drum Diameter	9"

CAPACITIES

Cooling System, Qts	10
Fuel Tank, Gals	17
Crank Case, Qts	5
Trans. Pints	3.75
Differential, Pts	2.5

WHEEL ALIGNMENT

Caster, Degrees	0 to +1
Camber, Degrees	+¼ to +¾
Toe in, Inches	1/16 to ⅛

The New Identity: 1949·1954

This is it folks! This is when it all broke loose. From this point forward, for better or for worse, America was to be inextricably bound to modern times. We waited three years for the economic lag to tense for the occasion. With the back burners finally rekindled, the melting pot of the world was about to boil over with new ideas and a new identity.

The vehicle of our journey into 1949 will, as usual, be the automobile. The resplendent symbol of 20th-century man has a lot to say as our guide. Taking us into the era of modern times meant relinquishing much of its conventionality. Oh pooh, it was ready to go anyway! The '49 cars took to their new skin like a shark takes to water. Cadillac even sprouted "fishtail fins" to cope with the big new pond. Others grew teeth like a Barrucada, and chromed them to the gills! Oldsmobile sponsored a screaming new type of engine that declared supremacy over a suddenly impotent past. These were new cars, built to fulfill new dreams.

Too bad for Studebaker. Too bad for Packard. Too bad for Mr. Kaiser and Mr. Frazer, in spite of their ingenuity. All these cars missed the big style boat. Only perseverance was able to borrow back some of the time lost in their rush to present the all-new leftover dreamcar. That dream never materialized, leaving these manufacturers in the unfortunately precarious position of having to survive five years in a rough stream without a paddle. Five years was about how long their body shells had to last, you see, to offset the cost of retooling. None of the independents' woes, however, could match the heartbreak of Preston Tucker. His car, the Tucker, was too good to be allowed to live. This rear-engined hybrid looked like nothing ever seen, with its wandering Cyclopean headlight and its completely unorthodox blend of fastback and fantasy-land styling. It died in the courts, when they pulled the financial rug out from under Mr. Tucker before his creation could upset the whole apple cart of the automobile world. This is the stuff of legends. We don't really know how well the Tucker would have done on its own. What we do know is that it deserved the chance to find out.

What was this new breed of car that killed the Tucker? Where did it get its strength? To answer the latter, it relied on its ego, a prismatic array of things both opulent and ostentatious. The new cars embodied our recent peacock syndrome, but with the added flare of a thoroughly modern wardrobe. The power and the lines became an almost inseparable combination in most cases. Let me attempt to explain the feeling.

The new cars, in 1949, continued the squaring and the streamlining of their predecessors, except that the finishing touches, when applied to the mold, breathed life into the whole design. New for 1949 was the pillarless two-door hardtop, an open air offshoot of the convertible fad that was sweeping the country. The fender lines never quite evolved into the slab-sided renditions seen in the pre-war models. Instead, the rear fender hump was predominantly retained, giving the impression of a power bulge when accented with chrome spears. In the few instances (Ford Motor Company and some independents) where fenderlines entirely disappeared, a subtle curve, a dominant hoodline, or a crease of chrome marked their former location. This was a form of identity as surely as Buick's portholes or Ford's spinner grille.

Between 1949 and 1954, all cars swelled to meet the demands of a growing public appetite for status by size. But the appetite didn't come about until the cars were already bigger! It was a slow process at first, and went unnoticed in the beginning. The cars were merely ballooning to meet the perimeter of their new width, a result of those broad fenderless sides. Only by the end of this period was there an outward attempt to equate luxury with length.

Part of this movement toward open extravagance was contrived and part of it was an exponent of interchangeability. As the big three swung into high gear (with General Motors still leading the way) production efficiency became so refined that parts-standardization reached new limits. Some part on the Chevrolet were basically the same as those found on Cadillacs. Small and imperceptible at first, the list grew steadily, even until the present, and had the effect of making low-priced cars approach the larger luxury makes in size. The criterion of status by size was a valid sales pitch among luxury cars, but was gradually to diminish. There would have to be a substitute for class recognition.

The substitute came in the mechanical upheaval that purged the unglorious engineering lapse of the forties. As mentioned, Oldsmobile and Cadillac had pioneered the automatic transmission a decade earlier. When the 1949 cars arrived, G.M. added a kickdown device to insure that more torque would meet the road when it was needed. Suddenly, it was "automagic." Everyone rushed to produce a shiftless transmission. If they couldn't put one together quickly enough, they bought units from G.M. This was General Motor's grandest era. Ford was modern in approach, if not in definition, and Chrysler Corporation remained conservative while the independents tried anything that looked faintly hopeful for sales.

The biggest single push into modern times turned out to be that overhead V-8 engine. Oldsmobile, Cadillac's perennial testbed, beat big brother to the punch by a few days. What a punch! The power and efficiency of these new engines seemed limitless. By 1954, nearly everyone had a version of the overhead V-8. This became the new token of the status elite. The more expensive the car, the bigger the overhead; hence, the more powerful the image. Hot-rodders couldn't wait to stuff these outsized ego inflaters into their little deuce coupes. The torrid machines they created became dragsters and a new organized sport was born.

America the powerful was stirring the world with wheels — fast, sporty, colorful wheels. We blossomed then, and took a liking to anything that resembled our ego. More and more of those little European jobs dotted the landscape. America was not seeking the tired, the poor, the huddled masses. We were out to satisfy our position at the top of the pecking order. Even the sedate fell privy to an era of gadgets and conveniences that served notice of our renaissance.

Somewhere in the middle of all this fury, perhaps at the time of Ike's first heart attack, a certain indefinable weakness began to infect the American way. The moderate recession at this time did little to slow the wheels of progress, but it showed its stress in a more abstract way. Our introspection began to tell us that we were riding a false high. Had we begun to lose sight of the future again? Where would be the end to all that chrome and bulk and power?

The seeds of our contemplation were self-fulfilling. For the remainder of the period we would continue to fuel our extravagance while eroding the confidence that gave it to us. Joe McCarthy vocalized our fears to the point of giving ulcers to democracy. Was this the kind of balance we needed to temper our runaway opulence? The prescription of the day called for sane judgment and rational behavior. The original post-war effort that led us to this era was founded upon substantial effort toward preconceived goals. The effort was still there, but we were losing sight of the goals. They were becoming tarnished by the mortal aspect of their reality. We needed a new set of directives to supply reason for pumping the earth's resources into pleasure packages. By 1954 Europe was pretty well resettled and we could well afford to pause and ask ourselves what was next. The clues were all around us. We shall use our medium, the automobile, to analyze them.

Frazer having departed some time earlier, his partner, Kaiser, was about to bite the dust. The Henry J., of course, would follow its kin. Willys, the great war hero, was as forgotten as Ira Hayes, despite Bill Mauldin's elevating tales of its glory. Hudson, Nash and Packard were still captives of their own misdirected art. Of the independents, only Studebaker arrived at the finish line of this period with a proper concoction for the future. Something was wrong here, though. Critics the world over acclaimed Raymond Loewy's new (Studebaker) hardtop as the most aesthetically ideal car ever made. But it didn't click! Oh, sure, it had moderate success, but to find the real reasons for its lack of an overwhelming mandate, we must search the identity of the corporation.

I think what we find happening at this time (1949-54) is a loss of true individual identity. So drowned did it become in these years of rebuilding that we left it at the factory or at the office. Yes, we did have some expression of individuality in the glamour cars we drove, but they were inaccurate placebos sold by the corporate store. The dictates of their style were out of hand and out of reach for most of us. All we had to do was work hard enough to earn the right to choose from a preselected field. When a truly good idea (the 1953 Studebaker) hit the market with refreshing intrinsic appeal, we were afraid to react according to our own feelings. We were no longer even sure what these feelings were! Consequently, we preferred the security of the corporate wing over our own frail individuality. This may be an oversimplification of a complex situation. Neverthlesess, the auto industry had feelers of its own.

General Motor's Motorama shows were touring the country, collecting popular opinion about some new ideas. If we were lucky, the boats of the middle fifties would survive only a little while longer, simply because of the time lag involved in putting something new into effect. A couple of things seen at these roving dreamcar extravaganzas caught the public eye. While G.M. placated the people's demands in 1954 with a new upper body series, the industry quietly retooled for the biggest year of its lifetime. Panoramic (wraparound) windshields, racy dips at the beltline, and overt dual exhausts and dual color schemes portended the arrival of the big new year. A strange looking wagon, shrunken and plastic and inspired by the newly introduced Corvette, was to hold the key to a coming generation of cars. The new identity of 1949 was already largely outgrown. The time was ripe for instilling a little vigor into the American Dream Machine — very ripe.

1949 Crosley Hotshot

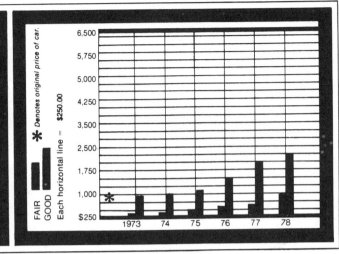

* Denotes original price of car.

FAIR
GOOD
Each horizontal line = $250.00

Crosley was not the first American built mini car, and from the looks of things, it won't be the last. Of all the minis (Bantam, American Austin, Metropolitan) it had the most extensive lineup, ranging from a station delivery model to a roadster-like version called the Hotshot. Quite a few Crosleys are still around. They have been for years an inexpensive source of interest and pleasure among appreciative car buffs. Except for the hard-to-find Hotshot, they will probably remain in this light, moving slowly but steadily upward in value. Some day, any Crosley will be redeemable for big bucks, but that is in the distant future. For the time being, only the Hotshot has favorable odds for success.

The car that couldn't make it at home went to England to become the basis of the Austin Healey Sprite. When it returned in that form it was better received, commanding today an excellent resale value. Not bad for a car that went almost unnoticed in its humble beginning!

The problem with finding a Hotshot today, as with any rare phenomenon, is finding enough good parts to put it together. By the time the expense of reassembly has been completed, the investment will probably necessitate a high exchange rate just to break even. Only a proficient craftsman of well-rounded ability stands a chance of coming out ahead with a Hotshot, unless the good fortune of finding a relatively intact specimen presents itself.

The Crosley is a good looking car, undoubtedly deserving of special interest in every sense of the word. It may be just the ticket for modern commuting. Aside from advantages of economy, this mini star looks bright as a hedge against inflation. Good things do still come in small packages.

SPECIFICATIONS

Wheelbase ....80"
Tread; Front, Rear ....40", 40"
Overall Length ....145"
Overall Width ....49"
Overall Height ....57"
Weight, Lbs 1210
Tire Size ....4.50 x 12"

ENGINE

Type ....In-line 4 cyl.
Bore & Stroke....................2.50" x 2.25"
Displacement, Cu. In. 44
Compression Ratio ....7.80 to 1
Horsepower @ RPM...............26.5 @ 5400
Max. Torque @ RPM ....33.5 @ 3000
Electrical ....6 Volt, pos. grd.

TRANSMISSION

Type ....3 speed manual
Available ....—

REAR

Type....................¼ elliptic, hypoid
Ratio ....5.17 to 1

TUNE UP

Spark Plug Gap ....025"
Point Gap ....020"
Cam Angle, Degrees 45
Timing ....12° B.T.D.C.
Firing Order 1342
Tappet Clearances:
    Intake ....005"
    Exhaust ....007"
Compression Pressure,
Lbs 135
Idle Speed, RPM 400

BRAKES

Type ....Hydraulic, int. exp.
Drum Diameter ....

CAPACITIES

Cooling System, Qts 4
Fuel Tank, Gals 6.5
Crank Case, Qts 2
Trans. Pints 1
Differential, Pts 1.5

WHEEL ALIGNMENT

Caster, Degrees............................+10
Camber, Degrees ....+2
Toe in, Inches ....3/64 to 1/16

1949 Dodge Wayfarer Roadster

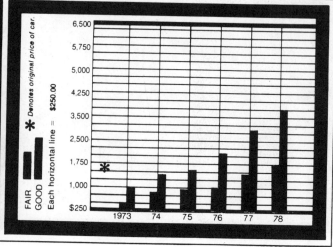

* Denotes original price of car.

Each horizontal line = $250.00

FAIR
GOOD

This is not a car you see every day. Nor is it typical of the kind of car you find forgotten in the corner of an old gas station. For that matter, it is not even a little old lady's car. It is rather rare on all these counts. Not many people ever owned one. In fact, few are aware that they ever existed.

But here it is. The 1949 Dodge Roadster was just that. It had plastic side curtains and a hand operated convertible top that covered its single bench seat. As you know, true roadsters never had roll-up side windows. If you were not aware of this fact, it's probably because there have been no roadsters produced in America in the last generation or more — except this one.

When Chrysler Corporation fitted Dodge and Plymouth with new bodies for 1949, Plymouth made a neat little business coupe, one version of which is discussed later on. Dodge took the same car and removed the top. They placed it with canvas and, as this was a roadster, did not even need concern themselves with the side windows! It made a spiffy package. Apparently not enough people felt it spiffy to cope with the removable plexiglass side curtains, though, and it sold very little. Toward the end, Dodge gave this model roll-up side windows; but it was too late to salvage the project.

Being a standard Dodge in every other respect (at a time when standard meant no deviations and precious few options), the Roadster's obvious

claim to fame is in its name. It's amazing how these cars have been overlooked for so long by so many. Now that prices of all 1949 models are rising, the Roadster is no longer a "cheap pick up." It still has not crested any wave of popularity, but sooner or later it's bound to be noticed. The car actually has no weaknesses. It is meek, but the old Ford roadsters of the thirties were also intended to be humble conveyances. As a point of comparison, a rough 1930 Ford Roadster is worth a quick couple of grand. That should inspire enough incentive to organize your own scavenger hunt.

Keep your eyes open. These Dodges pop up in the darnedest places and at the darnedest times. And if you ever get hold of one, it's for sure you'll have the most special-interest car to come along in twenty-five years. If you like your automobiles, you should also get the darnedest thrills of your life out of this obscure little roadster. Happy hunting!

SPECIFICATIONS

Wheelbase	123.5"
Tread; Front, Rear	56", 57"
Overall Length	204"
Overall Width	73"
Overall Height	66"
Weight, Lbs	3385
Tire Size	7.10 x 15"

ENGINE

Type	L-Head 6 cyl.
Bore & Stroke	3.25" x 4.625"
Displacement, Cu. In.	230.2
Compression Ratio	7.00 to 1
Horsepower @ RPM	103 @ 3600
Max. Torque @ RPM	184 @ 1200
Electrical	6 Volt, pos. grd.

TRANSMISSION

Type	Semi-automatic
Available	3 speed manual, overdrive

REAR

Type	Hypoid, semi-floating
Ratio	4.10 to 1

TUNE UP

Spark Plug Gap	.035"
Point Gap	.020"
Cam Angle, Degrees	38
Timing	T.D.C.
Firing Order	153624
Tappet Clearances:	
Intake	.008"
Exhaust	.010"
Compression Pressure, Lbs	160
Idle Speed, RPM	450

BRAKES

Type	Hydraulic, int. exp.
Drum Diameter	11"

CAPACITIES

Cooling System, Qts	15
Fuel Tank, Gals	17
Crank Case, Qts	5
Trans. Pints	2.75"
Differential, Pts	3.25"

WHEEL ALIGNMENT

Caster, Degrees	−1 to +1
Camber, Degrees	0 to +¾
Toe in, Inches	0 to 1/16"

1949 Ford 2-Door Coupe

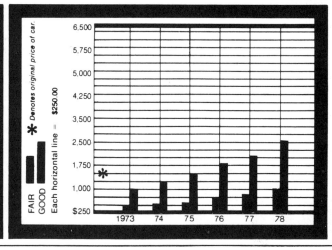

The "shoebox" Ford will now stand on its own merit. Its form in metal has always inspired the personal refinement of customizers. Slab sides with smoothed hood-fender junctions, the boxy shape just looked like an unfinished mold too good for a young designer to pass up. The original custom car kit came on a 1-to-1 scale. You really could transform it with ease into any personality of your choosing — and then drive it away. In this respect, it is quite similar to the 1957 Chevy Bel Air. In terms of getting an early start on a reputation, it is similar to its ancestor, the 1940 Ford Coupe. Neither of these analogies is detrimental to its health. Today, with chopping and sectioning and lowering blocks a thing of the past (engine swaps are still happening), the pasture of this Ford looks greener than ever. It is probably the tint of money that lends it this hue. Certainly time has been favorable to the 1949-50 Ford Coupes. There is a surprising number of intact survivors.

With nothing to break the reflection on the side, a good coat of paint will magnify the beauty of this car many fold. That's what the shoebox Ford is all about. People see many things in it, most of which it is not. The illusion of a proportioned car with an unproportioned reputation is an awesome combination. Nobody ever said it was bland looking, unless I just did. It is all things to all people.

The 1949-50 Ford Coupe has been collected for a long time now, even though it is relatively young. For this reason any imaginable part can be had for it. Only it will cost a fortune. This is the price of an early success. By the time you refurbish this cute coupe you picked up for a song, your wallet is empty. You have invested in it as much as it is worth. This is when the sum of the parts becomes greater than the whole. It also is a general truth that because of the scarcity of old parts, the credibility of the car stands on the value ceiling created by their demand. In other words, you can't build one for less. Money is too expensive now.

SPECIFICATIONS

Wheelbase	114"
Tread; Front, Rear	56", 56"
Overall Length	197"
Overall Width	72"
Overall Height	65"
Weight, Lbs	3030
Tire Size	6.00 x 16"

ENGINE

Type	Flathead V-8
Bore & Stroke	3.4375" x 3.75"
Displacement, Cu. In.	239.4
Compression Ratio	6.80 to 1
Horsepower @ RPM	100 @ 3600
Max. Torque @ RPM	181 @ 2000
Electrical	6 Volt, pos. grd.

TRANSMISSION

Type	3 speed manual
Available	overdrive

REAR

Type	Hypoid, ½ floating
Ratio	3.73 to 1

TUNE UP

Spark Plug Gap	.032"
Point Gap	.016"
Cam Angle, Degrees	.30
Timing	2° B.T.D.C.
Firing Order	15486372
Tappet Clearances:	
Intake	.011"
Exhaust	.015"
Compression Pressure,	
Lbs	110
Idle Speed, RPM	475

BRAKES

Type	Hydraulic, int. exp.
Drum Diameter	10"

CAPACITIES

Cooling System, Qts	22
Fuel Tank, Gals	16
Crank Case, Qts	4
Trans. Pints	4
Differential, Pts	3.5

WHEEL ALIGNMENT

Caster, Degrees	−¾ to +¼
Camber, Degrees	−¼ to +¾
Toe in, Inches	1/16 to 1/8

1949 Lincoln Cosmopolitan

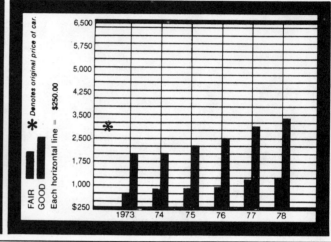

The Cosmopolitan was the real Lincoln in 1949, the standard Lincoln series consisting of warmed-over Mercury components. Not that the standard Lincolns for 1949 were not good looking or well built cars, for they were. So were the 1949 Mercurys, for that matter. But Lincoln, the perennial choice of the status elite, was the beautiful Cosmopolitan in 1949. Differentiated by a continuous sweeping fender line, front to rear, and an interesting chrome-bordered window line, the Cosmopolitan was for Lincoln what the 98 was for Oldsmobile. Or, if you prefer, the standard Lincoln was to the Cosmopolitan as the Clipper was to the big Packards.

All Cosmopolitans came from the factory with standard power windows and a power-operated front seat. Ironically, this was the same spring-loaded hydraulic system used on the Mercury convertibles. For the Cosmopolitan, there was also a spiffier interior, complemented by a few other standard niceties.

Those sweeping chrome spears that brow Lincoln's wheel cutouts may look familiar. They were heralded as the brutish epitome of Teutonic flair when Mercedes reintroduced them in 1955 on their unparalleled 300 SL gullwing coupe and roadster models. There really is nothing new under the sun! At the upper corners of a massive, but vaguely harmonious grille, there can be found another distinguishing feature of '49-51

Lincolns: tunnelled headlights. Lined with chrome, the recessed luminaries were duplicated in simplicity by large round taillights. Somehow the car looked as if it were a fresh clay mold streamlined in the Chrysler Thunderbolt school of philosophy, and sweepingly knifed with the accent of its final character by some anonymous master.

This is a Lincoln that came from nowhere and went nowhere. It was not at all like previous or later Lincolns. The ghost-like car that appeared and astonished post-war America vanished as quickly, leaving many to rephrase that famous Lone Ranger query, "Say, what was that car?" The answer, my friend, is a Lincoln, and you'll have to trade in all your silver bullets to get one.

SPECIFICATIONS

Wheelbase	125"
Tread; Front, Rear	59", 60"
Overall Length	220"
Overall Width	79"
Overall Height	65"
Weight, Lbs	4315
Tire Size	8.20 x 15"

ENGINE

Type	Flathead V-8
Bore & Stroke	3.50" x 4.375"
Displacement, Cu. In.	336.7
Compression Ratio	7.00 to 1
Horsepower @ RPM	152 @ 3600
Max. Torque @ RPM	265 @ 2000
Electrical	6 Volt, pos. grd.

TRANSMISSION

Type	3 speed manual
Available	overdrive

REAR

Type	Hypoid, semi-floating
Ratio	3.91 to 1

TUNE UP

Spark Plug Gap	.030"
Point Gap	.015" - .018"
Cam Angle, Degrees	26-30
Timing	4° B.T.D.C.
Firing Order	15486372
Tappet Clearances:	
Intake	Zero, hydraulic
Exhaust	Zero, hydraulic
Compression Pressure, Lbs	110
Idle Speed, RPM	500

BRAKES

Type	Hydraulic, int. exp.
Drum Diameter	12"

CAPACITIES

Cooling System, Qts	34.5
Fuel Tank, Gals	19.5
Crank Case, Qts	6
Trans. Pints	3.2
Differential, Pts	4

WHEEL ALIGNMENT

Caster, Degrees	0 to +1/2
Camber, Degrees	0 to +3/4
Toe in, Inches	0 to 5/32

1949 Mercury Coupe

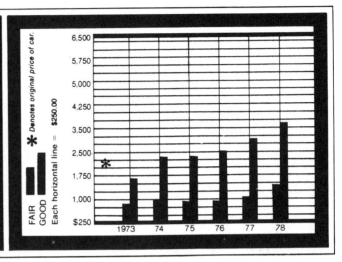

James Dean may have died in a Porsche, but he lived in a Mercury Coupe. The black leather jacket set immortalized the 1949-50 Merc Coupes, and James Dean was their hero. These Mercurys are also among the most customized of all times. Early renditions popularized the chopped top and flamed paint jobs as well as frenched headlights and grille area. With lakes pipes and lowering blocks all the way around, these cars were more show than go.

Yet the venerable flatheat served many a '49-50 Merc quite well. Available speed parts covered the gamut of a hot-rodder's needs, and many needed all they could get to keep up with the Olds and Cadillac overhead engines. Some chose to switch rather than fight, and installed the overhead in their Mercs.

The car that created all this sensation was a heartbeat ahead of the crowd, even in bone stock form. The first all-new body for Mercury in many a year was mean and modern, but not the least bit disproportioned or distasteful. The rakish slope of the coupe's quarter windows was more in the eye of the beholder than the actual metal of the car. But there was no illusion about the low, wide stance of the new Mercury. That was as real as the wide rounded hood and the flushed fender lines that enhanced it.

These cars were as sweet to drive as they were to look at. Surging with confidence at virtually any speed, the

feelings inspired by driving this car seem insanely logical, in keeping with its character. Insane, because it doesn't seem real to know such joy on wheels. But then that's where James Dean came in. Even now, there's probably a good five hundred dollar's worth of James Dean inspiration in the price of every sanitary '50 Merc Coupe. And nobody is being short-changed!

SPECIFICATIONS

Wheelbase	118"
Tread; Front, Rear	58.5", 60"
Overall Length	207"
Overall Width	77"
Overall Height	65"
Weight, Lbs	3430
Tire Size	6.00 x 16"

ENGINE

Type	Flathead V-8
Bore & Stroke	3.1875" x 3.75"
Displacement, Cu. In.	239.4
Compression Ratio	6.80 to 1
Horsepower @ RPM	110 @ 3600
Max. Torque @ RPM	200 @ 2000
Electrical	6 Volt, pos. grd.

TRANSMISSION

Type	3 speed manual
Available	overdrive

REAR

Type	Hypoid, semi-floating
Ratio	3.78 to 1

TUNE UP

Spark Plug Gap	.030"
Point Gap	.015"
Cam Angle, Degrees	28
Timing	2° B.T.D.C.
Firing Order	15486372
Tappet Clearances:	
Intake	.014"
Exhaust	.014"
Compression Pressure,	
Lbs	115
Idle Speed, RPM	440

BRAKES

Type	Hydraulic, int. exp.
Drum Diameter	11"

CAPACITIES

Cooling System, Qts	21
Fuel Tank, Gals	16
Crank Case, Qts	4
Trans. Pints	4
Differential, Pts	3.5

WHEEL ALIGNMENT

Caster, Degrees	−¼ pref.
Camber, Degrees	+½ pref.
Toe in, Inches	⅛ to 3/16 (early cars), 1/16 to ⅛ (late cars)

1949 Oldsmobile 88 Fastback

As spacious as a sedan—as convenient as a coupe—it's the streamlined Futuramic Oldsmobile Club Sedan. Wide doors and the divided front seat offer easy access to the rear seat. There's plenty of room for six big people in the roomy, ultra-modern Fisher Body. It's a "New Thrill" in riding comfort.

FUTURAMIC "76" AND "88" 2-DOOR CLUB SEDAN

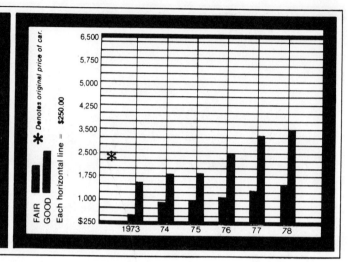

Recent enthusiasm for 1949 and 1950 Oldsmobiles is kicking up almost as much dust as the cars did when they were new. At that time, nothing could catch them on the NASCAR circuit. They had too much of an edge with their new overhead, oversquare V-8 engine. As if this were not enough, the lower series shared a body with Chevrolet, making them both light and powerful. I chose to highlight the 88 Fastback model because it is lean and lithe in looks as well as spirit. The coupe and convertible models are currently as popular if equipped with the proper drivetrain. Convertibles and coupes are common attractions, though, in the world of special-interest autos. The Fastback, on the other hand, is a totally uncommon car.

The quiet ride and well-mannered response of this Olds are due to its tight, aerodynamically efficient body being fitted to an all coil suspension, stiffened by stabilizer bars plus front and rear-mounted anti-roll bars. A rear axle ratio of 3.64 to 1 provides energetic response, even with the four-speed hydramatic transmission. This is because it had the now familiar kickdown device to add the punch of a lower gear when the throttle was stomped.

The standard grey broadcloth interior was nice to look at and comfortable to sit on. The firm seats sat you up high where you could get a commanding feeling of the road. A rich but not overworked dash layout placed the optional clock into the nacelle in the center of its top. There was no power steering to be had in 1949 or 1950, so the large steering wheel at least had the effect of reducing the pull required to turn this massive car.

Some cars have the honor of introducing a new idea to the public. Seldom does it become either universal or enduring. At its usual best, it kicks off a fad that dies down in a few years. The Fastback body on this Olds is a good example of such short-lived status. But, beyond fad and fancy lies the true contribution of the 1949 Oldsmobile. After more than twenty-five years, the engine it introduced (along with Cadillac) is still the undisputed number-one power plant of the American automobile. You can't argue with this kind of success.

SPECIFICATIONS

Wheelbase	120"
Tread; Front, Rear	57", 59"
Overall Length	202"
Overall Width	75"
Overall Height	64"
Weight, Lbs	3515
Tire Size	7.60 x 15"

ENGINE

Type	Overhead V-8
Bore & Stroke	3.75" x 3.4375"
Displacement, Cu. In.	303.7
Compression Ratio	7.25 to 1
Horsepower @ RPM	135 @ 3600
Max. Torque @ RPM	263 @ 1800
Electrical	6 Volt, neg. grd.

TRANSMISSION

Type	3 speed manual
Available	Automatic

REAR

Type	Hypoid, semi-floating
Ratio	3.64 to 1

TUNE UP

Spark Plug Gap	.030"
Point Gap	.0145"
Cam Angle, Degrees	15
Timing	2.5° B.T.D.C.
Firing Order	18736542
Tappet Clearances:	
Intake	Zero, hydraulic
Exhaust	Zero, hydraulic
Compression Pressure,	
Lbs	183
Idle Speed, RPM	375

BRAKES

Type	Hydraulic, int. exp.
Drum Diameter	11"

CAPACITIES

Cooling System, Qts	21.5
Fuel Tank, Gals	18
Crank Case, Qts	5
Trans. Pints	3
Differential, Pts	3.75

WHEEL ALIGNMENT

Caster, Degrees	0 to −¾
Camber, Degrees	−¼ to −¾
Toe in, Inches	1/16 to 1/8

1949 Packard Station Wagon

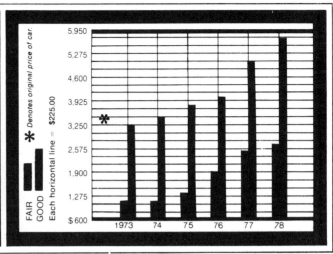

As woodies go, this was not a sensation. As styles go, this was not a sensational one. Yet, as Packards go, this was, and is, a sensational car. It doesn't seem to add up, but let me explain.

After the war, Packard was fighting an uphill battle to continue its long-established standards of quality and excellence. The great classic era of the thirties was the pinnacle of its success. In those years when craftsmanship was at its zenith, the great cars embodied the kind of dedication and aspiration that the cathedrals of the Renaissance had depicted hundreds of years before. And the resultant perfection of accomplishment was no less revered. The only way to go from there was down. The Depression years forced the consolidation and elimination of many fine names. Then came the technological surge brought about by World War II, and by the time the post-war autos were rolling out, it was a whole new ball game.

Packard's post-war energies were dedicated to design rather than quality of craftsmanship. Escalating costs prompted the decision to moderate previous standards of achievement. New goals meant new ideals, and for Packard it meant the beginning of the end. There was no way this John Henry could beat the machinery of progress. In 1949, the Packard body was a smoothed, rounded lump of streamlining with only a hint of its former stately grille

recalling any majesty. The quality was there, even if the engineering was becoming dated. The problem was that Packard was lost in this new world. It couldn't cope and it couldn't quit.

Even the newest aspect of the 1949 Packard, its appearance, was keyed in on a pre-war concept of streamlining, similar to the Chrysler Thunderbolt dreamcar that never materialized and did not even exist after the war! The wagon looked pretty graceful, though. The slope and taper of its rear was pleasing as a Packard's should be, trading the boxiness of contemporary wagons for a muted reminder of the great boat-tail bodies of its heyday. Though the wood was real, the car was mostly formed of metal: again the product of evolution. This station wagon is very, very rare, which makes it very, very expensive. Ask the man who owns one!

SPECIFICATIONS

Wheelbase	127"
Tread; Front, Rear	60", 61"
Overall Length	212"
Overall Width	77"
Overall Height	64"
Weight, Lbs	3870
Tire Size	7.60 x 15"

ENGINE

Type	L-Head, straight 8 cyl.
Bore & Stroke	3.50" x 4.25"
Displacement, Cu. In.	327
Compression Ratio	7.00 to 1
Horsepower @ RPM	145 @ 3600
Max. Torque @ RPM	266 @ 2000
Electrical	6 Volt, pos. grd.

TRANSMISSION

Type	3 speed manual
Available	overdrive

REAR

Type	Hypoid, semi-floating
Ratio	3.90 to 1

TUNE UP

Spark Plug Gap	.028"
Point Gap	.017"
Cam Angle, Degrees	27
Timing	6° B.T.D.C.
Firing Order	16258374
Tappet Clearances:	
Intake	.007"
Exhaust	.010"
Compression Pressure, Lbs	110
Idle Speed, RPM	400-450

BRAKES

Type	Hydraulic, int. exp.
Drum Diameter	12"

CAPACITIES

Cooling System, Qts	19
Fuel Tank, Gals	20
Crank Case, Qts	7
Trans. Pints	2
Differential, Pts	4

WHEEL ALIGNMENT

Caster, Degrees	+1½ to +2½
Camber, Degrees	−¼ to +¼
Toe in, Inches	0

1949 Plymouth Wooden Wagon

The Special De Luxe Station Wagon

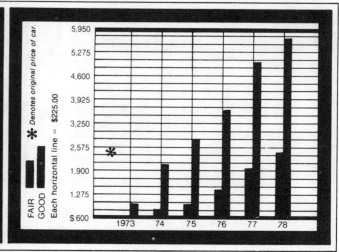

* Denotes original price of car.

FAIR GOOD
Each horizontal line = $225.00

The name of this book is Real Steel. For this car, it could as well have been "Real Wood." In the last two years, wood has been the quickest rising, quickest moving item on the market. Wooden station wagons have doubled or better in value. Woodies that were literally unheard of in 1973 now command thousands of dollars if in "restorable condition." Ford Sportsmans are rare and have always been valuable. The same is basically true of Chrysler Town & Countrys; at least of the earlier variety. But 1949-51 Ford and Mercury wagons, 1949-50 Chrysler Corporation woodies, Chevy, Pontiac, Buick and Olds woodies, and, understandably, even Packards are climbing out of sight.

Well, Ford and Mercury no longer have the woody market cornered. In truth, they never should have. The Plymouth Station Wagon pictured above is every bit up to the standards of its peers, both in looks and in construction. It is very similar, in fact, to the 1949 Ford Wagon, except that the front end metal says Plymouth. That means it shares standard components with the rest of the Plymouth lineup, and it has the same L-head six-cylinder engine. The rest of the car is an exercise in art. The thing that makes woodies so appealing is the combination of the natural, aesthetic quality of wood with the precision of man-made metal. Two different worlds meet in a matrix of harmony.

The feelings of both man the animal and man the master are satisfied with a woody — any woody. If you seek a three dimensional thrill, this has to be as close as you can come in the world of materialism. And, if you get materialistic about it, you're apt to be equally rewarded. You just can't lose with a woody!

SPECIFICATIONS

Wheelbase . . . . .119"
Tread; Front, Rear .55", 58"
Overall Length . . . . .193"
Overall Width . . . . .74"
Overall Height . . . . .65.5"
Weight, Lbs 3062
Tire Size . . . . .6.70 x 15"

ENGINE

Type . . . . .L-Head, in-line 6 cyl.
Bore & Stroke . . . . .3.25" x 4.375"
Displacement, Cu. In. 217.8
Compression Ratio . . . . .7.00 to 1
Horsepower @ RPM . . . . .97 @ 3600
Max. Torque @ RPM . . . . .175 @ 1200
Electrical . . . . .6 Volt, pos. grd.

TRANSMISSION

Type . . . . .3 speed manual
Available . . . . .Semi-automatic

REAR

Type . . . . .Hypoid, semi-floating
Ratio . . . . .3.90 to 1

TUNE UP

Spark Plug Gap . . . . .038"
Point Gap . . . . .020"
Cam Angle, Degrees 38
Timing . . . . .T.D.C.
Firing Order 153624
Tappet Clearances:
    Intake . . . . .008"
    Exhaust . . . . .010"
Compression Pressure,
Lbs 160
Idle Speed, RPM 450

BRAKES

Type . . . . .Hydraulic, int. exp.
Drum Diameter . . . . .10"

CAPACITIES

Cooling System, Qts 15
Fuel Tank, Gals 17
Crank Case, Qts 5
Trans. Pints 2.75
Differential, Pts 3.25

WHEEL ALIGNMENT

Caster, Degrees . . . .−1 to +1
Camber, Degrees . . . . .0 to +¾
Toe in, Inches . . . . .0 to ¹/₁₆

1950 Willys Jeepster

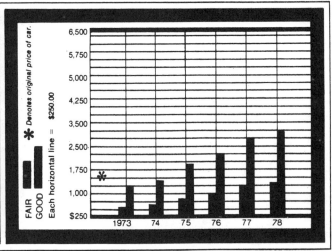

There is a little doubt that a healthy government contract kept Willys alive through the war years. That "general purpose" vehicle (from which we get the initials G.P., and hence the phoneme "jeep") emerged in 1945 as a national byword for a strong utility vehicle. So why not make it available to the public? The personification of this good idea was unveiled as the 1950 Jeepster.

The Jeepster resembled its fighting father in many ways. It had the same abbreviated fenders on all four corners and the same distinctively Willys flat hood that narrowed in front to house the unpretentious grille and headlights. The extra tire wasn't on the side like the jeep, but the Jeepster also carried its spare outside the confines of the body. This is because it had no trunk.

What it did have was an extra seat inside its lengthier body. Rarely has it been classified as such, but with its full canvas top and side curtains, this car is eligible to be called a phaeton — or at least a roadster of sorts. You can bet such a classification would drive the prices up!

Alas! The Jeepster receives no such honor. It is as it always has been, a hard-working, fun-to-drive replica of its father. It has earned the recognition it is attaining of late, but be quick. Prices are in a state of flux, leaning, as always, toward the higher extremes.

The Jeepster is a direct descendant of the Audie Murphy of the auto world. If there is an analogy to be made by his precedent, remember that Mr. Murphy was unable to cash in on his popularity for stardom. How much stardom the Jeepster will attain depends on the role it is expected to play. If prices go too high, the worthy little four-banger will find itself outclassed.

SPECIFICATIONS

Wheelbase	.104"
Tread; Front, Rear	.55", 57"
Overall Length	.176"
Overall Width	.69"
Overall Height	.72"
Weight, Lbs	.2587
Tire Size	.6.70 x 15"

ENGINE

Type	.Flathead, 4 cyl.
Bore & Stroke	.3.125" x 4.375"
Displacement, Cu. In.	.134.2
Compression Ratio	.7.40 to 1
Horsepower @ RPM	.72 @ 4000
Max. Torque @ RPM	.114 @ 2000
Electrical	.6 Volt, neg. grd.

TRANSMISSION

Type	.3 speed manual
Available	.overdrive

REAR

Type	.Hypoid, semi-floating
Ratio	.5.38 to 1

TUNE UP

Spark Plug Gap	.030"
Point Gap	.020"
Cam Angle, Degrees	.51
Timing	.T.D.C.
Firing Order	.1342
Tappet Clearances:	
Intake	.012"
Exhaust	.012"
Compression Pressure,	
Lbs	.135
Idle Speed, RPM	.350

BRAKES

Type	.Hydraulic, int. exp.
Drum Diameter	.9.9"

CAPACITIES

Cooling System, Qts	.11
Fuel Tank, Gals	.15
Crank Case, Qts	.4
Trans. Pints	.1.5
Differential, Pts	.2

WHEEL ALIGNMENT

Caster, Degrees	.−1 to +1
Camber, Degrees	.+1 to +1½
Toe in, Inches	.1/16 to 1/8

1950 Mercury Convertible

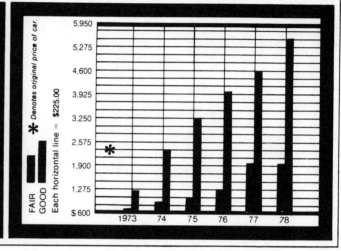

Cars are a lot like dogs in some ways. Both experience popularity peaks and both have steady favorites. For a while, cocker spaniels were in vogue, followed by poodles, shepherds and so on. With cars, the fad runs a lot quicker, with only the truly timeless favorites consistently in the winner's circle. In the last twenty-five years, cars like the '40 Ford Coupe and the '55 Chevy Hardtop have dominated the scene. Yet, there always looms a Mercury convertible in the nearby scenario. Usually it is a '49 or a '50 (there's not much difference except to nit-pickers) and the only thing holding it back is its limited availability.

The '49-50 Merc Convertible is not vulgar in the sense of its performance-oriented company. When it is hopped up, it is done with class, relying on a pair of finned aluminum heads and a couple or three Strombergs atop its much ogled flathead engine. Today, it won't win many races in such form, but that is not the position of this retired heavyweight. This Mercury never stepped down, you see; it only moved aside gracefully.

To return for a moment to canine similarities: much of what makes a champion is in the breeding — that is basically why the '50 Mercury Convertible is a perennial favorite. It has the lithe, spirited lines of a pedigree and the obedient heart of a well-trained watchdog. Few cars can better its well-proportioned display of classic characteristics. Overt cars,

such as the '40 Ford and '55 Chevy, ascend to great things. Etherial masterpieces like this Mercury are born there. Price tags that are the match of anything overt tell you so.

What kind of dog is the 1950 Mercury Convertible? A retriever, of course! Capable of retrieving more than mere dollars, it is the kind of car that retrieves and even recreates dreams. It is a constant reflection of its owner's impeccable taste. More than that, it is the embodiment of it!

SPECIFICATIONS

Wheelbase	.118"
Tread; Front, Rear	.58.5", 60"
Overall Length	.207"
Overall Width	.77"
Overall Height	.65"
Weight, Lbs	.3458
Tire Size	.6.00 x 16"

ENGINE

Type	.Flathead V-8
Bore & Stroke	.3.1875" x 3.75"
Displacement, Cu. In.	.239.4
Compression Ratio	.6.80 to 1
Horsepower @ RPM	.110 @ 3600
Max. Torque @ RPM	.200 @ 2000
Electrical	.6 Volt, pos. grd.

TRANSMISSION

Type	.3 speed manual
Available	.overdrive

REAR

Type	.Hypoid, semi-floating
Ratio	.3.78 to 1

TUNE UP

Spark Plug Gap	.030"
Point Gap	.015"
Cam Angle, Degrees	.28
Timing	.2° B.T.D.C.
Firing Order	.15486372
Tappet Clearances:	
Intake	.014"
Exhaust	.014"
Compression Pressure,	
Lbs	.115
Idle Speed, RPM	.440

BRAKES

Type	.Hydraulic, int. exp.
Drum Diameter	.11"

CAPACITIES

Cooling System, Qts	.21
Fuel Tank, Gals	.16
Crank Case, Qts	.4
Trans. Pints	.4
Differential, Pts	.3.5

WHEEL ALIGNMENT

Caster, Degrees	.−¼ pref.
Camber, Degrees	.+½ pref.
Toe in, Inches	.³/₁₆

1950 Nash Rambler Convertible

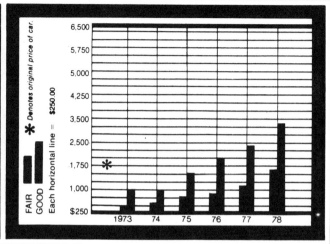

This car appeared twice on the market. Few noticed it either time. After some success, it fell victim to a glutted market. It was expanded from a 100" to a 108" wheelbase, but still fell quietly by the wayside after 1955. The second time around, none other than George Romney was responsible for its debut. This time (1958) it was called the American. It did well for a few more years, but the zesty, zippy feel of the original Rambler was lost.

That cute little convertible with the continental kit was the right car at the wrong time. Nash-Kelvinator beat the rush by a few too many years when it tried to undersell the low-priced three with its glamorous little car. They provided the industry with more than one definition of foresight, though, in putting the car together. Ideas such as unit body construction were new in 1950, pioneered by the Rambler. To make the car ride softer, the front coil springs were placed exceptionally high — an idea seen later on the Ford Mustang. Extruded aluminum upper window moldings lowered production costs and strengthened the body to accept the unique convertible top. Finally, by destroking the standard statesman engine, Nash had a reliable and economical powerplant.

It's a shame not enough people wanted to give a home to a Rambler. They were sold factory-equipped with options costing as much as $300 on other cars in an effort to make it the second choice of luxury car owners. Ramblers didn't have a lot of

trunkspace, but they were large enough inside to seat five adults comfortably. Even a hardtop and a station wagon were offered by 1951. Poor handling may have accounted for some loss of sales but probably not as much as the timing of its introduction.

The timing is quite good now for these cars. They are a bit rare, but suddenly after twenty-five years of oblivion, have returned as eye-catching knockouts. The lines are unmistakably Nash, with fully skirted front wheels and fake air scoop at the hood-fender confluence. The sporty convertible top and outside mounted spare are touches of finesse not seen in a while. Yes, they look good now. They won't pass a Cadillac in second gear, but they may soon pass it in resale value.

SPECIFICATIONS

Wheelbase ....100"
Tread; Front, Rear ....53", 53"
Overall Length ....176"
Overall Width ....74"
Overall Height ....60"
Weight, Lbs 2430
Tire Size ....5.90 x 15"

ENGINE

Type ....L-Head, in-line 6 cyl.
Bore & Stroke ....3.125" x 3.75"
Displacement, Cu. In. 172.6
Compression Ratio ....7.25 to 1
Horsepower @ RPM ....82 @ 3800
Max. Torque @ RPM ....138 @ 1600
Electrical ....6 Volt, pos. grd.

TRANSMISSION

Type ....3 speed manual
Available ....overdrive

REAR

Type ....Hypoid, semi-floating
Ratio ....3.80 to 1

TUNE UP

Spark Plug Gap ....030"
Point Gap ....020"
Cam Angle, Degrees 35
Timing ....T.D.C.
Firing Order 153624
Tappet Clearances:
  Intake ....015"
  Exhaust ....015"
Compression Pressure,
  Lbs 120
Idle Speed, RPM 475

BRAKES

Type ....Hydraulic, int. exp.
Drum Diameter ....8"

CAPACITIES

Cooling System, Qts 14
Fuel Tank, Gals 20
Crank Case, Qts 5
Trans. Pints 1
Differential, Pts 3

WHEEL ALIGNMENT

Caster, Degrees ....+¾ to +1¼
Camber, Degrees ....−¼ to +¾
Toe in, Inches ....1/16 to 3/16

1950 Plymouth Business Coupe

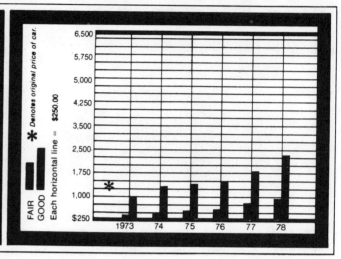

In 1950, as you know, the car industry was collectively pursuing the first modern stage of design. Front fenders were already faired into the body and rear fenders retained only a token image of their former bulging shape. Since World War II, when materials again became abundant, styles lavished chrome plating. The bright stuff was mostly up front in 1950, on the ornate grilles and on increasingly massive bumpers. It took a while to subdue the over-use of chrome, much as it takes a while to stop pampering a new baby.

When Detroit's new babies arrived, they left behind many interesting variations of the older bodies. A few others died more slowly. One of these old soldiers was the one-seat business coupe. A typical example of its adaptation to the new bodies is illustrated by the 1950 Plymouth model. Lines that were formerly pleasing because of more proportionate dimensions (for this application) suddenly looked like a small box placed in the center of a large box. The staggered protrusions of the older fenders and hood were fairly balanced with the long, graceful slope of the trunk. The new box styles were an inevitable advance in concept: the lower hood and slab sides created a squared image that was duplicated at the rear by boxing the trunk shape.

In spite of the fact that they look funny, these cars are conspicuous enough to be "neat." They are also the last

representatives of a style that was always admired by collectors. These are the primary sources of the value of the Plymouth Business Coupe. A standard Plymouth sedan of this vintage is just now approaching the point of recognition by collectors; but if it isn't clean, it isn't worth it — whereas the coupe is!

Certainly, the source of value cannot be found in the mechanics of this car. For 1950 Plymouth offered nothing to lift the engineers' eyebrows. The truth is, it hadn't for years and wouldn't for years; it preferred the solid reliability of its proven L-head six. Even at a time when automatics were the rage, Plymouth would go no more than half way with its semi-automatic transmission.*

History has a way of correcting the assumptions of the present. Detroit corrected the assumption that there was a demand for business coupes in 1953 by allowing their demise. Time has shown us that the popularity of the business coupe is still alive and well and living in old Plymouths.

*It's not fair to be demeaning about this transmission. The semi-automatic was indeed one of the easiest, most enjoyable types to use. It gave the driver the choice of shifting. This is a much missed alternative.

SPECIFICATIONS

Wheelbase ....111"
Tread; Front, Rear ....55", 58"
Overall Length ....188"
Overall Width ....73"
Overall Height ....63"
Weight, Lbs 2975
Tire Size ....6.40 x 15"

ENGINE

Type ....L-Head, in-line 6 cyl.
Bore & Stroke ....3.25" x 4.375"
Displacement, Cu. In. 217.8
Compression Ratio ....7.00 to 1
Horsepower @ RPM ....97 @ 3600
Max. Torque @ RPM......................175 @ 1200
Electrical ....6 Volt, pos. grd.

TRANSMISSION

Type ....3 speed manual
Available ....Semi-automatic

REAR

Type ....Hypoid, semi-floating
Ratio ....3.73 to 1

TUNE UP

Spark Plug Gap ....035"
Point Gap ....018" - .020"
Cam Angle, Degrees 38
Timing ....T.D.C.
Firing Order 153624
Tappet Clearances:
   Intake ....008"
   Exhaust ....010"
Compression Pressure,
Lbs 150
Idle Speed, RPM 450

BRAKES

Type ....Hydraulic, int. exp.
Drum Diameter ....10"

CAPACITIES

Cooling System, Qts 13
Fuel Tank, Gals 17
Crank Case, Qts 5
Trans. Pints 2.75
Differential, Pts 3.25

WHEEL ALIGNMENT

Caster, Degrees ....−1 to +1
Camber, Degrees ....0 to +¾
Toe in, Inches ....0 to 1/16

1950 Plymouth Special Deluxe

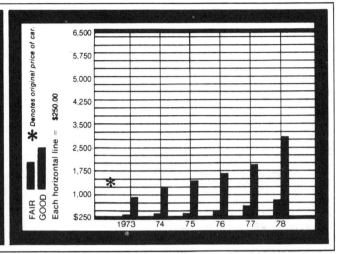

This car is turning out to be a dark horse. Years ago, when Dodges and Plymouths of this shape were abundant I always thought they would go places. I know that cars are made for going to places — and you know the places I had in mind, so let's get on with it! They seemed to have a dutiful type of character that made you want to take one home and be its friend. They were much nicer looking than the standard, boxy sedans, and worlds apart from the coupes and convertibles. They just seemed to have a pleasant, inviting message of their own.

In those years, Hudson had a notchback; G.M. had its torpedo coupes and its fastbacks; and Nash had its bathtub, or cucumber, or whatever it was. Even the Henry J. had a sloping roofline between its fins. Surely, somewhere in this company there was room for one more hunchback! The Plymouth Turtleback deserved, at least, the respect of its peers.

They were stout-hearted cars, those Plymouths and Dodges. They could take a lot of punishment. Unfortunately, they usually got it. This is because nobody cared to care for them. Here it is twenty-five years later, and all the other members of the fastback fraternity have gone on to better things. It just doesn't add up. If the same year Plymouth and Dodge sedans weren't selling, I would say, alright, the timing is off. But those shapeless, emotionless sedans are

bringing big bucks now, while the gentle, innocent Turtleback awaits its turn, unnoticed.

Not only that! Car collectors are shrewd. They are quick to pick up on someone's oversight, or undersight. They calculate so well that they sometimes jump the gun. It is surprising, then, to see them overlook a less common car for the want of a sedan. It is almost as if someone switched the price signs and nobody noticed.

I have refrained from using the specific names of Wayfarer and Cranbrook in this discussion of the turtleback cars for a few reasons. Obviously, the name implies the shape. Therefore, it reinforces a more singular identity. Also, it's easier to relate to a turtle than to a wayfarer or a cranbrook, whatever that is. The identity seems accurate in another way, too. Somebody once told a story about how tortoises get off to a slow start. As it turned out, the turtle was a good bet. It seems it had the stamina of a dark horse.

SPECIFICATIONS

Wheelbase . . . . .118.5"
Tread; Front, Rear . . . . .56", 58.5"
Overall Length . . . . .193.875"
Overall Width . . . . .73.375"
Overall Height . . . . .64.375"
Weight, Lbs 3110
Tire Size . . . . .6.70 x 15"

ENGINE

Type . . . . .L-Head, 6 cyl.
Bore & Stroke . . . . .3.25" x 4.375"
Displacement, Cu. In. .217.8
Compression Ratio . . . . .7.00 to 1
Horsepower @ RPM . . . . .97 @ 3600
Max. Torque @ RPM . . . . .175 @ 1200
Electrical . . . . .6 Volt, pos. grd.

TRANSMISSION

Type . . . . .3 speed manual
Available . . . . .semi-automatic

REAR

Type . . . . .Hypoid, semi-floating
Ratio . . . . .3.73 to 1

TUNE UP

Spark Plug Gap . . . . .035"
Point Gap . . . . .020"
Cam Angle, Degrees 38
Timing . . . . .T.D.C.
Firing Order 153624
Tappet Clearances:
   Intake . . . . .008"
   Exhaust . . . . .010"
Compression Pressure,
  Lbs 160
Idle Speed, RPM 450

BRAKES

Type . . . . .Hydraulic, int. exp.
Drum Diameter . . . . .10"

CAPACITIES

Cooling System, Qts 15
Fuel Tank, Gals 17
Crank Case, Qts 5
Trans. Pints 2.75
Differential, Pts 3.25

WHEEL ALIGNMENT

Caster, Degrees . . . .−1 to +1
Camber, Degrees . . . . .0 to +¾
Toe in, Inches . . . . .0 to ¹/₁₆

1950 Pontiac Sedan

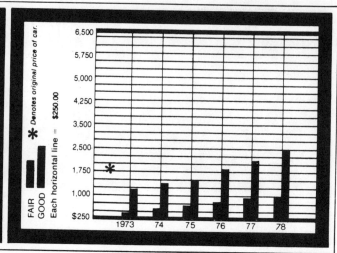

Special-interest cars, or milestone cars, or whatever you want to call them, exist in a sheltered world. They are separated from their less fortunate counterparts in price and purpose. These factors themselves are both unredeeming and irreversible. They are bestowed, as rites of initiation, upon cars judged meritorious for one reason or another. Generally, there is some distinction about such cars that warrants their inclusion in this select group. A certain vagueness in the definition, however, permits questionable entries.

The limbo-like status of special-interest autos is an invisible veneer of higher prices and functional immunity. Sometimes it acts like a white market, effectively condoning its own existence. This is the situation that arises when a car that is not outstanding, and never was, appears in its ranks. Granted a pristine anything is worth a lot of money, but when it is not yet uncommon on the road, the suspicion of a double market casts shadows on one value or the other.

In a free enterprise system, supply and demand maintain market stability, forcing such cars to seek their own level. Just beware of marginal entries. They may bob before they weave into their final price niche.

The integrity of the 1952 Pontiac Sedan is not contested here. Its price is basically equitable with its demand. In fact, the car is only a barometer of value for any of several similar sedans. A 1954 Plymouth could as well have been that gauge. The point is that none of these cars is particularly old or unique, but there are a few excellent surviving examples. These deserve high prices. To be sure, they will be worth even more in the future. It is the lesser survivors that should arouse caution, because they tend to appreciate beyond their means once the snowball starts rolling. No harm is intended these fine cars or their pursuit of fame. In the pursuit of fortune, caution is intended.

SPECIFICATIONS

Wheelbase	120"
Tread; Front, Rear	58", 59"
Overall Length	203"
Overall Width	76"
Overall Height	63"
Weight, Lbs	3384
Tire Size	7.10 x 15"

ENGINE

Type	L-Head, in-line 8 cyl.
Bore & Stroke	3.375" x 3.75"
Displacement, Cu. In.	268.2
Compression Ratio	6.50 to 1
Horsepower @ RPM	108 @ 3600
Max. Torque @ RPM	208 @ 1800
Electrical	6 Volt, neg. grd.

TRANSMISSION

Type	Automatic
Available	3 spd. manual

REAR

Type	Hypoid, semi-floating
Ratio	3.63 to 1

TUNE UP

Spark Plug Gap	.023" - .028"
Point Gap	.016"
Cam Angle, Degrees	21-31
Timing	4° B.T.D.C.
Firing Order	16258374
Tappet Clearances:	
Intake	.012"
Exhaust	.012"
Compression Pressure,	
Lbs	156
Idle Speed, RPM	450

BRAKES

Type	Hydraulic, int. exp.
Drum Diameter	11"

CAPACITIES

Cooling System, Qts	20
Fuel Tank, Gals	17.5
Crank Case, Qts	5
Trans.	12 Qts.
Differential, Pts	3.25

WHEEL ALIGNMENT

Caster, Degrees	−¾ to −1
Camber, Degrees	0
Toe in, Inches	0 to 1/16

1951 Chevrolet Hardtop

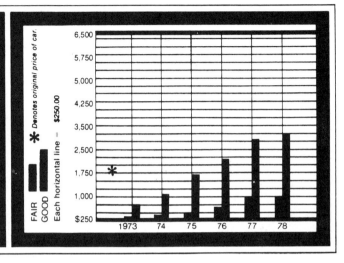

Crewcuts appeared in the early fifties. With the big war over, Korea was making men out of the rest of our boys. These indelible experiences boosted a reticent nation into an era of comparative opulence. True, the beginnings are hard to see; but in 1951 there was work to be done and the technology was present to transform hard-earned dollars into dreams. In 1951 these dreams were seething for personification. The recent wars had fortified the male power syndrome and loosened conservative morals.

Most students of design will agree that the impact of these factors is what led to the sweeping success of the hardtop invasion of 1949-1952. Somehow, the absence of a center pillar and rear window metamorphosized even the sleepiest sedan into a modern ego-screaming status symbol.

The rush was on and Chevrolet enjoyed no less of this fascination than the next car. It could well have enjoyed more, were it not for a growing distinction for lack of power. It's not that the reliable "stovebolt" six was so weak. Rather, the overhead V-8's were by now fulfilling the spirit of the youth market and all of its macho needs.

Actually, there was little to be impressed with in the '51-52 Chevrolet Hardtop after the initial sex appeal mellowed. Maybe this is why brighter colors (yes, even brighter than grey) and two-tone paints that added to the illusion of lightness were offered. Regardless, a turn of the key told you quite unmistakably that you were in a lamb in wolf's clothing! At least you could order the powerglide automatic transmission in your Chevy Hardtop. That was good, because the early fifties was also the era of convenience and power gadgets.

These years were also typical of the cold war, replete with bomb shelters and fear of nuclear attack. A man named McCarthy was transcending this paranoia into the old adage that one is guilty until proven innocent. The shock waves of these events filtered down into daily life in obtuse ways. It was a time to be extroverted and it was a time to be restrained. This is why the Chevy Hardtop was successful. It was a proven and conservative car with an acceptable amount of flair, because flair was acceptable then.

With Dinah Shore singing, "See the U.S.A. in your Chevrolet," it was hard to go wrong. It would still be a few years before Chevrolet would assert its magnificent potential. Meanwhile, Dinah is still around and so are a lot of these nifty Chevy Hardtops.

SPECIFICATIONS

Wheelbase ....115"
Tread; Front, Rear ....57", 59"
Overall Length ....198"
Overall Width ....74"
Overall Height ....66"
Weight, Lbs 3300
Tire Size ....6.70 x 15"

ENGINE

Type ....Overhead in-line 6 cyl.
Bore & Stroke ....3.5625" x 3.9375"
Displacement, Cu. In. 235.5
Compression Ratio ....6.70 to 1
Horsepower @ RPM ....105 @ 3600
Max. Torque @ RPM ....193 @ 1100-2200
Electrical ....6 Volt, neg. grd.

TRANSMISSION

Type ....Automatic
Available ....3 spd. manual

REAR

Type ....Hypoid, semi-floating
Ratio ....3.55 to 1

TUNE UP

Spark Plug Gap ....035"
Point Gap ....018"
Cam Angle, Degrees 39
Timing ....5° B.T.D.C.
Firing Order 153624
Tappet Clearances:
    Intake ....Auto adj.
    Exhaust ....Auto adj.
Compression Pressure,
Lbs 110
Idle Speed, RPM 440

BRAKES

Type ....Hydraulic, int. exp.
Drum Diameter ....11"

CAPACITIES

Cooling System, Qts 16
Fuel Tank, Gals 16
Crank Case, Qts 5
Trans. ....9 Qts.
Differential, Pts 3.5

WHEEL ALIGNMENT

Caster, Degrees ....0 to +1
Camber, Degrees ....0 to +1
Toe in, Inches ....0 to ⅛

1951 Chrysler Windsor Newport

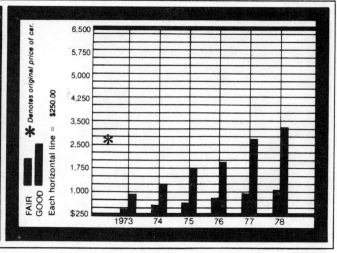

Hardtops are easy money. Between 1949 and 1952, everyone introduced one. Some manufacturers produced new bodies during those years, giving a choice of two distinctive hardtops for the period (1951 v. 1952 Ford). Others were altered in trim only, and offered for a couple of years, such as this Chrysler. Either way, any 1949-52 hardtop is a milestone car and quite collectible. To put the icing on the cake, their respective sedan models are still comparatively plentiful and cheap, presenting an ideal solution to the parts problem.

The factors that make the 1951 Chrysler Hardtop desirable are the same denominators of value for all these hardtops. Only the specific intrinsic qualities that comprise the actual character of each car's nomenclature will cause any final deviation in 1949-52 hardtop prices (plus, of course, the actual condition of the car being considered.) Conceived as a more practical alternative to the convertible, the hardtop met with immediate success. Being second only to its stepfather in automobile pecking order gave it the advantage of instant admiration. It was, after all, the stylists' best effort their coup de grace.

The 1951 Chrysler version had the prevalent quarter circle rear window shape and paned rear glass that arced fully to the beltline to meet it. Chrome roof slats were the universal complement of early hardtops. They were supposedly reminiscent of the bows in the convertible tops, but were actually as much in vogue because of the contemporary obsession with things both bright and flashy. As did the rest of the industry, Chrysler distinguished its hardtops by a two-tone paint job.

In those final years of the long period when Chrysler Corporation preached conservative styling, this hardtop was an oasis. Not until Virgil Exner's "Flightsweep" influence beginning in 1955 would Chrysler take the styling offensive. But the one thing that made Mr. Exner's cars possible was introduced in 1951. That is the much renowned hemi-head engine. Still, it mattered little in 1951, as most of Chrysler's hardtops that year were equipped with the old L-head six. Apparently that was more in keeping with the conformity of the package.

SPECIFICATIONS

Wheelbase	126″
Tread; Front, Rear	56″, 60″
Overall Length	207″
Overall Width	75″
Overall Height	65″
Weight, Lbs	3855
Tire Size	7.60 x 15″

ENGINE

Type	L-Head, in-line 6 cyl.
Bore & Stroke	3.0625″ x 4.50″
Displacement, Cu. In.	250.6
Compression Ratio	7.00 to 1
Horsepower @ RPM	116 @ 3600
Max. Torque @ RPM	208 @ 1600
Electrical	6 Volt, pos. grd.

TRANSMISSION

Type	3 speed manual
Available	automatic, semi-automatic

REAR

Type	Hypoid, semi-floating
Ratio	3.73 to 1

TUNE UP

Spark Plug Gap	.035″
Point Gap	.020″
Cam Angle, Degrees	34.5-38
Timing	2° B.T.D.C.
Firing Order	153624
Tappet Clearances:	
Intake	.008″
Exhaust	.010″
Compression Pressure, Lbs	120
Idle Speed, RPM	450

BRAKES

Type	Hydraulic, int. exp.
Drum Diameter	12″

CAPACITIES

Cooling System, Qts	17
Fuel Tank, Gals	17
Crank Case, Qts	5
Trans. Pints	2.75
Differential, Pts	3.25

WHEEL ALIGNMENT

Caster, Degrees	-1 to -3
Camber, Degrees	-⅜ to +⅜
Toe in, Inches	0 to 1/16

1951 Nash Ambassador Sedan

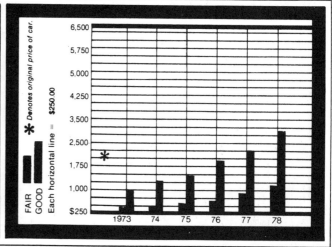

Denotes original price of car. = $250.00

Each horizontal line = $250.00

FAIR GOOD

6,500 / 5,750 / 5,000 / 4,250 / 3,500 / 2,500 / 1,750 / 1,000 / $250

1973 74 75 76 77 78

If you were going to be in the back seat "kissin' and a huggin' with Fred," as the song went, this was the car to be in. It was commonly known as the Bathtub Nash. I saw a green one many years ago, and since then these cars have more closely resembled cucumbers to me! To the folks in the back seat, I'm sure it was more of a bedroom than either of these anomalies.

Fortunately, the uniqueness of this Farina styled car exists in more ways than one. As long as we're fooling around inside, we may as well observe some of the Ambassador's peculiarities . . . like the unorthodox instrument cluster. I'm not sure if it resembles a huge pod or a sawed-off bomb shell, but somehow it adds up in a car that is unequivocal about being a cucumber or a bathtub! By contrast, the rest of the interior appointments are mild, even average, for the day.

In spite of the fact that its slippery aerodynamic design permitted excellent economy on the highway, the fifties saw the most demand for this Nash on the eve before the prom. In the sixties, the supercars would deliver their occupants to the scene with a reckless abandonment for energy that was the antithesis of Nash's philosophy. But the seventies are again conservative and suddenly there is a fondness for the good old days when the Nash was new.

If you choose to relive 1951 in this car, you will be noticed. You'll be noticed like the chicken watched by the fox. In other words, people envious of your flirtation with the fifties will barter dollars for the thrill. How many dollars depends, of course, on the condition of the car and the strength of memories sought v. memories parted.

I don't think these cars have reached their peak value yet. It seems they're sleepers in more ways than one! One thing is for sure: no amount of time will make them worth less, so just let down the front seat and relax awhile. Contemplate your choices. This is the real gratification in having an old car. Sometimes in life you get to feel like you're sitting in the catbird seat. In this case you can lay in it and gloat. Forget the first song. Carly Simon says it better in her song. "These are the good old days."

SPECIFICATIONS

Wheelbase	114.5"
Tread; Front, Rear	55.5", 59.6875"
Overall Length	202.75"
Overall Width	78"
Overall Height	61.75"
Weight, Lbs	3410
Tire Size	7.10 x 15"

ENGINE

Type	L-Head, 6 cyl.
Bore & Stroke	3.125" x 4.25"
Displacement, Cu. In.	195.6
Compression Ratio	7.10 to 1
Horsepower @ RPM	88 @ 3800
Max. Torque @ RPM	150 @ 1600
Electrical	6 Volt, pos. grd.

TRANSMISSION

Type	3 speed manual
Available	overdrive

REAR

Type	Hypoid, semi-floating
Ratio	4.40 to 1

TUNE UP

Spark Plug Gap	.030"
Point Gap	.022"
Cam Angle, Degrees	35
Timing	T.D.C.
Firing Order	153624
Tappet Clearances:	
Intake	.016"
Exhaust	.018"
Compression Pressure, Lbs	120
Idle Speed, RPM	500

BRAKES

Type	Hydraulic, int. exp.
Drum Diameter	9"

CAPACITIES

Cooling System, Qts	14
Fuel Tank, Gals	20
Crank Case, Qts	5
Trans. Pints	2.25
Differential, Pts	3

WHEEL ALIGNMENT

Caster, Degrees	0 to +½
Camber, Degrees	0 to +¼
Toe in, Inches	⅛ to 3/16

1952 Cadillac Sedan

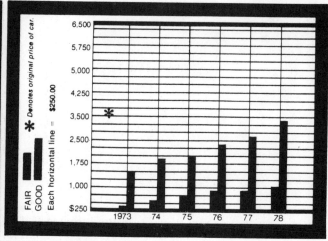

Cadillac entered its fiftieth year with only a modicum of hoopla. It really didn't need to dress up its three year old body with the gold token images it displayed at the corners of its grille any more than a king would require a new castle to celebrate such a milestone.

And king it was! Heir apparent to the luxury car crown, the 1952 Cadillac was witness to competition from an ailing Packard, a non-existent Continental, and an Imperial that was more rumor than real. The success of Cadillac was no overnight event, though. The dynamism of the nation's largest and healthiest corporation had much to do with its outcome.

Cadillac management was bold enough to be better. Cadillac novelty repeatedly became popular aspiration and then the industry norm. Power steering, power brakes, air conditioning, virtually all the convenience devices pioneered in the early fifties, trace their origins to Cadillac. True, there are isolated examples of these conveniences in earlier cars. Air conditioning, for example, made a brief debut in the 1941 Packard — but it was offered by Cadillac as well in 1941. What I'm talking about is the development of functional, marketable units that survive because of engineered simplicity and durability. The awesome totality with which the overhead engine and automatic transmission swept the industry should provide convincing argument to this point.

Not to be cosmetically outdone, Cadillac also provided the stimulus for external emulation. The fins and the vee crest were not new, but bumper tip dual exhausts were in 1952. In five years it would be hard to find a car without them. Similarly, the origins of the frenched headlight fad are traceable to the discreetly dipped bezels on this Cadillac.

Sedans are never beauty queens, but they are plentiful and, perhaps, most acceptable in the luxury car field. 1950 to '53 Cadillacs, therefore, represent a solid opportunity to the investor. They are well seasoned now, and it appears that they will ripen quickly. Such cars bear their age with utmost dignity. They don't get older — they get better.

SPECIFICATIONS

Wheelbase	126"
Tread; Front, Rear	59", 63"
Overall Length	220"
Overall Width	80"
Overall Height	63"
Weight, Lbs	4151
Tire Size	8.00 x 15"

ENGINE

Type	Overhead V-8
Bore & Stroke	3.8125" x 3.625"
Displacement, Cu. In.	331
Compression Ratio	7.50 to 1
Horsepower @ RPM	190 @ 4000
Max. Torque @ RPM	322 @ 2400
Electrical	6 Volt, neg. grd.

TRANSMISSION

Type	Automatic
Available	3 speed manual

REAR

Type	Hypoid, semi-floating
Ratio	3.36 to 1

TUNE UP

Spark Plug Gap	.035"
Point Gap	.015"
Cam Angle, Degrees	31
Timing	5° B.T.D.C.
Firing Order	18436572
Tappet Clearances:	
Intake	Auto adj.
Exhaust	Auto adj.
Compression Pressure, Lbs	150
Idle Speed, RPM	430

BRAKES

Type	Hydraulic, int. exp.
Drum Diameter	12" front, 11" rear

CAPACITIES

Cooling System, Qts	19
Fuel Tank, Gals	20
Crank Case, Qts	5
Trans.	12 Qts.
Differential, Pts	5

WHEEL ALIGNMENT

Caster, Degrees	−½ to +½
Camber, Degrees	−3/8 to +3/8
Toe in, Inches	1/32 to 3/32

1952 Henry J. Corsair 6

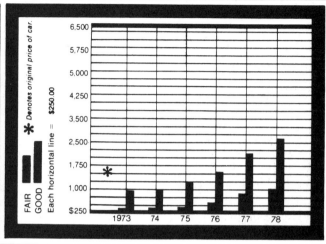

Henry J. is the other half of Mr. Kaiser's name. In a spirit becoming of the familiarity of a first name rapport, the Henry J. is a friendly little car. It is, perhaps, too cute to have been taken seriously. The turned-up tips of its rear fenders were certainly reminiscent of Cadillac's fishtail fins, yet it was permissible because the car no more stole Cadillac's character than it extolled its virtues. Had Packard or Lincoln sprouted fins in 1952, the threat would have been more somber. For Henry J., it was more like a little boy wearing his father's shoes.

Henry J. was not intended to be a laughing matter. Mr. Kaiser perceived it as an inexpensive solution to the problem of basic transportation. Indeed, its stark utilitarian efficiency left little to smile about. Before long, the car succumbed to pressures beyond its meager capacity to endure. The independents, especially the small cars, were not destined to survive the decade.

The present situation for Henry J., beyond the scarcity of its numbers, is optimistic. It is ripe for rehabilitation, or even reuse, if the parts can be found to restore its condition. It gives every indication of appreciating quickly in the near future, but even a drastic increase in value will not put it on a par with the big cars of its day. It simply is not good enough for that on the basis of its original purpose. The growth of the Henry J. will be realized more on a percentage basis than a dollar basis.

Nowadays, a Henry J. is a heartwarming sight as well as an attractive one. Its cuteness is more thorough since acquiring the nonobligatory function of a special-interest car. As an investment, there is nothing to prevent it from being very friendly.

SPECIFICATIONS

Wheelbase	.100″
Tread; Front, Rear	.54″, 54″
Overall Length	.176″
Overall Width	.69″
Overall Height	.60″
Weight, Lbs	.2405
Tire Size	.5.90 x 15″

ENGINE

Type	L-Head, in-line 6 cyl.
Bore & Stroke	3.125″ x 3.50″
Displacement, Cu. In.	.161
Compression Ratio	.7.00 to 1
Horsepower @ RPM	.80 @ 3800
Max. Torque @ RPM	.133 @ 1600
Electrical	.6 Volt, pos. grd.

TRANSMISSION

Type	.3 speed manual
Available	.overdrive

REAR

Type	Hypoid, semi-floating
Ratio	.4.10 to 1

TUNE UP

Spark Plug Gap	.030″
Point Gap	.020″
Cam Angle, Degrees	.38
Timing	.T.D.C.
Firing Order	.153624
Tappet Clearances:	
Intake	.016″
Exhaust	.016″
Compression Pressure,	
Lbs	.130-140
Idle Speed, RPM	.550

BRAKES

Type	Hydraulic, int. exp.
Drum Diameter	.9″

CAPACITIES

Cooling System, Qts	.9
Fuel Tank, Gals	.13
Crank Case, Qts	.5
Trans. Pints	.1.5
Differential, Pts	.2.5

WHEEL ALIGNMENT

Caster, Degrees	−1 to +1
Camber, Degrees	+¼ to +1
Toe in, Inches	.0 to ¼

1952 Hudson Commodore

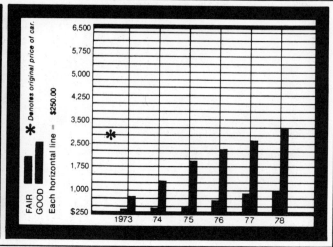

One of the most identifiable cars ever made was the Hudson Hornet of this era. The car that was made possible by the step-down frame turned out to be the final glory for Hudson. When it passed, in 1955, into conventionality, along with it went the fame and glory of its identity. It shouldn't be surprising that the sleek Hudsons of the early fifties established an enviable record of performance and durability on the stock car circuit. The hefty twin-horsepower overhead straight eight was the scourge of NASCAR and a constant nemesis even to the Oldsmobile V-8's.

Hudson was cashing in on the fame gained in these events. Despite a body that was five years old in 1953, the twin-horsepower campaign was an effective one. It may be, too, that the novelty of its banana-like body would not easily wear away. The worst thing that happened to it in those five years was the addition of a little chrome, which seemed only to enhance the Hudson, while having a debilitating effect on other cars. The chopped side glass and visored windshield created an illusion beyond the actual lowness of the car. This vision was further dramatized by a long, tapering roofline and super-smooth metal below the beltline. The slippery Hudson deliberately lacked noticeable rear wheel cutouts to preserve continuity of form.

Originality was preserved inside as well. The wood-based dash with its

huge oval dials resembled no other control panel. Sumptuous interiors, inspired by the totally different atmosphere of Hudson's recessed floor interior, were both cozy and exciting. An interesting combination, indeed!

The revolutionary impact of these Hudsons turned out to be an evolutionary dead end. The only car ever made that looked better with four doors than two had an incurable allergy to conventionality, a disease not uncommon among great cars.

SPECIFICATIONS

Wheelbase	.124"
Tread; Front, Rear	.59", 56"
Overall Length	.208"
Overall Width	.77"
Overall Height	.60"
Weight, Lbs	.3605
Tire Size	.7.10 x 15"

ENGINE

Type	L-Head, in-line 8 cyl.
Bore & Stroke	.3.00" x 4.50"
Displacement, Cu. In.	.254
Compression Ratio	.6.70 to 1
Horsepower @ RPM	.128 @ 4200
Max. Torque @ RPM	.198 @ 1600
Electrical	.6 Volt, pos. grd.

TRANSMISSION

Type	.3 speed manual
Available	Automatic, overdrive

REAR

Type	Hypoid, semi-floating
Ratio	.4.10 to 1

TUNE UP

Spark Plug Gap	.032"
Point Gap	.017"
Cam Angle, Degrees	.27
Timing	T.D.C.
Firing Order	.16258374
Tappet Clearances:	
Intake	.008"
Exhaust	.010"
Compression Pressure,	
Lbs	.119
Idle Speed, RPM	.600

BRAKES

Type	Hydraulic, int. exp.
Drum Diameter	.11"

CAPACITIES

Cooling System, Qts	.18
Fuel Tank, Gals	.20
Crank Case, Qts	.7
Trans. Pints	.2
Differential, Pts	.3.5

WHEEL ALIGNMENT

Caster, Degrees	+½ to +1½
Camber, Degrees	+½ to +1½
Toe in, Inches	.0 to 1/16

1953 Buick Skylark

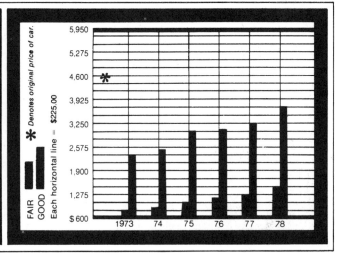

The 1953 Skylark arrived on Buick's 50th anniversary. It brought with it a host of better ideas from the builder of better cars. Most notable of these must be the oversquare (4.0 x 3.2) overhead V-8 engine. For those who mourned the loss of the venerable straight eight, Buick retained it in the lower series. An improved twin turbine Dynaflow helped the new engine's power reach the rear wheels. Power steering finally got to Buick in 1953, and more than a few appreciated the assistance on this massive car.

These and every other conceivable option were at the command of some 1,690 Skylark owners in 1953. But, better than the standard conveniences and the gadgets (like foot-operated radio tuning) was the distinctive style of this car. The chopped top, dipped belt line and radiused wheel openings were intended to convey a sporty image to the genteel. The Borrani wire wheels and close-ribbed leather interiors may have hit the mark, but, as anybody could see, this car would intimidate no one at Watkins Glen. Obviously, the car was too large to be a sporty car.

The Skylark was built at a time when dreamcars were exhibited to test public opinion of the latest designs. Buick's experimental XP-300 was the styling lab for the Skylark. Though successful in G.M.'s Motorama shows, the people who approved the design failed to appear in the

showrooms. But anybody knows you don't have to buy a car to know it looks good! So now we're in a situation where there are many admirers and few cars. Simple supply and demand laws say this car has to be valuable. And it is! The Borrani wheels alone will fetch up to $500 today.

The original Skylark must also be considered as the first of the luxury road cars. Cars like the El Dorado, Carribean, and later the Grand Prix and even some Thunderbirds owe their existence to Buick's ill-fated Skylark. For the record, only about half as many 1954 Skylarks were sold. This situation resulted from the fact that Buick remodeled all its cars for 1954 in such a way that the standard Century Convertible (which was the basis of the '54 Skylark) was now as racy looking as the Skylark at half the price. It seems that Buick did, indeed, build a better car!

SPECIFICATIONS

Wheelbase	.126"
Tread; Front, Rear	.60", 62"
Overall Length	.211"
Overall Width	.80"
Overall Height	.63"
Weight, Lbs	.4315
Tire Size	.8.00 x 15"

ENGINE

Type	.Overhead V-8
Bore & Stroke	.4.00" x 3.20"
Displacement, Cu. In.	.322
Compression Ratio	.8.50 to 1
Horsepower @ RPM	.188 @ 4000
Max. Torque @ RPM	.300 @ 2400
Electrical	.12 Volt, neg. grd.

TRANSMISSION

Type	.Dynaflow automatic
Available	.—

REAR

Type	.Hypoid, semi-floating
Ratio	.3.62 to 1

TUNE UP

Spark Plug Gap	.035"
Point Gap	.015"
Cam Angle, Degrees	.Not recommended
Timing	.5° B.T.D.C.
Firing Order	.12784563
Tappet Clearances:	
Intake	.Auto. adj.
Exhaust	.Auto. adj.
Compression Pressure,	
Lbs	.160
Idle Speed, RPM	.450

BRAKES

Type	.Hydraulic, int. exp.
Drum Diameter	.12"

CAPACITIES

Cooling System, Qts	.19.5
Fuel Tank, Gals	.19
Crank Case, Qts	.6
Trans. Pints	.10
Differential, Pts	.4.5

WHEEL ALIGNMENT

Caster, Degrees	.+¼ to +1½
Camber, Degrees	.+⅞ to −⅝
Toe in, Inches	.¹/₁₆ to ⅛

1953 Hudson Jet

A compact, economical wonder car
in the low price field, with performance

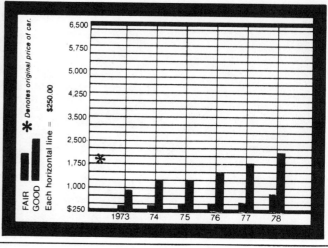

The small American car has historically been shrouded in an enigma that defies unraveling. Certainly, the compact is no newcomer to North America. It did not arrive with the Rambler or the Corvair, as many suspect. Its origins are traceable well beyond these memorable cars to less memorable names such as Crosley, Bantam and American Austin. Conceivably, the list could go back as far as the birth of the automobile itself, covering periods of economic growth and stagnation, recession and depression. Yet, for all its varied attempts, the struggle for survival has been a most elusive one for small cars. Strangely, almost without exception, the failure of the compact has been vindicated after a period of dormancy by an absurdly high resale value. The Hudson Jet, if for no other reason than being out of production for more than twenty years, should be ready for a comeback.

The Hudson Jet was originally intended to be a lower, sleeker car. By the time the final dies were set, upper management had altered the design just enough to remove its aesthetic appeal. Convincingly, they argued that more conventional lines would lend further spaciousness to the car. Bearing the car's purpose in mind, the assumption was correct; but the complexity of the compact problem proved itself unsolvable by this simplistic approach.

As the Jet turned out, it didn't look like other Hudsons. Its cubic dimensions

prohibited such style. The four-door Jet was less than beautiful outside, but it did have a conformity of concept throughout. It was a good car, but not a great car. Compacts, by their very nature, though, preclude such finesse. With cost a major factor, greatness must be traded off for utility. In this respect, the Jet did approach a happy medium. The old American hangups of conspicuous identity and fear of the faltering independent doubtless contributed to the Jet's demise. With full-sized Chevrolets and Fords selling at about the same price, the advantages of owning a Hudson Jet were negligible, if not nil, in 1953. The Jet is still a forgotten car. It will not escape the watchful eye of the collector much longer. All things considered, it is a better bargain now than ever.

SPECIFICATIONS

Wheelbase	105″
Tread; Front, Rear	54″, 52″
Overall Length	180″
Overall Width	67″
Overall Height	61″
Weight, Lbs	2650
Tire Size	5.90 x 15″

ENGINE

Type	L-Head, 6 cyl.
Bore & Stroke	3.007″ x 4.75″
Displacement, Cu. In.	202
Compression Ratio	7.50 to 1
Horsepower @ RPM	104 @ 4000
Max. Torque @ RPM	158 @ 1400
Electrical	6 Volt, pos. grd.

TRANSMISSION

Type	3 speed manual
Available	overdrive, automatic

REAR

Type	Hypoid, semi-floating
Ratio	4.10 to 1

TUNE UP

Spark Plug Gap	.032″
Point Gap	.020″
Cam Angle, Degrees	39
Timing	1°-6° U.D.C.
Firing Order	153624
Tappet Clearances:	
Intake	.010″
Exhaust	.012″
Compression Pressure, Lbs	100
Idle Speed, RPM	500

BRAKES

Type	Hydraulic, int. exp.
Drum Diameter	11″

CAPACITIES

Cooling System, Qts	15
Fuel Tank, Gals	15
Crank Case, Qts	5
Trans. Pints	1.5
Differential, Pts	2.5

WHEEL ALIGNMENT

Caster, Degrees	+½ to +1½
Camber, Degrees	+¼ to +1¼
Toe in, Inches	0 to 1/16

1953 Packard Sedan

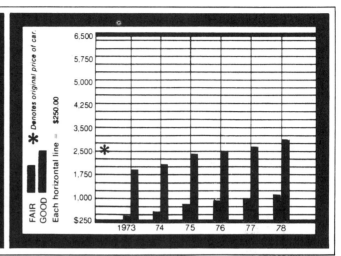

The Packard name in the early fifties was placed on cars that otherwise would have little value to the collector. The big, square cars that bore this insignia not only lacked style, but compounded the error by the distasteful application of trim. There was still the traditional Packard owner, who purchased confidence in quality; but the dwindling number of repeat owners was not enough to counter a serious shortage of Packard converts. There just wasn't enough to entice them!

The conservative appearance was in no way pretentious of a beauty more than skin deep. It was matched in mediocrity by a smooth, but outdated, straight eight engine and an elegant but unimaginative interior. The Packard was just hanging on out of principle, instead of applying principle to leadership as it had done in its glory days.

All of this is moot testimony anyway. Anything made by Packard is, and has been for eons, collectible material. This situation will only improve as time enhances a reputation turned legend by the cessation of production. With a fair amount of sedans remaining, it would seem logical to assume they possess an excellent investment potential. They do, in the sense of blue chip stocks. High to begin with, the price rise promises to be as steady and as conservative as the cars themselves. If you have time, or prefer security over moderate profit potential, this is the car for you.

Watch out for Packard's Ultramatic transmission. The cost of repairing a defective unit will eliminate any margin of profit on an average sedan. A valve job, which is not an infrequent expense on these engines, will have nearly the same results. It is better to see the red flag of caution than the red ink of an imbalanced account. When scouting Packards, a simple guide is to search for dignity. That has always been the outstanding quality in these cars. It is not likely to change.

SPECIFICATIONS

Wheelbase	122"
Tread; Front, Rear	60", 61"
Overall Length	213"
Overall Width	78"
Overall Height	62"
Weight, Lbs	3725
Tire Size	7.60 x 15"

ENGINE

Type	L-Head, straight 8
Bore & Stroke	3.50" x 4.25"
Displacement, Cu. In.	327
Compression Ratio	8.00 to 1
Horsepower @ RPM	160 @ 3600
Max. Torque @ RPM	295 @ 2000
Electrical	6 Volt, pos. grd.

TRANSMISSION

Type	Automatic
Available	3 spd. manual

REAR

Type	Hypoid, semi-floating
Ratio	3.90 to 1

TUNE UP

Spark Plug Gap	.030"
Point Gap	.017"
Cam Angle, Degrees	30
Timing	6° B.T.D.C.
Firing Order	16258374
Tappet Clearances:	
Intake	.007"
Exhaust	.010"
Compression Pressure,	
Lbs	120
Idle Speed, RPM	400

BRAKES

Type	Hydraulic, int. exp.
Drum Diameter	12"

CAPACITIES

Cooling System, Qts	20
Fuel Tank, Gals	20
Crank Case, Qts	7
Trans.	12 Qts.
Differential, Pts	4

WHEEL ALIGNMENT

Caster, Degrees	−½ to −1
Camber, Degrees	0 to +¾
Toe in, Inches	0

1953 Studebaker Hardtop

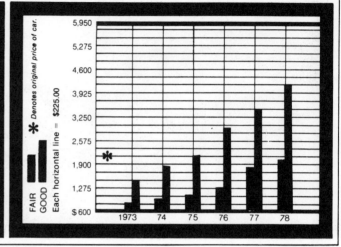

This car is alphabetically toward the end of the book. It is also one of the last cars I wrote about when compiling the book. But I thought about it most of all because I like it so much. I had trouble justifying my feelings with words of description. Words are too rigid, too permanent, to capture the timelessness of this hardtop. It has been proclaimed by everyone everywhere as the most illustrious example of automotive art in modern times. I can't add to that.

This car hit me like a sledge hammer in 1953. More than any car before or since, it made me aware of my feelings, and its feelings. In high school I couldn't believe the naiveté of the people who had let the prices drop so low. For $65 I stole a Venus de Milo before I graduated. The love affair has never ended, though we've been estranged for a long while. The feeling is warmed by the fact that I know I will have another. The price is no longer so important to me as the preservation. It's like buying a Picasso.

The 1953 and 1954 Hardtop models are nearly identical, but the original is a bit cleaner in a grille and bumper guard area. The pillared coupes are as nice looking. The pastel colors available on these cars blend perfectly with their timeless attitude. They are hues, not colors. They are vague in the spectrum, as ideas are in time. Its basic design was so good it graced several Studebakers for more than a decade. Every one of them is a valuable variation of this original, as

the next three cars will evidence.

In my mind this Studebaker Hardtop Coupe is still underpriced. The chart reflects the general opinion of the market and is probably more accurate than my feelings. Nevertheless, that day in 1953 when I first laid eyes on the new Studebaker Hardtop, Raymond Loewy replaced the Lone Ranger as my hero. He may not ride a white stallion, but he surely rides in the most beautiful car ever made.

SPECIFICATIONS

Wheelbase . . . . .120"
Tread; Front, Rear . . . . .56", 56"
Overall Length . . . . .202"
Overall Width . . . . .71"
Overall Height . . . . .61"
Weight, Lbs 3075
Tire Size . . . . .7.10 x 15"

ENGINE

Type . . . . .Overhead V-8
Bore & Stroke . . . . .3.375" x 3.25"
Displacement, Cu. In. 232.6
Compression Ratio . . . . .7.00 to 1
Horsepower @ RPM . . . . .120 @ 4000
Max. Torque @ RPM . . . . .190 @ 2000
Electrical .6 Volt, pos. grd.

TRANSMISSION

Type . . . . .3 speed manual
Available . . . . .overdrive, automatic

REAR

Type . . . . .Hypoid, semi-floating
Ratio . . . . .3.54 to 1

TUNE UP

Spark Plug Gap . . . . .035"
Point Gap . . . . .015"
Cam Angle, Degrees 34
Timing . . . . .4° B.T.D.C.
Firing Order 18436572
Tappet Clearances:
    Intake . . . . .022"
    Exhaust . . . . .022"
Compression Pressure,
Lbs 130
Idle Speed, RPM 550

BRAKES

Type . . . . .Hydraulic, int. exp.
Drum Diameter . . . . .11"

CAPACITIES

Cooling System, Qts 19
Fuel Tank, Gals 18
Crank Case, Qts 6
Trans. Pints 2.5
Differential, Pts 3

WHEEL ALIGNMENT

Caster, Degrees . . . .−1¾ to −2½
Camber, Degrees .0 to +1
Toe in, Inches . . . . .¹/₁₆ to ⅛

1953 Willys Aero Eagle

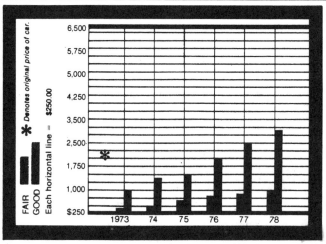

In 1954, it was easy to tell the high-priced cars from the low-priced cars. All that was needed was one glance. The pecking order of prestige was directly related to the size of the package. There were some good, even excellent, smaller cars made then that never sold well because they bore the indelible mark of lower class distinction. The Hudson Jet, the Henry J. and the Willys Aero Sedan were all sturdy, economical, inexpensive means of transportation. They were also small and marketed by the small auto companies.

In other words, the odds of success were unfavorable from the beginning. No one needed the advantages these cars offered more than the stereotype that went with their purchase. Gasoline was cheap and plentiful. Status was not. Status, therefore, necessitated the display of its position. It was never necessary to insure a position of lower class, though. It is for this reason that the Willys never attained the kind of respect it deserved.

Even today, you can't get a man to pay Cardin prices for a Robert Hall suit, even though the difference might be negligible without the labels. On the other hand, if you know that clothes do not a personality make, you will see the real beauty of this Aero Sedan. Certainly man should have learned by now that classic beauty is not always baroque. Some of the clearest expressions of form and function are revered for their uncomplicated

simplicity. Simplicity is an element we will see more of as labor and resources leave us little alternative. Why not beat the rush and pick up a functional car and a rare jewel in the same package. It is this combination of usefulness and identity that will serve mankind in the near future.

SPECIFICATIONS

Wheelbase	.108"
Tread; Front, Rear	.58", 57"
Overall Length	.180"
Overall Width	.72"
Overall Height	.60"
Weight, Lbs	.2588
Tire Size	.5.90 x 15"

ENGINE

Type	L-Head, in-line 6 cyl.
Bore & Stroke	.3.125" x 3.50"
Displacement, Cu. In.	.161
Compression Ratio	.6.90 to 1
Horsepower @ RPM	.75 @ 4000
Max. Torque @ RPM	.125 @ 2000
Electrical	.6 Volt, pos. grd.

TRANSMISSION

Type	.3 speed manual
Available	.overdrive, automatic

REAR

Type	.Hypoid, semi-floating
Ratio	.4.10 to 1

TUNE UP

Spark Plug Gap	.030"
Point Gap	.020"
Cam Angle, Degrees	.39
Timing	.T.D.C.
Firing Order	.153624
Tappet Clearances:	
Intake	.016"
Exhaust	.016"
Compression Pressure, Lbs	.105
Idle Speed, RPM	.550

BRAKES

Type	.Hydraulic, int. exp.
Drum Diameter	.9"

CAPACITIES

Cooling System, Qts	.12
Fuel Tank, Gals	.15
Crank Case, Qts	.5
Trans. Pints	.1.5
Differential, Pts	.2

WHEEL ALIGNMENT

Caster, Degrees	+½ to +1½
Camber, Degrees	+¾ to +1¼
Toe in, Inches	.3/32 to 5/32

1954 De Soto Sportsman

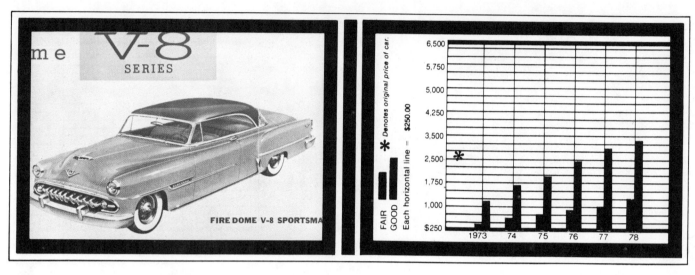

FIRE DOME V-8 SPORTSMA

The thrill, the joy of re-igniting the breath of life in some long forgotten memory is matchless for its intrinsic reward. And aren't we — all of us — victims of our past, searching to recreate the fabric of former experience in a meaningful, contemporary image? You bet, and the risk of such a gamble is eliminated when dealing in old iron. An old car is a coat of many colors. It invokes in people a multitude of sensations and dreams, all of them different but equally meaningful to the lost chord of their individual past. To contribute to the faintest inkling of a man's soul is to be the Walter Mitty of a thousand hearts. Yes, the price of pride is measured more in the diffusion of its effect than in the concentration of its effort. Why look to an edifice of the present to be the decaying vehicle of your human dynamism? Resurrect a temple of old and you will find the timeless reward of being all things to all people. Truly, there is no greater panacea for the wanderlust of the mind!

The cover car, a 1954 De Soto Hardtop, transmits this message loud and clear. In 1954, it was just another car, not exceptional and not inferior. It was hardly noticed in the showroom, much less on a crowded street. Yet it survived the vagueness of our memories to become an eye-catching hunk of yesteryear. If seen on the streets today, the reaction is strong enough to be distracting to the driver.

It is well to recall the perspective of our past. It helps us to plant our feet more firmly in the present. If you see a 1954 De Soto Hardtop gliding through your town some day, be assured that the person inside is enjoying the best of two worlds.

SPECIFICATIONS

Wheelbase	125.5"
Tread; Front, Rear	56", 59"
Overall Length	214.5"
Overall Width	77.625"
Overall Height	62.5"
Weight, Lbs	3705
Tire Size	7.60 x 15"

ENGINE

Type	Overhead V-8
Bore & Stroke	3⅝" x 3¹¹/₃₂"
Displacement, Cu. In.	276.1
Compression Ratio	7.5 to 1
Horsepower @ RPM	170 @ 4400
Max. Torque @ RPM	255 @ 2400
Electrical	6 Volt

TRANSMISSION

Type	3 spd manual
Available	Automatic, overdrive

REAR

Type	Hypoid, semi-floating
Ratio	3.73 to 1

TUNE UP

Spark Plug Gap	.035"
Point Gap	.018"
Cam Angle, Degrees	34
Timing	4° B.T.D.C.
Firing Order	18436572
Tappet Clearances:	
Intake	Zero, hydraulic
Exhaust	Zero, hydraulic
Compression Pressure, Lbs	120
Idle Speed, RPM	475

BRAKES

Type	Hydraulic, int. exp.
Drum Diameter	12"

CAPACITIES

Cooling System, Qts	22
Fuel Tank, Gals	17
Crank Case, Qts	5
Trans. Pints	2¾
Differential, Pts	3½

WHEEL ALIGNMENT

Caster, Degrees	−1 to −3
Camber, Degrees	−⅜ to +⅜
Toe in, Inches	0 to ¹/₁₆

1954 Kaiser Manhattan

'54 Kaiser Manh[...]

This two-door version o[...]
enough safety plate glas[...]
4½ feet, with glass to s[...]
much glass — or uses it [...]
visibility and roominess[...]

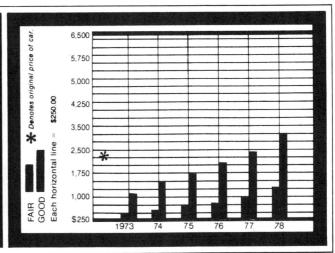

There are several Kaisers that are more collectible than the 1954 Manhattan, but none of them is likely to be found on less than the most ardent expedition. Even then, the price will either be too high or the condition too poor for purchase. With the '54 Manhattan, availability is by far a lesser problem. Naturally, parts will also be more abundant. The only sad part about all this is that the typical Manhattans don't bring the prices of the more exotic Virginians and Vagabonds.

The Manhattan is not a hatchback or a four-door convertible. The 1954 model does have a supercharger atop its undernourished Lycoming engine, as does the more valuable 1955 version. But what gives it worth is more in its name than anything else. The style never seemed to impress anyone. Not even safety features such as a pop-out windshield and padded dash attracted great response. America was not safety conscious in those years. The car that was surrounded by a broad band of stainless trim died the unwanted orphan of an industrialist in 1955. As with many other displaced personalities, the Kaiser is alive and well in Argentina.

For those Kaisers that still exist in America, the future is getting brighter. The nostalgia wave is not hurting them any. All of Kaiser's cars are doing well, in fact. Henry J. and Frazer are enjoying a spirited revival, if not a revival in spirit. The concave grille

with its vertical bars and the Darrinesque taillights are looking better all the time on the Kaiser sedans. And the heartshaped dip in the center of their windshields suddenly has a warmth of character about it.

These Kaiser peculiarities are nothing to get excited about. They simply spell out the name of the car, for it is still the name, more than any other factor, that is making the comeback. A rose by any other name may be able to cut it, but for the Kaiser Manhattan, that's all it's got going for it!

SPECIFICATIONS

Wheelbase . . . . .119″
Tread; Front, Rear . . . . .58″, 59″
Overall Length . . . . .211″
Overall Width . . . . .75″
Overall Height . . . . .60″
Weight, Lbs 3210
Tire Size . . . . .6.70 x 15″

ENGINE

Type . . . . .L-Head, in-line 6 cyl.
Bore & Stroke . . . . .3.3125″ x 4.375″
Displacement, Cu. In. 226.2
Compression Ratio . . . . .7.30 to 1
Horsepower @ RPM . . . . .118 @ 3650
Max. Torque @ RPM . . . . .200 @ 1800
Electrical . . . . .6 Volt, pos. grd.

TRANSMISSION

Type . . . . .3 speed manual
Available .Automatic, overdrive

REAR

Type . . . . .Hypoid, semi-floating
Ratio . . . . .3.91 to 1

TUNE UP

Spark Plug Gap . . . . .030″
Point Gap . . . . .022″
Cam Angle, Degrees 37
Timing . . . . .4° B.T.D.C.
Firing Order 153624
Tappet Clearances:
    Intake . . . . .014″
    Exhaust . . . . .014″
Compression Pressure,
Lbs 120
Idle Speed, RPM 500

BRAKES

Type . . . . .Hydraulic, int. exp.
Drum Diameter . . . . .11″

CAPACITIES

Cooling System, Qts 13.5
Fuel Tank, Gals 17
Crank Case, Qts 5
Trans. Pints 2.5
Differential, Pts 3

WHEEL ALIGNMENT

Caster, Degrees . . . .−1 to +1
Camber, Degrees . . . . .0 to +¾
Toe in, Inches . . . . .0 to ¹/₁₆

1954 Lincoln Capri Hardtop

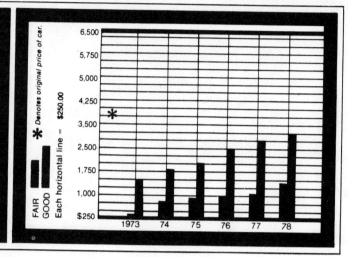

This is the car that tore 'em up on the Mexican Road Race circuit. By so doing, it emblazoned its name in the journals of history, to speak nothing of its reputation. Lincoln was an all new car in 1952, remaining virtually unchanged through 1954. But the big push — the one that sent it to Mexico — was the powerful new overhead engine. Gone were the days of the flathead and gone was the image of old.

The new body for Lincoln included a hardtop version that looked light and modern. It was as pleasing as motion itself, a notion suggested by the forward rake of the atrophied rear fenders. Actually, this was more of a fake scoop, as the fenders were no more than a crease intended to further the lithe horizontal lines of the car. To the front and the rear, the placement of the lights beyond each fender's edge was different looking and kept the lines uncluttered. The hardtop, with no vertical pillars to break the continuity, easily became the most beautiful Lincoln in the lineup.

The Lincoln name was still a synonym for quality, in spite of its new-found success at the races. Interiors of genuine leather and very fine pattern were among the best to be found. As a luxury car, Lincoln offered the full range of power options known in 1954, making driving as effortless as possible.

It may, however, take some effort to find one of these fine road cars.

Relatively speaking, they are not very old. They never were very common, being reserved by price and prestige for the uncommon man. All of which means the value today of a Capri Hardtop is pretty high. It's a collector's car that can be used — even abused — without fear of modern traffic conditions. Quite the exception, it's one of the few collector's cars that will actually give you a run for your money!

SPECIFICATIONS

Wheelbase	.123"
Tread; Front, Rear	.58.5", 62.3"
Overall Length	.214.8"
Overall Width	.77.4"
Overall Height	.62.7"
Weight, Lbs	.4245
Tire Size	.8.00 x 15"

ENGINE

Type	.Overhead V-8
Bore & Stroke	.3.80" x 3.50"
Displacement, Cu. In.	.317
Compression Ratio	.8.00 to 1
Horsepower @ RPM	.205 @ 4200
Max. Torque @ RPM	.205 @ 2300
Electrical	.6 Volt, pos. grd.

TRANSMISSION

Type	.Automatic
Available	.—

REAR

Type	.Hypoid, semi-floating
Ratio	.3.31 to 1

TUNE UP

Spark Plug Gap	.035"
Point Gap	.015"
Cam Angle, Degrees	.26-28
Timing	.3° B.T.D.C.
Firing Order	.15486372
Tappet Clearances:	
Intake	.Zero, hydraulic
Exhaust	.Zero, hydraulic
Compression Pressure, Lbs	.140
Idle Speed, RPM	.425

BRAKES

Type	.Hydraulic, int. exp.
Drum Diameter	.12"

CAPACITIES

Cooling System, Qts	.24
Fuel Tank, Gals	.20
Crank Case, Qts	.5
Trans.	.11 Qts.
Differential, Pts	.4

WHEEL ALIGNMENT

Caster, Degrees	.—1½ to 0
Camber, Degrees	.0 to +¾
Toe in, Inches	.³/₃₂ to ⁵/₃₂

From Horsepower to Rockets: 1955·1959

The new identity that metamorphosed the American car in 1949 was nearly seven years old and beginning to show signs of decay. To the doctors of Detroit, there were two ways to go in 1955. Either the patient could be saved by a stronger dose of the same medicine, or there were complications which would require different treatment. Actually, it was a combination of ills that afflicted the automobile at this time. The prognosis became equivocal. The treatment was decided to be massive exploratory surgery.

If you look at the results of this operation in the light of 1956, it will show that the image transplant was nothing short of miraculous. Sales reached ten million that year (1955), a zenith as touted as the four-minute mile. Sadly, if you step back a few more years and adjust the perspective, the outcome of the operation seems less radiant. The surgery was, indeed, successful; the new cars actually looked new. But by 1958, the new look was becoming macabre, distorted by the cancer of the real disease, which went untended.

Toward 1954, cars had been getting fat and complacent. As they grew, stylists covered their paunch with silver buckles. Swapping the chrome for a bonanza of creases, dips, and fins rendered the defect less glaring, but did nothing to correct the new cars' creeping inflation. As they continued to grow, the symmetry of their rejuvenated bodies collapsed from the swelling, finally causing the balloon to burst in 1960. Let us look at some of the reasons why the operation was a success as we determine how the patient died.

Chrysler had been playing the conservative role too long now. In 1953, it was obvious that something must be done to put the corporation in a position of leadership. Management contracted an Italian body builder, Ghia, to create a series of modern, European style road cars. The designs were very pleasing. Coupled with variously tuned versions of the awesome hemi V-8, which Chrysler had recently developed, some of them were downright threatening. Under the styling leadership of Virgil Exner, 1955-56-57 witnessed a three-part explosion which hurled at the public a series of mollified, Americanized versions of the basic Ghia concept. By the time it was all over, Chrysler had a parade of wedge-shaped cars and the styling leadership it had sought. Unused to this kind of respect and with nowhere else to go, it abdicated the position, preferring to busy itself with trivia. In a short while the jet age fins grew hideous. Of the escapede, only the original Chrysler 300 approximated the message intended by the Ghia experiment. As a sidelight, one of the original Ghia cars, the D'Elegance, ended up at the Karmann factory, where it received a new front end and lived happily ever after as a Volkswagen!

Ford could do little better with the hot potato. 1955 to 1959 saw the company range from hot to cold and cold to hot again in its search for the automobile's true identity. Perhaps the Mercury story illustrates the most tragic example of the wild guesswork going on at Ford during this time. What was a sensible, understandable car in 1954 received the costume of a clown in 1955. There was no cohesion to its lines. To compound matters, Ford Motor Company embarked on a popularity crusade the following year and nicknamed Mercury "The Big M." That formula may have worked for Elvis. But for Mercury, the Big M came to stand for "misfit." True to form, Ford countered in 1957 with an all-new approach for its middle-priced offering. The message of the new Mercury was lost in an amalgam of unrelated styling devices. The top of the line Turnpike Cruiser became the first modern dreamcar-inspired fiasco. This pile of gadgets and gizmos waltzed Mercury right to the end of the automotive pecking order by 1960.

Undaunted, Ford planned a new assault on the identity crisis. The Edsel was to be a completely new car; an entire series, chock full of the very latest American ideals. Such confidence! Some of these ideals turned out to be about twenty years late, such as the vertical grille theme and the rolling digit speedometer. Other ideas were too advanced, creating an overall sensation of confusion. The Edsel was not the savior America needed, but it made a great dancing partner for Mercury!

In the midst of all this fumbling around, the success of some of its cars escaped almost unnoticed by Ford. The Thunderbird did well as a two-seater and in 1958 became a well-received personal luxury car. Just when this stunning, sculptured four-seater was announcing the proper size and status to solve the identity crisis, deaf ears at Dearborn gave America the biggest, heaviest boat of them all — the Continental Mark III! This giant step backward succeeded the nicely proportioned Mark II Continental of 1956-57, and epitomized an era of gluttony.

With Ford failing to recognize the results of its own strategy, General Motors won a crack at the crown by default. Old numero uno certainly did get off to a flying start in 1955, but failed, too, to capitalize on the proper aspects of its success. Chevrolet was a beautiful car in 1955 and the possessor of the best V-8 in town. By proving this fact at the expense of Ford and Plymouth, among others, G.M. initiated the horsepower race. Unfortunately, the rest of the General Motors lineup came to rely upon progressively ornate trimmings for personality differentiation. By 1958, the situation was out of hand. The bulk and the chrome were too much for John Q. Public. Is it any wonder the little foreign cars were becoming familiar?

As we approach the present on our journey through time in the automobile, we find things happening at an expanded rate. It is almost impossible to simplify the influence of the myriad factors brought about by our command over technology. Depicting trends in black and white leaves lingering doubts about the grey areas that are the real world in which we live. Casting our own suspicions about enemies both real and imagined only clouds matters more. During the period from 1955 to 1960, the United States was not involved in any foreign war. The best we could do to vent our doubts was create a war — a cold war. The real villain was not Communism or fear of atomic attack. The Suez crisis of 1955 should have told us that. This politically volatile situation contained all the elements of our cold war fear, yet it was resolved not by force, but by U.N. intervention. Nor did nuclear holocaust follow the Hungarian Revolt, to the chagrin of our misguided logic.

The real feeling of unrest probably stemmed from our lives at home. The populace was swept into a glamour world on the crest of the great post-war economic boom. Now stagnation was setting in. People were finding the tinsel tarnished. They tried to look beyond it for a purpose but found there was none! It was like decorating for a party and finding no cause to celebrate. A sense of direction was lacking. We needed someone or something that could take our sorry shape and whip it into a strong, unified cause. Yes, we needed someone with charisma! Time was getting short. In truth, the weight of so many of the auto industry's dismal failures crashing on the G.N.P. amounted to another recession on our hands. After eight years of the Eisenhower administration it was obvious that General MacArthur's farewell speech about old soldiers who fade away was really a reference to the man who fired him!

Late in 1957 Russia launched the first Sputnik, while in America the jet age was suffering from jet lag. Neither fuel-injection, nor super-chargers, nor all Detroit's horses could hope to outrace a rocket. Something new was in the air. The time for change was again ripening. Soon there would be a new man in Washington and he would give us the strength and conviction to find ourselves.

1955 Chevrolet Nomad

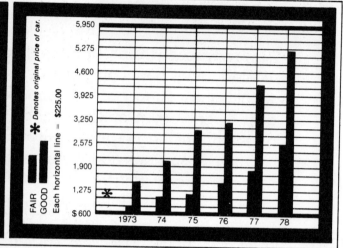

The war babies were pushing ten years old now and the jet influence had filtered down to man's most intimate totem: his car. Power and sleekness came of age in 1955 and the young family man needed to be flashy too. Basic black was losing ground to brighter, multiple color schemes. The racy lines of exotic European sport cars could no longer be ignored, so in 1955 Detroit broke away from the stodginess of preceding years and took aim at an enlightened market.

One of the finest examples of this era was the Chevrolet Nomad. The design was light looking and flowed from bumper to bumper, with the egg-crate grille reminiscent of the great Ferarri. The wraparound windshield, frenched headlights and lower silhouette sounded the death-knell for the great custom era.

Chevrolet now offered an overhead, oversquare V-8 engine, of the type pioneered in 1949 by Olds and Cadillac. This is the engine that set the way for the great horsepower race of the late fifties, and it was available with an optional "power pac" (dual exhaust and a four-barrel carb) to let the world know Chevrolet was in the race.

By now, even Chevrolet offered power steering, power brakes, air conditioning and power windows. Coupled with an efficient drivetrain, this means that the car is practical to use as well as restore. This car was

produced through 1957 with such rare and pleasing facelifting that any original example of this marque has tremendous value and appeal today. However, many of the war babies grew up in the next ten years and modified the old family sport wagon. Most of it is tasteful, consisting primarily of ridding the car of any gaudiness by dechroming and modifying the power train. These conditions are easily restored to original, but many of the '56 and '57 models have had their rear wheel openings radiused to accept larger tires. This is costly to correct and depreciates the car.

Nomads are so popular now that some manufacturers have begun to reproduce hard-to-find parts, such as the waffle pattern interior and the chrome strips for the tail-gate. They are available, but they can be expensive.

SPECIFICATIONS

Wheelbase . . . . .115"
Tread; Front, Rear . . . . .58", 58.8"
Overall Length . . . . .197.1"
Overall Width . . . . .74.0"
Overall Height . . . . .60.7"
Weight, Lbs 3335
Tire Size . . . . .6.70 x 15"

ENGINE

Type . . . . .Overhead 90° V-8
Bore & Stroke . . . . .3.75" x 3.00"
Displacement, Cu. In. .265
Compression Ratio .8.0 to 1
Horsepower @ RPM . . . . .162 @ 4400
Max. Torque @ RPM . . . . .257 @ 2200
Electrical .12 Volt, neg. grd.

TRANSMISSION

Type . . . . .3 speed manual
Available . . . . .Automatic, overdrive

REAR

Type . . . . .Hypoid, spiral bevel gears
Ratio . . . . .3.70 manual
                                             3.55 powerglide
TUNE UP
                                             4.11 overdrive

Spark Plug Gap . . . . .035"
Point Gap . . . . .019" new, .016" used
Cam Angle, Degrees 36-33
Timing . . . . .Second mark before "0"
Firing Order 18436572
Tappet Clearances:
    Intake . . . . .008"
    Exhaust . . . . .016"
Compression Pressure,
Lbs 140
Idle Speed, RPM . . . . .475 (manual trans.)

BRAKES

Type . . . . .Hydraulic, int. exp.
Drum Diameter . . . . .11"

CAPACITIES

Cooling System, Qts 17
Fuel Tank, Gals 16
Crank Case, Qts 4
Trans. Pints 2
Differential, Pts 3½

WHEEL ALIGNMENT

Caster, Degrees . . . .+1½
Camber, Degrees . . . . .0 to +1°
Toe in, Inches . . . . .⅛ to 3/16

1955 Corvette

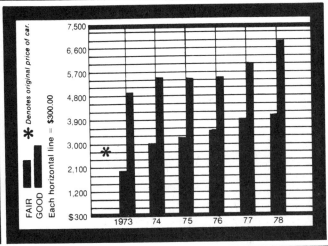

Otherwise the same as the 1954 model, the Corvette in 1955 featured Chevy's new 265 cubic-inch V-8. This was the move that shaped the future for Corvette. By the following year, it would irreversibly assume the role of the only American sports car. But in 1955, the fiberglass bodied roadster was already unique. From its wire mesh headlight screens to its abbreviated split rear bumpers, it conveyed the sensation of sportiness, if not the finality of it. The transmission fitted to most early Corvettes was powerglide, a floor-mounted carryover from the six-cylinder progenitor of the series.

The Corvette became one of few G.M. motorama inspired success stories. This was one time the people wanted what they got and got what they wanted. Strangely, the Waldorf Nomad, which led to the full size Chevrolet wagon of the same name, was originally a Corvette-based prototype. The two-seater Corvette was supposed to pave the way for the future of fiberglass. In the early fifties, many foresaw fiberglass as the salvation of the auto industry. Of course, it didn't turn out that way, but plastic in many forms has been assuming an ever-growing role in the creation of our newer cars. While plastic is generally looked upon with disdain, the Corvette remains highly praised for its rust-free fiberglass body. The panels that would crack rather than crease are responsible for the preservation of so many early Corvettes.

Inside this low-slung beauty, the driver was at the command of the most enviable machine in America. With a fiberglass canopy totally enveloping the convertible top mechanism, the sporty character of the Corvette was sustained in fair weather or foul. Bucket seats and an imaginative dash layout were the complements of this car.

With only a few thousand of these 1954-55 Corvettes ever reaching production, it is no wonder the price is so high. Production always seemed to run behind demand of the early versions. Only briefly, when the super fast fuel-injected models kept America preoccupied, did the prices sag low enough for a commoner to pick one up. That momentary lapse of attention is long gone, though. Today, expect to pay in the neighborhood of $5,000 for a decent 1955 specimen. Tomorrow, with the memories becoming even fonder, it will be among the strongest investments in the material world, barring none.

SPECIFICATIONS

Wheelbase	.102"
Tread; Front, Rear	.57", 59"
Overall Length	.167"
Overall Width	.72.2"
Overall Height	.52.1"
Weight, Lbs	.2850
Tire Size	.6.70 x 15"

ENGINE

Type	.Overhead V-8
Bore & Stroke	.3.75" x 3.00"
Displacement, Cu. In.	.265
Compression Ratio	.8.00 to 1
Horsepower @ RPM	.195 @ 5000
Max. Torque @ RPM	.260 @ 3000
Electrical	.12 Volt, neg. grd.

TRANSMISSION

Type	.3 speed manual
Available	.Automatic

REAR

Type	.Hypoid, semi-floating
Ratio	.3.70 to 1

TUNE UP

Spark Plug Gap	.035"
Point Gap	.019" (new) .016" (used)
Cam Angle, Degrees	.26-33
Timing	.2nd line before "O" mark
Firing Order	.18436572
Tappet Clearances:	
Intake	.008"
Exhaust	.016"
Compression Pressure,	
Lbs	.165
Idle Speed, RPM	.425

BRAKES

Type	.Hydraulic, int. exp.
Drum Diameter	.11"

CAPACITIES

Cooling System, Qts	.17
Fuel Tank, Gals	.17.25
Crank Case, Qts	.5
Trans. Pints	.5
Differential, Pts	.4

WHEEL ALIGNMENT

Caster, Degrees	.0 to +1
Camber, Degrees	.0 to +1
Toe in, Inches	.0 to 1/8

1955 Ford Crown Victoria

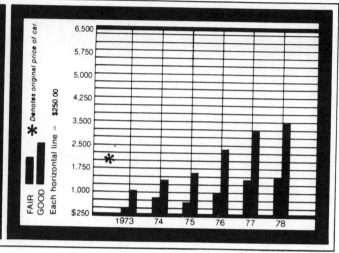

The sweeping chrome sash arcing gracefully over the roofline tells you immediately that this is a Crown Victoria. It is a stylized Fairlane that extrolled the virtues of the dreamcar for many Americans. The inspirational effect of this roofline was just the right complement to Ford's lower body lines of 1955 and 1956. It looks good and its good looks are unmistakably Ford. Of course, the real crowning glory of these Victorias was the glasstop model that saw even more limited production. The tinted plexiglass panel that replaced the steel roof forward of the chrome sash breathed immortality into the Victoria. Even though the glasstop option was available in 1954 (Ford and Mercury), the superior execution of its design in the 1955 and '56 versions makes them far more valuable to the collector.

All Crown Victorias had a uniqueness that has never been begrudged. Unlike some statements of form whose peculiarities command value beyond reason, the Victorias' traditionally high prices mirror their desirability. This was a good year for Ford in general. The new body more aptly conveyed the message of the overhead V-8 introduced in 1954. The image was complete now: clean and racy and consciously extroverted. The "kissin' cousin of the Thunderbird" was no joke.

It is not yet difficult to find the Crown Victorias (except for the glasstop version), but the effects of twenty years will undoubtedly necessitate some refurbishing. With many '55 and '56 Fords still in some state of existence, the problems of physical and mechanical restoration are limited. Just make sure the Crown Victoria lettering on the front fenders is intact, as there is no place to find it other than on another Crown Victoria.

A really prized combination is the stick shift and overdrive mated to the four-barrel engine with dual exhausts. It was a flashy car in 1955 and it has lost little ground since. The thrill of driving one can only be expressed as an indescribable chuckle brought about by the personification of the mind and spirit of 1955 and powered by the adrenalin of that era.

SPECIFICATIONS

Wheelbase	115.5"
Tread; Front, Rear	58", 56"
Overall Length	198.5"
Overall Width	75.9"
Overall Height	61"
Weight, Lbs	3236
Tire Size	6.70 x 15"

ENGINE

Type	Overhead V-8
Bore & Stroke	3.625" x 3.60"
Displacement, Cu. In.	272
Compression Ratio	7.60 to 1
Horsepower @ RPM	162 @ 4200
Max. Torque @ RPM	258 @ 2200
Electrical	6 Volt, pos. grd.

TRANSMISSION

Type	3 speed manual
Available	Automatic

REAR

Type	Hypoid, semi-floating
Ratio	3.78 to 1

TUNE UP

Spark Plug Gap	.034"
Point Gap	.015"
Cam Angle, Degrees	26-28
Timing	3° B.T.D.C.
Firing Order	15486372
Tappet Clearances:	
Intake	.019"
Exhaust	.019"
Compression Pressure, Lbs	135
Idle Speed, RPM	475

BRAKES

Type	Hydraulic, int. exp.
Drum Diameter	11"

CAPACITIES

Cooling System, Qts	21
Fuel Tank, Gals	17
Crank Case, Qts	5
Trans. Pints	3
Differential, Pts	3.5

WHEEL ALIGNMENT

Caster, Degrees	+½ to +1½
Camber, Degrees	+¼ to +1¼
Toe in, Inches	¹/₁₆ to ⅛

1955 Hudson Hornet Hollywood

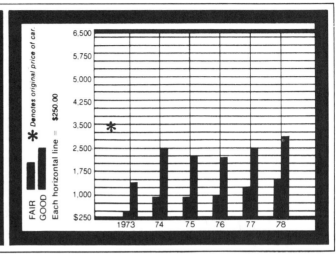

1955 ushered in the Davy Crockett fad for the children. It was destined for a short life, as the parent of any ten-year-old well knew. In the world of automobiles, a few fads were also brought to public attention. It was just harder to see that they, too, were temporary. Two-tone paint jobs intended for contrast more than accent found their way onto most of the new cars. In 1955, if it was bright, it was right. So the color rage caught on. Headlights had to be frenched, peaked or browed that year for a car to be accepted. And if your car didn't have a wraparound windshield, it was as out of place as a Tex Ritter gun in the company of a coonskin cap.

The Hudson Hornet Hollywood had all of this and more. This top-of-the-line hardtop had a factory standard continental kit to clinch the approval of the most demanding connoisseur. With a V-8 engine and all the usual options, it was a shoo-in to win the hearts of the people. It didn't, for a few reasons. The first reason is the unforgivable assumption that any car — especially a good one — produced by an independent must be viewed with skepticism. The merger that year with Nash-Kelvinator fooled no one into believing the whole was greater than the sum of its parts. The next reason is the nature of the product itself. While it was equipped with all of the hot-selling items and had no appreciable lack of quality, the Hollywood looked like a gimmick. It was like no previous Hudson with this new body it shared with Nash. It had

no identity strong enough to assimilate the components of its structure into a singular essence. In effect, it was a laughable potpourri of all of the gimmicks of 1955 that were successful in the guise of more traditional namesakes.

As always, the uncommon sight of the name becomes the prime factor of such a car's value. This Hudson gave us a look at ourselves as we really were in 1955 and no one liked the starkness of that reality. In light of that response, the price of a good specimen today may seem high. You never can tell about fads. Sometimes they return and sometimes they don't. That seems to be the way it is with these Hudsons. Sometimes they sell and sometimes they don't.

SPECIFICATIONS

Wheelbase	121.25"
Tread; Front, Rear	59.5", 60.5"
Overall Length	209.25"
Overall Width	78"
Overall Height	62.25"
Weight, Lbs	3550
Tire Size	7.10 x 15

ENGINE

Type	Overhead V-8
Bore & Stroke	3.8125" x 3.50"
Displacement, Cu. In.	320
Compression Ratio	9.55 to 1
Horsepower @ RPM	208 @ 4200
Max. Torque @ RPM	300 @ 2000
Electrical	12 Volt, pos. grd.

TRANSMISSION

Type	Automatic
Available	3 speed manual, overdrive

REAR

Type	Hypoid, semi-floating
Ratio	3.54 to 1

TUNE UP

Spark Plug Gap	.035"
Point Gap	.020"
Cam Angle, Degrees	27
Timing	5° B.T.D.C.
Firing Order	18436572
Tappet Clearances:	
Intake	Zero, hydraulic
Exhaust	Zero, hydraulic
Compression Pressure, Lbs	140
Idle Speed, RPM	425

BRAKES

Type	Hydraulic, int. exp.
Drum Diameter	11"

CAPACITIES

Cooling System, Qts	21
Fuel Tank, Gals	20
Crank Case, Qts	5
Trans.	11 Qts.
Differential, Pts	4

WHEEL ALIGNMENT

Caster, Degrees	0 to +½
Camber, Degrees	−¼ to +¼
Toe in, Inches	1/16 to 3/16

1955 Oldsmobile Holiday 88

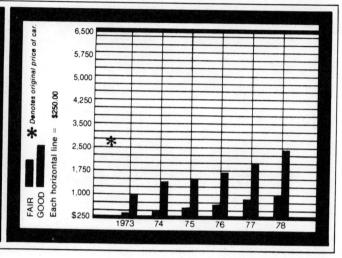

The 1955 Oldsmobile Holiday 88 was a good car, but not a great car. It had no distinct idiosyncrasies that could guarantee its place in destiny. With no abundance of any particular quality, it was forced to earn any reputation it got. The piece of the automotive spectrum it represents is more general than particular. Since the majority of cars shares this definition, it is necessary to illustrate their ranks from time to time to maintain a proper perspective on automobiles. The typical sedans and coupes of all eras comprise the backbone of the industry. Eventually, they all get old enough to be collected, so it is wise to understand their roles.

The Oldsmobile name has always enjoyed a sound reputation. In the years between 1949 and 1957, some of the soundest Oldsmobiles were built. This is in no small way responsible to its rocket V-8 engine. Big news in 1949, the 1955 version was still among the most potent in the industry. At least in this application, Oldsmobile was respected for its performance. The sporty hardtop styling made it the darling of the young at heart, a family car that left the fun in driving.

The polychromatic flair that swept across its profile was duplicated in harmony by matching interior colors. The oval grille cavity and teardrop shrouds surrounding the headlights were distinctively Oldsmobile, with origins traceable to the Cutlass dreamcar of Motorama fame. The

scalloped rear wheel openings went well with this package, as did the fender tip taillights.

That's the way the 88 was in 1955 — good looking, well built and not uncommon. A tight, clean car will bring a good price today, but anything less than that would be too . . . er . . . common to be worth much. It will be another decade before the importance of the condition factor will diminish. It's always been that way for average cars. It's the other ones that are exceptions to the rule.

SPECIFICATIONS

Wheelbase . . . . .122"
Tread; Front, Rear . . . . .59", 58"
Overall Length . . . . .203.4"
Overall Width . . . . .77.8"
Overall Height . . . . .60.5"
Weight, Lbs 3711
Tire Size . . . . .7.60 x 15"

ENGINE

Type . . . . .Overhead V-8
Bore & Stroke . . . . .3.875" x 3.437"
Displacement, Cu. In. 324
Compression Ratio . . . . .8.50 to 1
Horsepower @ RPM . . . . .202 @ 4000
Max. Torque @ RPM . . . . .332 @ 2400
Electrical .12 Volt, neg. grd.

TRANSMISSION

Type . . . . .Automatic
Available . . . . .3 spd. manual

REAR

Type .Hypoid, semi-floating
Ratio . . . . .3.23 to 1

TUNE UP

Spark Plug Gap . . . . .030"
Point Gap . . . . .016"
Cam Angle, Degrees 26-33
Timing . . . . .Slot on pulley
Firing Order 18736542
Tappet Clearances:
    Intake . . . . .Zero, hydraulic
    Exhaust . . . . .Zero, hydraulic
Compression Pressure,
Lbs 150
Idle Speed, RPM 375

BRAKES

Type .Hydraulic, int. exp.
Drum Diameter . . . . .11"

CAPACITIES

Cooling System, Qts 21.5
Fuel Tank, Gals 20
Crank Case, Qts 5
Trans. . . . . .11 Qts.
Differential, Pts 4.75

WHEEL ALIGNMENT

Caster, Degrees . . . .−¾ to 0
Camber, Degrees . . . .−¾ to +¾
Toe in, Inches . . . . .¹/₁₆ to ⅛

1955 Packard Caribbean

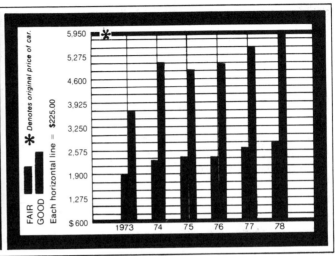

1955 was one of the biggest years the auto industry has ever had. Almost every car was new that year. This factor pushed sales to the magic ten million mark for the first time. For Packard, 1955 was to be the last big splash into the pool of modern times.

No one can say that Packard didn't go down swinging. In the Caribbean model, the ailing independent conjured up all the modern magic it could assemble. The car was a sensational departure, even from previous Caribbean models. At a time when two colors were in, this Packard had a three-color paint scheme. At a time when people were conscious of the number of horses under the hood, the Caribbean coralled the largest herd. And, as always, Packard was to lead the parade of engineering developments. A self-leveling torsion bar suspension was offered on the big Packards in 1955. Before the Caribbean was finished, it would be available with an electric push-button automatic transmission selector. One would think this was the ultimate in one-upmanship.

Reversible seat cushions that snapped in place gave the owner the choice of leather or fabric interiors in his Caribbean. This is something others have yet to discover. Outside, courtesy lights marked the rear fenders, while huge wraparound taillights were visible from the sides as well as the rear. In front, the parking lights wrapped around also, making the Caribbean safer than its 1955

counterparts. Twin rear-mounted antennae capped the essence of its long, nearly radical, looks.

The list of achievements could continue. The point is, though, that the strength of the company was not able to match the precedent of the car. Packards had been so somber in the early part of the decade that the contrast was too much of a jolt, even for Packard afficianados. The big convertible also saw ample competition from Cadillac's Eldorado in a severely restricted market. But the Caribbean said exactly what it meant. It was an opulent, if unforeseen, exit for one of the great marques of all time. The Predictor dreamcar kept alive the flicker of its imagination a while longer, but the ill wind of fate soon snuffed the breath of these breathtaking Packards. By 1957, after a merger with Studebaker, the bark of its name would be bigger than its bite on the market.

It is fitting that Packard Caribbeans command such high prices today. No Packard is really inexpensive; but these showboats, as the corporeal embodiment of luxury, stand in lasting testimony to the mid-fifties' ideal of unlimited expense in transportation. It would cost far more to build one today.

SPECIFICATIONS

Wheelbase	127"
Tread; Front, Rear	60", 60.9"
Overall Length	217.5"
Overall Width	78"
Overall Height	62.3"
Weight, Lbs	4355
Tire Size	8.00 x 15"

ENGINE

Type	Overhead V-8
Bore & Stroke	4.00" x 3.50"
Displacement, Cu. In.	352
Compression Ratio	8.50 to 1
Horsepower @ RPM	275 @ 4800
Max. Torque @ RPM	355 @ 2400
Electrical	12 Volt, pos. grd.

TRANSMISSION

Type	Automatic
Available	—

REAR

Type	Hypoid, semi-floating
Ratio	3.07 to 1

TUNE UP

Spark Plug Gap	.035"
Point Gap	.016"
Cam Angle, Degrees	27
Timing	5° B.T.D.C.
Firing Order	18436572
Tappet Clearances:	
Intake	Zero, hydraulic
Exhaust	Zero, hydraulic
Compression Pressure, Lbs	120
Idle Speed, RPM	425

BRAKES

Type	Hydraulic, int. exp.
Drum Diameter	12"

CAPACITIES

Cooling System, Qts	24
Fuel Tank, Gals	20
Crank Case, Qts	5
Trans.	11 Qts.
Differential, Pts	4.5

WHEEL ALIGNMENT

Caster, Degrees	−½ to −1½
Camber, Degrees	−¾ to +¾
Toe in, Inches	0 to +1/16

1955 Studebaker President Speedster

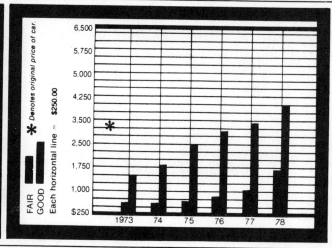

"Rev 'er up to 8500, we're coming through." You may recognize this James Thurber line from *The Secret Life of Walter Mitty*. Walter Mitty was a meek little character who daydreamed his way in and out of daring adventures. We all have a little Walter Mitty in us. Occasionally, we too confuse the commonness of reality with the illusion of our mind. And while the mind is the vehicle of our ascent, the automobile is often the scapegoat of our travels.

In 1955, Studebaker put forth the sheer image of such a vehicle. The Speedster was low, lithe and full of the spirit that tempts the Walter Mitty in us to indulge in fantasy. An extension of the original Raymond Loewy design of 1953, the Speedster was bold and daring. The drooping nose now sported a splash of chrome; the aggressive pattern found its way to the sculpted sides of the car. The delicate pastel colors that adorned the original were swapped for a contrasting pair of colors that were so loud they screamed for attention. The engine-turned dash and hopped-up V-8 certified the authority for such insolence. Available with strong looking wire-type wheels and overdrive transmission, the Speedster could back its sassiness with action — even while standing still.

Yes, the action of its lines and the threat of its indignant scowl at the contemporary boxcars made in America were responsible for placing more than one Walter Mitty in the

driver's seat. James Thurber would wink if you told him how hard it was to separate the fun from the fantasy in the Studebaker Speedster. So would Walter Mitty!

SPECIFICATIONS

Wheelbase	120.5"
Tread; Front, Rear	56.6875", 55.6875"
Overall Length	206"
Overall Width	71"
Overall Height	57"
Weight, Lbs	3165
Tire Size	7.10 x 15"

ENGINE

Type	Overhead V-8
Bore & Stroke	3.5625" x 3.25"
Displacement, Cu. In.	259
Compression Ratio	7.50 to 1
Horsepower @ RPM	185 @ 4500
Max. Torque @ RPM	258 @ 2800
Electrical	6 Volt, pos. grd.

TRANSMISSION

Type	3 speed manual
Available	Automatic, overdrive

REAR

Type	Hypoid, semi-floating
Ratio	3.54 to 1

TUNE UP

Spark Plug Gap	.035"
Point Gap	.013"
Cam Angle, Degrees	28-34
Timing	I.G.N. mark on dmpr.
Firing Order	18436572
Tappet Clearances:	
Intake	.024"
Exhaust	.024"
Compression Pressure,	
Lbs	130
Idle Speed, RPM	550

BRAKES

Type	Hydraulic, int. exp.
Drum Diameter	11" front, 10" rear

CAPACITIES

Cooling System, Qts	18.75
Fuel Tank, Gals	18
Crank Case, Qts	6
Trans. Pints	2.5
Differential, Pts	3

WHEEL ALIGNMENT

Caster, Degrees	−1 to −2½
Camber, Degrees	0 to +1
Toe in, Inches	1/16 to 1/8

1956 Cadillac Coupe de Ville

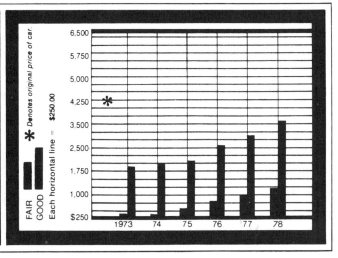

Picture yourself in 1956, riding on the crest of prestige, flaunting the opulence of success by the mere character of your Cadillac. From 1948 until 1956, the fishtail fins that graced every Cadillac were symbolic of this identity. It all happened when General Motors emerged after World War II as the uncontested engineering and styling leader of the industry. In this, their most prestigious product, we find the most empirical definition of this success. The Cadillac was the embodiment of the cumulative traits that earned for G.M. its hot reputation of the fifties. In these years, General Motors capped its creations with various symbols to preserve its identity. While others dared to emulate the broad vee crest that adorned its hood and trunk, no one ever adopted Cadillac's fishtail fins. To do so would have been both blasphemous and disastrous, as their success was more symbolic than physical.

In fact, by 1956, the physical limits of their inspiration were exhausted. This was to be the last year that the man in the grey flannel suit could defer the comparison of prestige. It also ended for a while the status by size that had served to differentiate the high priced cars from the rest of the crowd. And as the narrow-minded affluence that captioned these years drew to an end, along with it went other aspects of Cadillac's prominent character. No longer was the 60 Special the fastest thing on wheels. Cadillac's exclusive bumper tip exhausts were commonly

available, as was the overhead V-8 engine that began the era of its dominance. The middle class cars were even scoring gains in the area of power assists and options — an area that once was reserved for an elite few.

Still, the car that gave us "the Solid Gold Cadillac" was the star of 1956, barely surpassing the feats of Rock Hudson and Doris Day. The last reminder of a glamorous age when a man's car was his castle has been rediscovered. As with any complete castle, there is a ghost that haunts the domain. It is the spirit of past excellence, and, judging from the early returns of its redebut, it is still packing them in! If you intend to be the manager of a 1956 Coupe de Ville, be mindful of its condition. Otherwise, your star will have to work very hard to earn its keep.

SPECIFICATIONS

Wheelbase	.129"
Tread; Front, Rear	.60", 63.1"
Overall Length	.221.9"
Overall Width	.80"
Overall Height	.62"
Weight, Lbs	.4445
Tire Size	.8.00 x 15"

ENGINE

Type	.Overhead V-8
Bore & Stroke	.4.00" x 3.625"
Displacement, Cu. In.	.365
Compression Ratio	.9.75 to 1
Horsepower @ RPM	.285 @ 4600
Max. Torque @ RPM	.400 @ 2800
Electrical	.12 Volt, neg. grd.

TRANSMISSION

Type	.Automatic
Available	.—

REAR

Type	.Hypoid, semi-floating
Ratio	.3.36 to 1

TUNE UP

Spark Plug Gap	.035"
Point Gap	.Adj. screw
Cam Angle, Degrees	.30
Timing	.Mark "A"
Firing Order	.18436572
Tappet Clearances:	
Intake	.Zero, hydraulic
Exhaust	.Zero, hydraulic
Compression Pressure, Lbs	.165
Idle Speed, RPM	.420

BRAKES

Type	.Hydraulic, int. exp.
Drum Diameter	.12"

CAPACITIES

Cooling System, Qts	.19
Fuel Tank, Gals	.20
Crank Case, Qts	.5
Trans.	.11.5 Qts.
Differential, Pts	.5

WHEEL ALIGNMENT

Caster, Degrees	.0 to −1
Camber, Degrees	.−3/8 to +3/8
Toe in, Inches	.3/16 to 1/4

1956 Continental

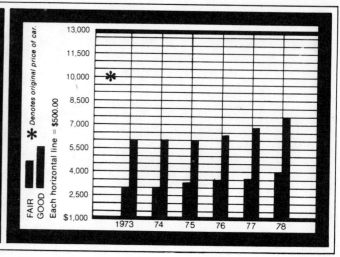

The success of the Lincoln Continental was never so remembered until after its departure. Within a few years after the last 1948 Continental was produced, feelings ran high in Dearborn for an able successor to the last classic. The original Continental was already legendary, so why not revive the theme with a modern projection of its essence?

At a time when Eldorados and Caribbeans were battling for the heavyweight crown of prestige, the new Continental Mark II was unveiled. It was to be the ultimate "chariot of the gods" and it *was* in many ways. What was most apparent was that it was a chic car compared to the gaudy, oversized Cadillac and Packard creations. Underneath this blueblood body, the obsession for perfection was carried to ridiculous extremes. The specially cast and plated hubcaps cost a fortune to build. So did the grille. They didn't look any better than those on any other car. The same is true for the heavy chrome plating used instead of stainless steel, and the horrendously expensive paint on the Continental. No wonder it cost $10,000 in 1956 — more than any other car in the country.

Comments on its reintroduction ranged through the extremes of accolade and hyprocrisy. After nearly twenty years, the impact of the Continental Mark II seems to be that a limited production car costing $10,000 new and bearing a noble

name, however bastardized, is still worth a great deal of money because no one is in a position to affirmatively deny its message. That is why its value is more static than erratic. The fulcrum of argument lies evenly balanced, as it always has. The fact that it does exist is the center of its position — the most tangible aspect of its definition. This fact alone is interchangeable with dollars. The rate of interchange must always be indicative of its spirit, or the car is either a fad or a phony. The Mark II is neither of these; it is what it is and it will cost you about $5,000 to find out if it is overrated or underrated. As purveyors of fine cars go, this one is a dealer's choice.

SPECIFICATIONS

Wheelbase	.126"
Tread; Front, Rear	.58.5", 60"
Overall Length	.218.5"
Overall Width	.77.5"
Overall Height	.56"
Weight, Lbs	.5190
Tire Size	.8.00 x 15"

ENGINE

Type	Overhead V-8
Bore & Stroke	.4.00" x 3.66"
Displacement, Cu. In.	.368
Compression Ratio	.9.00 to 1
Horsepower @ RPM	.N.A.
Max. Torque @ RPM	.402 @ 3000
Electrical	.12 Volt, neg. grd.

TRANSMISSION

Type	Automatic
Available	.—

REAR

Type	Hypoid, semi-floating
Ratio	.3.07 to 1

TUNE UP

Spark Plug Gap	.034"
Point Gap	.015"
Cam Angle, Degrees	.26-28
Timing	.5° B.T.D.C.
Firing Order	.15486372
Tappet Clearances:	
Intake	Zero, hydraulic
Exhaust	Zero, hydraulic
Compression Pressure,	
Lbs	.160
Idle Speed, RPM	.465

BRAKES

Type	Hydraulic, int. exp.
Drum Diameter	.12"

CAPACITIES

Cooling System, Qts	.25.2
Fuel Tank, Gals	.25
Crank Case, Qts	.5
Trans.	.10 Qts.
Differential, Pts	.4

WHEEL ALIGNMENT

Caster, Degrees	+3/4 to +1 1/4
Camber, Degrees	+1/2 to +1
Toe in, Inches	3/32 to 5/32

1956 Pontiac Safari

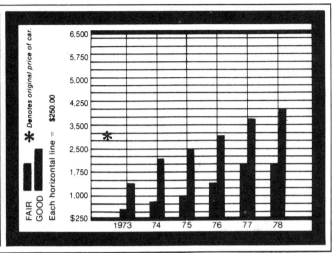

Back in 1955, things started to change at Pontiac. The aging straight eight became a V-8 and the familiar silver streak found itself atop a sporty new body. Gone were the staid image and the unmistakable sound of old Chief Pontiac.

It was a different car seeking a different image. It got it! Pontiac became the big name in racing over the course of about the next decade. Its style during those years reflected this aggressiveness. In fact, the earlier models flaunted it with excessive brightwork.

Over at Chevrolet, similar things were happening. When Chevy came out with the sporty Nomad wagon, Pontiac countered with its own version, the Safari. The cleaner looking Nomads went directly to fame and fortune. Safaris, being somewhat larger and heavier and gaudier, did not fare so well. In spite of the fact that they were nearly forgotten from sight and mind, it seems a curious oversight that they didn't start picking up in value years ago, when Nomads got hot. Only recently has the Safari received its just reward.

Pontiacs are more expensive than Chevrolets (when new, at least.) Since they share the same basic body, the Pontiac buyer usually ends up with a little bit more of whatever the public likes at any particular time. In 1956, the public liked, or was told it liked, flashy chrome, flashy colors, and the flash of extra horsepower. This is what

the Safari had to offer. It also had a more luxurious interior and came generally equipped with more driver conveniences than the lower-priced Nomad. At this point it became too good to be dirtied by the menial work of a station wagon. But it was a station wagon, one with only two doors. So it proved not good enough to serve the large family. The only other person it might have appealed to was buying the sportier, more spartan Nomad.

Today, neither of these cars is going to be used as a station wagon or a family car or a sporty runabout. The good original examples are show material and they bring corresponding prices. On this basis, the Safari really shines. If put in the same show with a Nomad, in equal condition, the Pontiac would get greater attention. This is because it is a fresh new star, seldom seen at such events. And, you know, all that leather and chrome looks pretty good now. It kind of gets to you after a while. There . . . I think I see the glitter in your eye!

SPECIFICATIONS

Wheelbase . . . . .122"
Tread; Front, Rear . . . . .58.67", 59.047"
Overall Length . . . . .206.7"
Overall Width . . . . .75.1"
Overall Height . . . . .59.6"
Weight, Lbs 3585
Tire Size . . . . .7.60 x 15"

ENGINE

Type . . . . .Overhead V-8
Bore & Stroke . . . . .3.9375" x 3.25"
Displacement, Cu. In. .316
Compression Ratio . . . . .8.90 to 1
Horsepower @ RPM . . . . .227 @ 4800
Max. Torque @ RPM . . . . .312 @ 3000
Electrical . . . . .12 Volt, neg. grd.

TRANSMISSION

Type . . . . .Automatic
Available . . . . .3 spd. manual

REAR

Type .Hypoid, semi-floating
Ratio . . . . .3.08 to 1

TUNE UP

Spark Plug Gap . . . . .035"
Point Gap . . . . .016"
Cam Angle, Degrees 26-33
Timing . . . . .First line under pointer
Firing Order 18436572
Tappet Clearances:
    Intake .Zero, hydraulic
    Exhaust .Zero, hydraulic
Compression Pressure,
Lbs 120
Idle Speed, RPM 440

BRAKES

Type .Hydraulic, int. exp.
Drum Diameter . . . . .12" front, 11" rear

CAPACITIES

Cooling System, Qts 24.5
Fuel Tank, Gals 17
Crank Case, Qts 5
Trans. . . . . .9.5 Qts.
Differential, Pts 3.25

WHEEL ALIGNMENT

Caster, Degrees . . . .−½ to −1½
Camber, Degrees . . . . .0 to +1
Toe in, Inches .0 to ¹/₁₆

1956 Thunderbird

The '56 FORD THUNDERBIRD

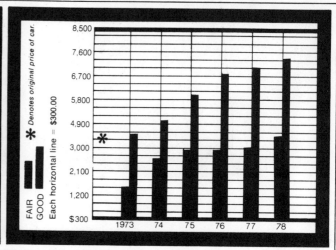

Denotes original price of car.

* Each horizontal line = $300.00

FAIR   GOOD

8,500
7,600
6,700
5,800
4,900
3,000
2,100
1,200
$300

1973   74   75   76   77   78

Built to capture the Corvette market, the original Thunderbird series lasted three years before changing its image. It never did intimidate America's only sports car, but it found a ready market just around the corner. In those three years of its two-seater production, not everyone who liked the T-bird got a chance to own one. Consequently, those still trying are at the heavy end of a resale price that never had a very light end.

The "personal car" always had a lot going for it. From the peaked headlight brows to the porthole hardtop to the continental kit, it imparted the elegance of its individuality. Even the optional fender skirts seemed to protect it from the carnal concept of a sports car. The lucky owner of a Thunderbird could have the comfort and convenience that lie on the fringe of the power spectrum and still be sassy with relative impartiality.

The overhead V-8 (Ford liked to call it a Y-8) was powerful and efficient with either the Fordomatic or the stick transmission. It had a four-barrel carburetor and bumper tip exhaust pipes that were the rage at the time. But the mechanical nuances of the Thunderbird are not as well remembered as the total image the car imparted. This is because the car was so well balanced that the parts did not stand out from the whole, just as the organs of the body do not exceed the nature of man.

In terms of this harmony there are few cars in history that stand equal to the Thunderbird. Those that do are called classics. In fairness befitting the breed, the price of such art is beyond the reach of the masses — a condition which leads them to aspire to such greatness. This is the way it was in 1955 and 1965 — and 1975. This is the Thunderbird mystique. It was created for an enlightened, affluent few and it has remained true to that ideal.

SPECIFICATIONS

Wheelbase . . . . .102"
Tread; Front, Rear . . . . .56", 56"
Overall Length . . . . .185"
Overall Width . . . . .71"
Overall Height . . . . .52"
Weight, Lbs 3570
Tire Size . . . . .6.70 x 15"

ENGINE

Type . . . . .Overhead V-8
Bore & Stroke . . . . .3.75" x 3.30"
Displacement, Cu. In. 292
Compression Ratio . . . . .8.40 to 1
Horsepower @ RPM . . . . .202 @ 4600
Max. Torque @ RPM . . . . .289 @ 2600
Electrical . . . . .12 Volt, neg. grd.

TRANSMISSION

Type . . . . .Automatic
Available . . . . .3 spd. manual

REAR

Type . . . . .Hypoid, semi-floating
Ratio . . . . .3.31 to 1

TUNE UP

Spark Plug Gap . . . . .034"
Point Gap . . . . .015"
Cam Angle, Degrees 26-28
Timing . . . . .6° B.T.D.C.
Firing Order 15486372
Tappet Clearances:
    Intake . . . . .019"
    Exhaust . . . . .019"
Compression Pressure,
Lbs 150
Idle Speed, RPM 450

BRAKES

Type . . . . .Hydraulic, int. exp.
Drum Diameter .11"

CAPACITIES

Cooling System, Qts 21
Fuel Tank, Gals .17
Crank Case, Qts .5
Trans. . . . . .10.25 Qts.
Differential, Pts .3

WHEEL ALIGNMENT

Caster, Degrees . . . .+½ to +1½
Camber, Degrees . . . .+¼ to +1¼
Toe in, Inches . . . . .1/16 to 1/8

1957 Cadillac Eldorado

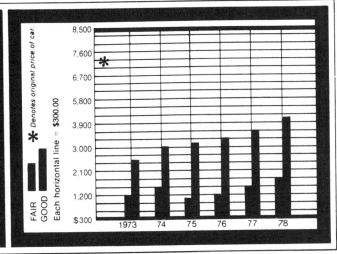

1957 was a strange year for General Motors. On the one hand, it offered the public perhaps the most timeless example of the box-shaped era of cars in the Chevrolet hardtop. On the other hand, the Cadillac Eldorado bordered on the bizarre. The Eldorado differed from other Cadillacs by its distinctive rear end treatment. Broken only by stubby fins, the rounded contour of the rear fenders flowed smoothly across the deck and from there continued its slope to the bottom of its rolled-under belly. It was a beautiful sculpt of metal, but it did not relate properly to the standard Cadillac front and side areas which comprised the rest of the body. Still, one cannot help but wonder how it would have looked without the obstruction of those fins.

The difference in the Eldorado was contrived to distinguish its personality. It was, after all, a step above the ordinary Cadillacs, both in status and price. Other contributions to its distinction ranged from a posh interior decor, to triple two-barrel carburetion, to exotic sabre-spoked wheels. Only the 1957 and 1958 Eldorados show any similarity in design, making them unique and somewhat rare production models. Nobody seems to think they are among the most beautiful cars made, even by Cadillac. Yet the strength of their merit on paper is too strong to be ignored. The situation this creates is obvious. There is a rush to buy them and a rush to sell them, with few people feeling any endearment to the actual essence of the car. Both the

hardtop and convertible versions of this hot potato can turn a profit for a foster owner.

To the man who owned an Eldorado in 1957, it was one asset among many — one that summarily spoke for his wealth. In this respect it was a disposable commodity. It had to be replaced annually to maintain the image it was created to fulfill. For the second and third owners of an Eldorado, the veneer of its mystique can work no charm. When this type of car becomes old enough so that there is no question of status in its ownership, it is ready to begin a new life, more enduring than the former. The 1957 Cadillac Eldorado offers you the chance of a lifetime.

SPECIFICATIONS

Wheelbase	129.5"
Tread; Front, Rear	61", 61"
Overall Length	222.1"
Overall Width	80"
Overall Height	57.9"
Weight, Lbs	4800
Tire Size	8.00 x 15"

ENGINE

Type	Overhead V-8
Bore & Stroke	4.00" x 3.625"
Displacement, Cu. In.	365
Compression Ratio	10.00 to 1
Horsepower @ RPM	325 @ 4800
Max. Torque @ RPM	400 @ 3200
Electrical	12 Volt, neg. grd.

TRANSMISSION

Type	Automatic
Available	—

REAR

Type	Hypoid, semi-floating
Ratio	3.36 to 1

TUNE UP

Spark Plug Gap	.035"
Point Gap	Adj. screw
Cam Angle, Degrees	30
Timing	Flywheel, mark "A"
Firing Order	18436572
Tappet Clearances:	
Intake	Zero, hydraulic
Exhaust	Zero, hydraulic
Compression Pressure,	
Lbs	165
Idle Speed, RPM	400

BRAKES

Type	Hydraulic, int. exp.
Drum Diameter	12"

CAPACITIES

Cooling System, Qts	21
Fuel Tank, Gals	20
Crank Case, Qts	5
Trans.	11.5 Qts.
Differential, Pts	5

WHEEL ALIGNMENT

Caster, Degrees	0 to −1
Camber, Degrees	−3/8 to +3/8
Toe in, Inches	3/16 to 1/4

1957 Chevrolet Bel Air Hardtop

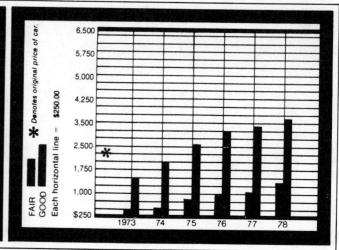

When is the last time you saw a 1957 Plymouth — or Ford, for that matter? The mortality tables say that they have surpassed their life expectancy. Then, why are all these '57 Chevys still around? Shouldn't they, too, have rusted and wheezed their way to the junkyards by now?

The answer is simple. Back in 1952, a man named Ed Cole was heading up a team to create the 1955 Chevrolets, with the intention of getting away from the stodginess that had befallen the car. So completely did they design this car that they literally outengineered the potential weaknesses that cause a car to debilitate. The finished product was a knockout, with beauty that was more than skin deep. It was good enough to last through 1957 with only minor changes. Beyond this, the endurance of the 1957 Chevrolet is attributable to an abnormal demand for it, which resulted in an undying concern for its well-being. This is the point where it parted company with the competition.

It had no fins to go out of style. It is closer to the epitome of the shoebox era of cars that was·at an end by 1957. It retained a balance of proportion that, even today, is nearly ideal. The style was refined enough to prevent it from looking boxy (no easy task) but not so overdone as to swap any class for a fleeting taste of glamour. The mechanics of the 1957 Chevy were so right that they survive today in a full range of variations. So many G.M. parts will bolt into this car that is a wild

card for both rodders and restorers. The car is a chameleon, able to adapt to any change without imposing an image of its own. It has probably been the extension of more ego variations than Freud thought existed!

And yet, when it stands by itself, it is a beautiful and timeless testimony to the definition of the automobile. It's not a lopsided balance of beauty and brawn, but a classic illustration approaching the perfection of the state of the art long after the era of classic cars was thought to have passed.

Prices of 1957 Bel Air Chevrolets are already out of reach for most. At $5,000 plus, there are alternatives to this elusive butterfly. The elements that give it value are negated when the car must be locked away to protect the investment. Prices should be lower. It might be well to remember the inflated Edsel prices in 1968. When people realized it was a decision based more on choice than demand, the hysteria abated, leaving the Edsel to ascend more slowly to a value based on merit.

SPECIFICATIONS

Wheelbase	.115″
Tread; Front, Rear	.58″, 58.8″
Overall Length	.202.8″
Overall Width	.73.9″
Overall Height	.59.1″
Weight, Lbs	.3296
Tire Size	.6.70 x 14″

ENGINE

Type	Overhead V-8
Bore & Stroke	.3.875″ x 3.00″
Displacement, Cu. In.	.283
Compression Ratio	.8.50 to 1
Horsepower @ RPM	.185 @ 4600
Max. Torque @ RPM	.275 @ 2400
Electrical	.12 Volt, neg. grd.

TRANSMISSION

Type	Automatic
Available	3 spd. manual, overdrive

REAR

Type	Hypoid, semi-floating
Ratio	.3.36 to 1

TUNE UP

Spark Plug Gap	.035″
Point Gap	.019″
Cam Angle, Degrees	.30
Timing	.4° B.T.D.C.
Firing Order	.18436572
Tappet Clearances:	
Intake	.Auto adj.
Exhaust	.Auto adj.
Compression Pressure,	
Lbs	.150
Idle Speed, RPM	.425

BRAKES

Type	.Hydraulic, int. exp.
Drum Diameter	.11″

CAPACITIES

Cooling System, Qts	.17
Fuel Tank, Gals	.16
Crank Case, Qts	.4
Trans.	.11 Qts.
Differential, Pts	.3.5

WHEEL ALIGNMENT

Caster, Degrees	+½ to +1½
Camber, Degrees	.0 to +1
Toe in, Inches	.⅛ to ³/₁₆

1957 Corvette

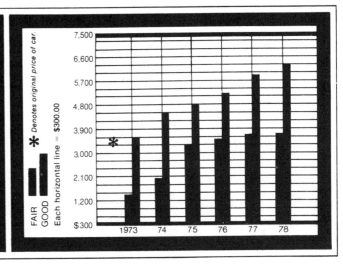

In 1954 and 1955 the Corvette was a sporty-looking novelty car, usually fitted with a near stock six-cylinder Chevrolet engine and powerglide transmission. Rival Thunderbird in 1955 was a little bit sleeker, but also sport-oriented. Under the influence of Zora Arkus Duntov, changes took place in 1956-57 that erased forever any similarities in the T–bird–Corvette definition.

The second generation fiberglass body of the Corvette was much more than sporty. Its intentions were serious. The concave fender flares and well contoured body curves signified the arrival of a modern American sport-racing design. By 1957, Mr. Duntov was producing an impressive one horsepower per cubic inch out of Corvette's high revving, fuel-injected V-8. With the first full syncromesh four-speed and numerous performance goodies under its belt, the 'Vette could outmuscle anything on the road. It was pure Kryptonite to the impunity of the Jaguar 120's and 140's.

That's when it dawned on Ford to go the glamour route with Thunderbird, thus ensuring Corvette's primacy in the sports car market. The 1956-57 models are venerated more for their engineering and macho appeal than for milestone accomplishment. That difference accounts for much of the price disparity between it and its special-interest predecessor. Because it survived relatively unchanged through 1960, and until

1963 in identifiable form, the 1957 Corvette is not considered as rare and unique as most milestone cars. The years between 1956 and 1960 have run together into one fuzzy image. There is no distinct partiality in price or prestige among these Corvettes. They are all highly regarded for the same legitimate reasons. If the '57 hadn't been such a good machine, this would not have been possible. Success, for the Corvette, is a non-specific synonym descriptive of its heritage.

SPECIFICATIONS

Wheelbase . . . . .102"
Tread; Front, Rear . . . . .57", 59"
Overall Length . . . . .168"
Overall Width . . . . .70.5"
Overall Height . . . . .51"
Weight, Lbs 2880
Tire Size . . . . .6.70 x 15"

ENGINE

Type . . . . .Overhead V-8
Bore & Stroke . . . . .3.875" x 3.00"
Displacement, Cu. In. 283
Compression Ratio . . . . .9.50 to 1
Horsepower @ RPM . . . . .270 @ 6200
Max. Torque @ RPM . . . . .285 @ 4200
Electrical . . . . .12 Volt, neg. grd.

TRANSMISSION

Type . . . . .3 speed manual
Available . . . . .Automatic, 4 speed manual

REAR

Type . . . . .Hypoid, Hotchkiss drive
Ratio . . . . .3.70 to 1

TUNE UP

Spark Plug Gap .035"
Point Gap . . . . .017"
Cam Angle, Degrees 30
Timing . . . . .12° B.T.D.C.
Firing Order 18436572
Tappet Clearances:
    Intake . . . . .012"
    Exhaust . . . . .018"
Compression Pressure,
Lbs 190
Idle Speed, RPM 475

BRAKES

Type . . . . .Hydraulic, int. exp.
Drum Diameter . . . . .11"

CAPACITIES

Cooling System, Qts 17
Fuel Tank, Gals .16.4
Crank Case, Qts 5
Trans. Pints 1.5
Differential, Pts 4

WHEEL ALIGNMENT

Caster, Degrees . . . . .0 to +1
Camber, Degrees . . . . .0 to +1
Toe in, Inches . . . . .0 to ⅛

1957 De Soto Adventurer

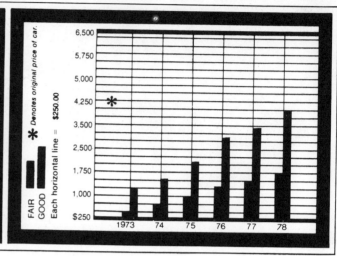

We leave everywhere significant reminders of our status. Totemic identification permeates our lives. Our office or desk has personal plaques or pictures that mark our territory and reinforce our credibility. Our dress, our homes, even if not our own, contain the marks of individuality. There is much to be learned from the choice of style and decor one utilizes to convey his worthiness. Studies have shown that color variations can lend powerful overtures to a particular setting — or they can dilute the strength of an object and decentralize its vantage point.

But nothing expresses power better than power itself. The offices of some executives are arranged to instill a feeling of subordination in visiting clients. The advantage is clearly in favor of the executive. As automobiles go, to be powerful means to display the symbol of such dominance even when it is not in use. The 1957 De Soto Adventurer showed quite clearly how to do this. Available only in limited colors and with certain outstanding deviations in decor, the car was recognizable as a symbol of power, whether it was used as a vehicle of power or not.

Indeed, the car was powerful. It earned an early reputation for that along with the Plymouth Fury, the Dodge 500, and the Chrysler 300. All of these cars used the same theme of distinctive trim and color schemes. They were good cars when it was

important to impress such an image. The peak of totemic potency was on the wane, though, even in 1957. When it reappeared in the mid-to-late sixties, a new breed of car would depict its character. For 1957, the identity of horsepower and fins was status enough. The limited production hot rods were a deviation not yet understood by the public. Now, after having gone full circle with the power game, these cars are emerging as unique memorials to man's strongest inner identity. They express an interesting combination of power muted by the wisdom of age. Like John Wayne, they command the respect of a tough guy through the media of charm and memories. Seldom is the brutality necessary to enforce the image. And seldom is the name taken lightly.

SPECIFICATIONS

Wheelbase .... 126"
Tread; Front, Rear .... 61", 59.7"
Overall Length .... 218.5"
Overall Width .... 78.3"
Overall Height .... 56.7"
Weight, Lbs 4235
Tire Size .... 8.50 x 14"

ENGINE

Type .... Overhead V-8
Bore & Stroke .... 3.794" x 3.794"
Displacement, Cu. In. 345
Compression Ratio .... 9.25 to 1
Horsepower @ RPM .... 345 @ 5200
Max. Torque @ RPM .... 355 @ 3600
Electrical .... 12 Volt, neg. grd.

TRANSMISSION

Type .... Automatic
Available .... —

REAR

Type .... Hypoid, semi-floating
Ratio .... 3.36 to 1

TUNE UP

Spark Plug Gap .... .035"
Point Gap .... .018"
Cam Angle, Degrees 29-32
Timing .... 6° B.T.D.C.
Firing Order 18436572
Tappet Clearances:
   Intake .... Zero, hydraulic
   Exhaust .... Zero, hydraulic
Compression Pressure,
Lbs 165
Idle Speed, RPM 475

BRAKES

Type .... Hydraulic, int. exp.
Drum Diameter .... 12"

CAPACITIES

Cooling System, Qts 20
Fuel Tank, Gals 23
Crank Case, Qts 5
Trans. .... 9 Qts
Differential, Pts 3.5

WHEEL ALIGNMENT

Caster, Degrees .... 0 to +1½
Camber, Degrees .... +⅜ left, 0 right
Toe in, Inches .... 3/32 to 5/32

1957 Ford Skyliner

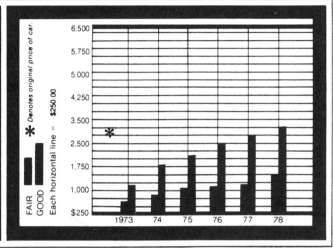

There is only one reason for the high value of the Ford retractable hardtops. That is, nobody else ever made one. I chose to illustrate the 1957 model because it has the additional appeal of being the first one made and it is also the best looking Ford of the three years of retractable production. No retractable really looked great, though, because of the short square roof and long high trunk that were necessary to achieve its purpose. Then there was that line across the roof where it had to fold to fit in the trunk.

There is no point in arguing the beauty of a car whose merit exists independently and regardless of its presence. That was only important in 1957 — and '58 and '59, when it influenced the purchase and subsequent production of the car. Now it is a moot question, the fate of the car having been decided by history. History such as limited trunk space and less than confident mechanics plus the increasing difficulty of incorporating the technology into later designs all spelled trouble for a car that could never match the symmetry of either the hardtop or convertible nature of its schizophrenic personality.

Now that Fords of these years are sufficiently old to be conspicuous in any variation, the uniqueness of the retractable models is icing on the cake. Many are still in hiding awaiting only the final seasoning of their dual nature to enjoy their rightful niche in

the market place. In the meantime, they are secure in the faith that no other car can claim the uniqueness of their territory. They have paid the price of admission to the ranks of the collectible. Nothing can prevent them from redeeming this reservation.

SPECIFICATIONS

Wheelbase	118"
Tread; Front, Rear	59", 56.4"
Overall Length	210.8"
Overall Width	78"
Overall Height	56.3"
Weight, Lbs	3597
Tire Size	8.00 x 14"

ENGINE

Type	Overhead V-8
Bore & Stroke	3.75" x 3.30"
Displacement, Cu. In.	292
Compression Ratio	9.10 to 1
Horsepower @ RPM	212 @ 4500
Max. Torque @ RPM	290 @ 2700
Electrical	12 Volt, neg. grd.

TRANSMISSION

Type	Automatic
Available	3 spd. manual, overdrive

REAR

Type	Hypoid, semi-floating
Ratio	3.56 to 1

TUNE UP

Spark Plug Gap	.034"
Point Gap	.015"
Cam Angle, Degrees	26-28
Timing	6° B.T.D.C.
Firing Order	15486372
Tappet Clearances:	
Intake	.019"
Exhaust	.019"
Compression Pressure,	
Lbs	150
Idle Speed, RPM	475

BRAKES

Type	Hydraulic, int. exp.
Drum Diameter	11"

CAPACITIES

Cooling System, Qts	20
Fuel Tank, Gals	19
Crank Case, Qts	5
Trans.	9.75 Qts.
Differential, Pts	4.5

WHEEL ALIGNMENT

Caster, Degrees	+½ to +1½
Camber, Degrees	+½ to +1½
Toe in, Inches	1/16 to 1/8

1957 Mercury Turnpike Cruiser

CED CAR YOU CAN BUY AT ANY PRICE

TURNPIKE CRUISER 4-DOOR

Most distinguished of the 1957 Mercurys, this gracefully sculptured 4-door hardtop represents the ultimate in advanced Dream-Car Design, features and luxury. Sophisticated styling is intriguingly combined with sedan spaciousness and comfort. There's a new kind of inspired performance that takes you in effortless strides over byway and superhighway. Power steering, power brakes, Merc-O-Matic Automatic Transmission with Keyboard Control, and padded instrument panel are standard equipment on Turnpike Cruisers.

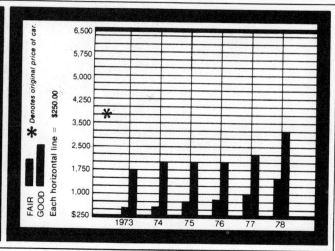

If there is a lesson to be learned from the 1957 Mercury Turnpike Cruiser, it is to be found in the 1934 Chrysler Airflow. That car, too, was advanced beyond the incremental differences of yearly disguise. Although they were radical when they arrived, time has shown both to be accurate, if distorted, innovators of later automotive philosophy. To the consumer who lives in a world of conspicuous consumption, it is dangerous to step ahead of the status quo. There is no strength in the diminished security of a leader who stands alone, facing the multitudes with a concept as yet untested.

Only hindsight can satisfy the accuracy of perception bequeathed to a "dream-car." Usually, the general ideas forwarded by such innovators of advancement prove correct, but the mode of normal application, coming a few years later, renders the original specimen grotesque by comparison. This is both a blessing and a curse. First comes the curse. It is figurative from the standpoint of sales records and literal to the ears of the misunderstood designer. The blessing comes in the form of a quick life cycle which emerges shortly in the favored form of nostalgia. It doesn't particularly appease the auto makers to find their products rising in value after the initial failure. They would much prefer the money to be in their pockets. They know too well, though, that this can never be the case when gambling on giant steps in a business whose success is built upon baby steps.

At any rate, we find the original idea car valuable because it is locked into an immovable world of grotesque over-characterization; a mutant that was less than perfect in form, if not in function. The question is, is it a laugh to own such a retroactive statement of the future — or is it the folly of the people for failing to recognize changes in large doses? Only the omnipresent dollar can give a clue to the worth of such a car. But in the world of dream-cars, misguided as they may be in their material form, there is another, aesthetic value, one whose satisfaction is not realized in terms of dollars. In this respect, the answer, my friend, is blowin' in the wind!

SPECIFICATIONS

Wheelbase	122"
Tread; Front, Rear	59.375", 59"
Overall Length	211.1"
Overall Width	79.1"
Overall Height	56.5"
Weight, Lbs	4005
Tire Size	8.00 x 14"

ENGINE

Type	Overhead V-8
Bore & Stroke	4.00" x 3.66"
Displacement, Cu. In.	368
Compression Ratio	10.00 to 1
Horsepower @ RPM	290 @ 4600
Max. Torque @ RPM	405 @ 2600
Electrical	12 Volt, neg. grd.

TRANSMISSION

Type	Automatic
Available	—

REAR

Type	Hypoid, semi-floating
Ratio	3.22 to 1

TUNE UP

Spark Plug Gap	.034"
Point Gap	.015"
Cam Angle, Degrees	26-28
Timing	5° B.T.D.C.
Firing Order	15486372
Tappet Clearances:	
Intake	Zero, hydraulic
Exhaust	Zero, hydraulic
Compression Pressure, Lbs	150
Idle Speed, RPM	450

BRAKES

Type	Hydraulic, int. exp.
Drum Diameter	11"

CAPACITIES

Cooling System, Qts	20
Fuel Tank, Gals	20
Crank Case, Qts	5
Trans.	10.5 Qts.
Differential, Pts	4.5

WHEEL ALIGNMENT

Caster, Degrees	−1½ to 0
Camber, Degrees	0 to +¾
Toe in, Inches	3/16 to 5/16

1958 Chevrolet Impala Coupe

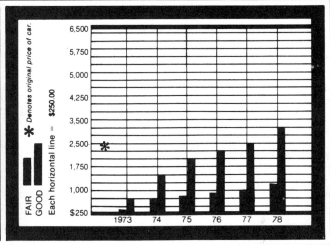

General Motors has an uncanny talent for coming up with the right car at the right time. The popularity of so many of their new cars has resulted in industry-wide revisions of design theory that G.M. seems almost psychic. Looking back, you can practically segment the last thirty years of automobile history into successive waves of influence, each originating with a General Motors product.* Consider the 1949 Buick Riviera (first hardtop), the 1953 El Dorado (first sporty luxury car, first wraparound windshield), the 1955 Cadillac Sedan de Ville (first 4-door hardtop), the 1958 Impala (first sculpted look), the 1964 GTO (first mid-size luxury-performance car), and others that have initiated everything from tailfins to rectangular headlights.

Now let's focus on the Impala. Chevy was due for a new body in 1958, having received only a facelift in 1957 to compete against radical new bodies from Ford and Plymouth. At a time when it appeared that the possessor of the finest fin would lead the parade, the Impala debuted with scooped and sculpted styling that was so sharp, it broke everybody's balloon. This was the first Chevy to sport quad headlights, turbohydramatic and the big 348 engine. It was a nice combination. So was the racing-type steering wheel and flashy, color-keyed interior decor.

But the big news was that sculpted rear fender design that curved auspiciously around the sexy triple taillights! Accented by a thin chrome strip, the effect was devastating. It was *the* focal point of the car. So much so that it counteracted the typical but disconcerting overuse of chrome that was dabbed over the rest of the car, including the roof.

Like the Nomad in 1955, the Impala shared its new body with Pontiac. Pontiac's version, called the Bonneville, was a little more obscure, just as the Safari was a few years before. This time it wasn't overshadowed by a brighter star. With fuel injection and bucket seats, it was more than a match for 1958.

The names of both these cars have been standards for several years now. Only for one year, though, did they actually live; for in 1959 G.M. restyled all its cars. This time each was awarded an entire model series which was based on the standard body and chassis. Thus, stripped of their autonomy, the cars survived in name only — a fate which, ironically, provided their immortality.

*Ford, Chrysler and the independents have all had "firsts" too, but for sheer number and consistent performance, the record goes to G.M.

SPECIFICATIONS

Wheelbase	117.5"
Tread; Front, Rear	58.8", 58.8"
Overall Length	209"
Overall Width	77.7"
Overall Height	57"
Weight, Lbs	3459
Tire Size	7.50 x 14"

ENGINE

Type	Overhead V-8
Bore & Stroke	4.125" x 3.25"
Displacement, Cu. In.	348
Compression Ratio	9.50 to 1
Horsepower @ RPM	250 @ 4400
Max. Torque @ RPM	335 @ 2800
Electrical	12 Volt, neg. grd.

TRANSMISSION

Type	Automatic
Available	3 speed manual

REAR

Type	Hypoid, semi-floating
Ratio	3.55 to 1

TUNE UP

Spark Plug Gap	.035"
Point Gap	.018"
Cam Angle, Degrees	30
Timing	4° B.T.D.C.
Firing Order	18436572
Tappet Clearances:	
Intake	Auto adj.
Exhaust	Auto adj.
Compression Pressure, Lbs	150
Idle Speed, RPM	450

BRAKES

Type	Hydraulic, int. exp.
Drum Diameter	11"

CAPACITIES

Cooling System, Qts	23
Fuel Tank, Gals	20
Crank Case, Qts	4
Trans.	3.5 Qts.
Differential, Pts	4

WHEEL ALIGNMENT

Caster, Degrees	−½ to +½
Camber, Degrees	0 to +1
Toe in, Inches	1/16 to 1/8

97

1958 Continental Mark III

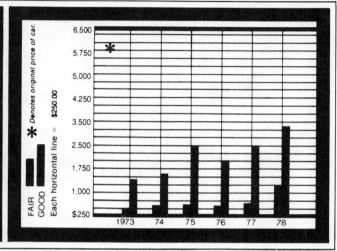

Between the years of 1958-60, Ford Motor Company produced some unorthodox automobiles. The Edsel and the Ford Retractable Hardtop, the Continental Mark III and the Thunderbird are some of the weightier relics of this era. The present is fast proving itself the success of Ford's earlier failure to gain widespread acceptance of these "iron butterflies."

The 1958 Continental was a far cry from the 1956-57 version. It was larger and heavier than anything on the road, thus giving it a whole new image. Powered by a monstrous 430 cubic inch engine, the unitized construction of its body provided a surprisingly durable harness for all this energy. This is the era when cars were outrageously overpowered and oversized. If these were the criteria for the mastery of mind over metal, the Continental Mark III was clearly the most opulent exponent of such success. Curiously, the price went down as the size grew up on this car. This is because of the economies achieved by mass production and sharing a body with the standard Lincoln.

In so doing, the Continental lost its charm. It was no longer different unto itself. Its identity became a study in group dynamics when the Thunderbird became the co-sponsor of its engine. Now it was no different from any other hollow token of upper class identity. This is not to say the car was a poor buy. From a resale point of view, yes; but the concern for luxury is evident throughout in the quality of workmanship of this behemoth.

Now that its glory days are past, the Mark III is enjoying the same revival of spirit that has befallen the other unique Ford products of the late fifties. The trend will be toward shorter, smaller luxury cars for the remainder of the seventies, about the size of Cadillac's Seville and the Mercedes sedans. From there, the illogical pursuit of change for the sake of selling a product will force these cars to exhale to their former size, if not their former greatness. The testimony of that greatness will not be recalled in the plastic and vinyl covered cars of the future. It will be revered in cars like this Continental — cars which today are popular because they represent the antithesis of modern design.

SPECIFICATIONS

Wheelbase	.131"
Tread; Front, Rear	.61", 61"
Overall Length	.227.1"
Overall Width	.80.1"
Overall Height	.56.7"
Weight, Lbs	.5330
Tire Size	.9.50 x 14"

ENGINE

Type	.Overhead V-8
Bore & Stroke	.4.30" x 3.70"
Displacement, Cu. In.	.430
Compression Ratio	.10.50 to 1
Horsepower @ RPM	.375 @ 4800
Max. Torque @ RPM	.490 @ 3100
Electrical	.12 Volt, neg. grd.

TRANSMISSION

Type	.Automatic
Available	.—

REAR

Type	.Hypoid, semi-floating
Ratio	.2.89 to 1

TUNE UP

Spark Plug Gap	.034"
Point Gap	.015"
Cam Angle, Degrees	.26-28
Timing	.6° B.T.D.C.
Firing Order	.15426378
Tappet Clearances:	
Intake	.Zero, hydraulic
Exhaust	.Zero, hydraulic
Compression Pressure,	
Lbs	.190
Idle Speed, RPM	.465

BRAKES

Type	.Hydraulic, int. exp.
Drum Diameter	.11"

CAPACITIES

Cooling System, Qts	.26
Fuel Tank, Gals	.23
Crank Case, Qts	.5
Trans.	.12 Qts.
Differential, Pts	.4

WHEEL ALIGNMENT

Caster, Degrees	.0 to −1½
Camber, Degrees	.0 to +¾
Toe in, Inches	.⅛ to 3/16

1958 Edsel Citation Hardtop

The Edsel Citation 2-Door Hardtop

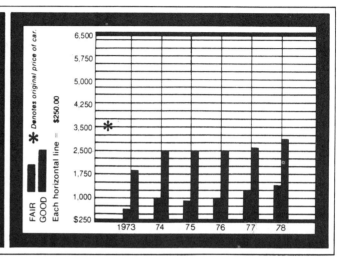

"The best laid plans of mice and men. . ." You know the rest of the cliché. So do the people at Ford Motor Company. They should! It cost them millions of dollars and years of marketing research to put wheels on these words. When they did, in 1958, they named it Edsel, after Henry's son. Unfortunately, no one knew who he was and the message of his car failed to serve notice.

The most unusual car of 1958 seemed destined to attract the oddball more than the Oldsmobile market, in spite of the fact that this was not a stellar year for Olds. The massive, chromy Oldsmobile was not so incongruous to compress thirty years of history into a ten foot wheelbase. Only a newcomer like the Edsel could put hindsight up front and foresight behind; but that's how it came out with its strong vertical grille of the thirties and those futuristic horizontal taillights that canted to break the contour of the trunk. The new (for '58) quad headlights cleverly confused the meaning of the grille even further, to say nothing of the Buck Rogers influence of the push-button transmission selector set inside the steering hub! If that didn't get you, the revolving dial of the cyclops speedometer was there to remind you of the thirties again. Now if only they had marked it with years, instead of miles per hour. . .

It was trimmed with an excess of anodized aluminum and fitted with many Ford components — no wonder we wondered who Mr. Edsel was.

Shortly into 1960, the Edsel was scratched entirely, leaving its limited numbers as monuments to a misfit. Surely enough, the same public that mocked it out of existence was back ten years later to let Edsel return the favor! Collecting the baroque behemoth became a fad that sent prices soaring. Now the wisdom of time has stabilized the Edsel market. The purging of the past has freed the Edsel to seek its own level of respect.

SPECIFICATIONS

Wheelbase . . . . .124"
Tread; Front, Rear . . . . .59.4", 59"
Overall Length . . . . .218.9"
Overall Width . . . . .79.8"
Overall Height . . . . .56.8"
Weight, Lbs 4136
Tire Size . . . . .8.50 x 14"

ENGINE

Type . . . . .Overhead V-8
Bore & Stroke . . . . .4.2031" x 3.703"
Displacement, Cu. In. 410
Compression Ratio .10.50 to 1
Horsepower @ RPM . . . . .345 @ 4600
Max. Torque @ RPM . . . . .475 @ 2900
Electrical . . . . .12 Volt, neg. grd.

TRANSMISSION

Type . . . . .Automatic
Available . . . .—

REAR

Type . . . . .Hypoid, semi-floating
Ratio . . . . .2.91 to 1

TUNE UP

Spark Plug Gap . . . . .034"
Point Gap . . . . .015"
Cam Angle, Degrees 26-28
Timing . . . . .6° B.T.D.C.
Firing Order 15426378
Tappet Clearances:
    Intake . . . . .Zero, hydraulic
    Exhaust . . . . .Zero, hydraulic
Compression Pressure,
Lbs 180
Idle Speed, RPM 475

BRAKES

Type . . . . .Hydraulic, int. exp.
Drum Diameter . . . . .11"

CAPACITIES

Cooling System, Qts 23
Fuel Tank, Gals 20
Crank Case, Qts 5
Trans. . . . . .10 Qts.
Differential, Pts 4.5

WHEEL ALIGNMENT

Caster, Degrees . . . . .0 to −1½
Camber, Degrees . . . . .0 to +¾
Toe in, Inches . . . . .¹/₁₆ to ³/₁₆

1958 Packard Hawk

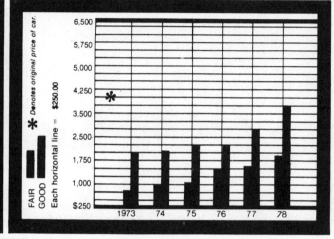

Those who were sad to see the once mighty Packard name on a slightly modified Studebaker body must have secretly admitted at some time that the 1958 Studebaker Packard Hawk is a pretty nice car. Uncharacteristic as it may be of the magnificent Packards of yesteryear, the 1958 Hawk is at least as memorable as any of Packard's own creations from the earlier fifties. The distinction of its size and shape is truly unbecoming of its stately tradition; but comparative judgment is equally demeaning to the analysis of the car itself. In fact, if it had any other name, this Packard would still be a valuable collector's item. This is evidenced by the Studebaker Golden Hawk, which was essentially the same car and which commands essentially the same esteem!

What makes the Packard Hawk a good car is its clean but racy design, augmented by a potent supercharged engine. The most remotely Packard concessions to public demand are the conspicuously highlighted fins atop the rear fenders. Don't blame this one on Studebaker, though, as much as the scapegoat presents itself. The quirk is merely the result of the sixth year of evolution of the beautiful, uncluttered 1953 Loewy Studebaker design — plus the forgivable assumption in 1958 that fins were the thing of the future. While the absence of fins has made the original design timeless, the Studebaker-Packard Hawks have proven it no sin to be dated by their inclusion. Quite to the contrary, fins are already making a nostalgic comeback!

Even so, the Packard Hawk is more prized for other reasons. As always with limited-production cars, one of these reasons is brought about by the scarcity of supply and the economics of demand. The real reason for the Hawk's appeal, though, is the sumptuous but sporty attitude it conveys. Not since the Darrin styled convertibles around 1940 did Packard offer the likes of such a car. This is the kind of enthusiasm the Hawk generates, with its sloping, wide-mouthed snout and sophisticated supercharged engine.

No, it was not the Hawk that signalled Packard's demise. Nor was it a baneful exit. The fate of Packard was sealed several years before when its leaders lost their imagination and daring. A spirited car like the Hawk became unthinkable to them — and without thought there can be no life.

SPECIFICATIONS

Wheelbase	120.5"
Tread; Front, Rear	56.7", 55.7"
Overall Length	205.1"
Overall Width	72.6"
Overall Height	55"
Weight, Lbs	3550
Tire Size	8.00 x 14"

ENGINE

Type	Overhead V-8
Bore & Stroke	3.56" x 3.63"
Displacement, Cu. In.	289
Compression Ratio	7.80 to 1
Horsepower @ RPM	275 @ 4800
Max. Torque @ RPM	333 @ 3200
Electrical	12 Volt, neg. grd.

TRANSMISSION

Type	Automatic
Available	3 spd. manual, overdrive

REAR

Type	Hypoid, semi-floating
Ratio	3.31 to 1

TUNE UP

Spark Plug Gap	.035"
Point Gap	.013" - .018"
Cam Angle, Degrees	31
Timing	4° B.T.D.C.
Firing Order	18436572
Tappet Clearances:	
Intake	.024"
Exhaust	.024"
Compression Pressure, Lbs	140
Idle Speed, RPM	550

BRAKES

Type	Hydraulic, int. exp.
Drum Diameter	11" front, 10" rear

CAPACITIES

Cooling System, Qts	17
Fuel Tank, Gals	18
Crank Case, Qts	5
Trans.	19 Qts.
Differential, Pts	3

WHEEL ALIGNMENT

Caster, Degrees	−2½ to −1
Camber, Degrees	.0 to +1
Toe in, Inches	1/16 to 1/8

1958 Studebaker Golden Hawk

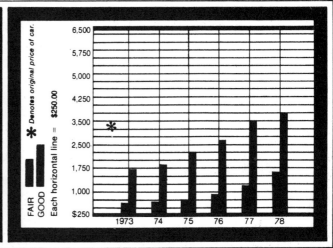

Golden Hawk. The name is the first clue that this is no ordinary car. The Hawk part stands for power and the intent is serious. The Golden part symbolizes the level of greatness and the inevitable desirability that accompanies it. Put the whole thing on wheels and you have one helluva car, 1958 style.

The fame may be in the name, but the glory is in the story. A protegé of the stunning '55 Speedster, the Hawk series debuted in 1956, when Studebaker remodeled its image. Available in series were the Power Hawk, Sky Hawk and Golden Hawk. The uphill progression was a facelifted triple entry of the original 1953 Studebaker Coupe. The sloping hood of the old Starlite Coupe was traded for a business-like bouffant. In this was housed an egg-crate grille, a concept forever analogous to racing, thanks to the Ferrari. By 1958, the straight, stubby portent of fins had become the real thing. The Hawk had sprouted gilded wings, to be sure.

In other ways, the refinement of the Golden Hawk is less apparent. The trunk received a bustle, which nicely balanced the effect of the raised front end. Mechanical and interior alterations over its life span kept the Hawk on a par with its rivals. Factory superchargers and fuel-injection units were in the experimental stage. Chevy and Pontiac toyed with the latter, while Ford (in 1957) and Studebaker deployed the former in a contest of one-upmanship. Reliability and production expenses were afterthoughts for most systems, although Studebaker's variable ratio setups have held up fairly well over the years. In fact, the entire car has proven quite durable. There are many fine examples remaining. Expect to find the usual Studebaker cancer on the front fenders, parallel to the door edge. This is a symptom almost axiomatic with Studebakers since 1953, including the Larks. Other than that, your expectations can be fond — and there is a car waiting to meet them.

SPECIFICATIONS

Wheelbase	.121"
Tread; Front, Rear	.56.7", 55.7"
Overall Length	.204"
Overall Width	.73"
Overall Height	.55"
Weight, Lbs	.3395
Tire Size	.8.00 x 15"

ENGINE

Type	Overhead V-8
Bore & Stroke	.3.5625" x 3.625"
Displacement, Cu. In.	.289
Compression Ratio	.7.80 to 1
Horsepower @ RPM	.275 @ 4800
Max. Torque @ RPM	.333 @ 3200
Electrical	.12 Volt, neg. grd.

TRANSMISSION

Type	Automatic
Available	.3 spd. manual, overdrive

REAR

Type	Hypoid, semi-floating
Ratio	.3.31 to 1

TUNE UP

Spark Plug Gap	.035"
Point Gap	.016"
Cam Angle, Degrees	.28-34
Timing	.4° B.T.D.C.
Firing Order	.18436572
Tappet Clearances:	
Intake	.026"
Exhaust	.026"
Compression Pressure,	
Lbs	.145
Idle Speed, RPM	.550

BRAKES

Type	Hydraulic, int. exp.
Drum Diameter	.11" front, 10" rear

CAPACITIES

Cooling System, Qts	.26.5
Fuel Tank, Gals	.18
Crank Case, Qts	.5
Trans.	.11 Qts.
Differential, Pts	.3

WHEEL ALIGNMENT

Caster, Degrees	−1 to −2½
Camber, Degrees	.0 to +1
Toe in, Inches	.1/16 to 1/8

1958 Thunderbird Hardtop

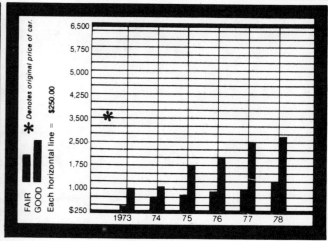

How often do you consider the other people on the road? Not the cars, the people. It's hard to imagine the personalities of the individuals, especially if we see no more of them than their passing totems. It doesn't take much imagination at 8:00 o'clock in the morning to realize that the majority of people on the road are commuters. The stereotypes can be stacked horizontally and vertically by the status shown in their cars. The clarity of the descriptions seems to intensify with the understanding of the car a man drives. There is a quiz show where contestants try to match a group of people with their occupations. Frequently they get it right. The same can be done for people and the cars they drive. In fact, there's no trick to it at all — until you get to the truly unique cars.

It was easier in 1958 to match the owner to the Thunderbird. By then it was a four-passenger luxury touring car. It was dashing and elegant and boldly new for 1958. The class of a Lincoln and the heritage of a sporty coupe made a nice combination. As the Thunderbird grew, the name became a cameo of its former greatness. By the end of the sixties, the original four-seater T-bird was an orphan in the sea of identity. It never found a resting place. It bobbed around enough to attract the curiosity of forgetful faces. Then someone realized it had a lot going for it and suddenly it became "chic" to own one. Prices began to rise accordingly. It is not the most demanded

special-interest car, but it has enough going for it to insure the endurance of its position.

You're not likely to see one on the way to work any more. If you do, chances are it will be going the other way. The man inside is not the typical commuter. He is more prone to hear the beat of a different drummer.

SPECIFICATIONS

Wheelbase	.113"
Tread; Front, Rear	.60", 56.4"
Overall Length	.205"
Overall Width	.77"
Overall Height	.53"
Weight, Lbs	.3869
Tire Size	.8.00 x 14"

ENGINE

Type	.Overhead V-8
Bore & Stroke	.4.00" x 3.50"
Displacement, Cu. In.	.352
Compression Ratio	.10.20 to 1
Horsepower @ RPM	.300 @ 4600
Max. Torque @ RPM	.395 @ 2800
Electrical	.12 Volt, neg. grd.

TRANSMISSION

Type	.Automatic
Available	.3 spd. manual

REAR

Type	.Hypoid, semi-floating
Ratio	.2.91 to 1

TUNE UP

Spark Plug Gap	.034"
Point Gap	.015"
Cam Angle, Degrees	.26-28
Timing	.4° B.T.D.C.
Firing Order	.15426378
Tappet Clearances:	
Intake	.Zero, hydraulic
Exhaust	.Zero, hydraulic
Compression Pressure,	
Lbs	.180
Idle Speed, RPM	.500

BRAKES

Type	.Hydraulic, int. exp.
Drum Diameter	.11"

CAPACITIES

Cooling System, Qts	.21
Fuel Tank, Gals	.20
Crank Case, Qts	.5
Trans.	.10 Qts.
Differential, Pts	.5.5

WHEEL ALIGNMENT

Caster, Degrees	.+½ to +1½
Camber, Degrees	.+½ to +1½
Toe in, Inches	.1/16 to 1/8

1959 Metropolitan Hardtop

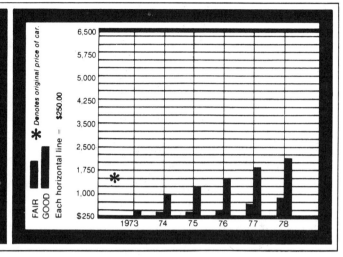

The result of placing an American body on an English chassis is the curious little Metropolitan. Distributed in the states by Nash and Hudson, the mini car was sold from 1954 to 1962 with only a few of those years meeting with lukewarm success. They are still around in good number and they all look basically alike, coming in either a hardtop or soft top form. It is only recently that Metropolitans have enjoyed the notoriety of a special interest car. Correspondingly, prices have shot up in the last year or so and the peak is yet to come.

When you think of it, why shouldn't you pay $500-$1,000 for a perky forty mile per gallon car with distinctive looks? The tiny Austin four-banger that propels it is one of the most prolific imported powerplants, existing in basic form in everything from the Austin America to the M.G. Midget. This helps keep the parts and maintenance problems to a minimum. The three-speed shifter on the column (actually there is no column, so the shifter emerges from a ball joint setup at the steering wheel/dash panel junction) has excellent ratios which provide the car with surprising performance.

The Metropolitan is truly the car for urban driving. It can zip around all day on a gallon of gas and be parked with ease in a space half the normal size. Of all the cars in this book, this one has got to be the most fun to drive. The feeling is so carefree it can make you feel like a kid in a bumper car at the amusement park. Don't get the idea that you can drive it that way, though, or you're liable to have a hazardous experience.

Relatively speaking, parts are not yet any obstacle for the Metropolitan. It's a pretty simple car and an easy one to work on. You can literally lift out the engine, if necessary, to work on it. Prices are going to continue to rise for a while, so if you have a yen to fulfill your second childhood, there's no time like the present. The little car with the big future is waiting for the chance to show you.

SPECIFICATIONS

Wheelbase ....85"
Tread; Front, Rear ....45.3125", 44.8125"
Overall Length ....149.5"
Overall Width ....61.5"
Overall Height ....54.5"
Weight, Lbs 1875
Tire Size ....5.20 x 13"

ENGINE

Type ....Overhead in-line 4 cyl.
Bore & Stroke ....2.875" x 3.50"
Displacement, Cu. In. 90.9
Compression Ratio ....7.20 to 1
Horsepower @ RPM ....52 @ 4500
Max. Torque @ RPM ....77 @ 2500
Electrical ....12 Volt, pos. grd.

TRANSMISSION

Type ....3 speed manual
Available ....—

REAR

Type ....Hypoid, semi-floating
Ratio ....4.30 to 1

TUNE UP

Spark Plug Gap ....024"
Point Gap ....015"
Cam Angle, Degrees ................................N.A.
Timing ....11° B.T.D.C.
Firing Order 1342
Tappet Clearances:
    Intake ....015"
    Exhaust ....015"
Compression Pressure,
Lbs 130
Idle Speed, RPM 625

BRAKES

Type ....Hydraulic, int. exp.
Drum Diameter ....8"

CAPACITIES

Cooling System, Qts 8
Fuel Tank, Gals 10.5
Crank Case, Qts 4
Trans. Pints 5.5
Differential, Pts 2

WHEEL ALIGNMENT

Caster, Degrees ....+2 to +3
Camber, Degrees ....+½ to +1½
Toe in, Inches ....0 to 1/16

All Things for All People: 1960·1969

The rockets' Red glare amply foretold the direction of American events for the coming ten years. Before this decade was over, we would go to the moon and to Southeast Asia and home again to civil unrest. The ultimate effect of these events would be the fostering of a global consciousness which enabled us to cope with the realities of the modern 20th Century. Let's put it into focus.

Whatever history discloses about John F. Kennedy, it cannot repudiate the power and the charm he displayed while president. Whether the country was hypnotized by his dynamism or not is irrelevant except to historians, because the people believed in something and the country made progress. Under his direction America responded to the Russian rocket race with a program dedicated to placing the first man on the moon. Though the success of that goal was posthumous, it spoke as decisively as the president himself for the intense dedication he instilled in the country. To achieve this singular purpose meant the recruiting of crisp new engineering talent. In a few years the response began to overflow. Some of this able personnel ended up in the employ of the auto industry, destined to influence our lives in a different way.

Along with J.F.K. in 1960 came the compact cars. Both were overdue and both were an instant success. The compact need was made apparent by a steadily increasing influx of those little foreign cars. The Corvette, and to some extent the early T-birds, did much to give American cars a sporting image. However powerful, they could use little of the potency found in a German strain of beetle that was infesting our country. The fact is, they couldn't even contain the Jag XK's or the Triumph TR's or the MG's, let alone the economy cars.

Rising to the occasion was a variety of home-bred gas-misers. They were just what America needed to escape the monotonous gluttony of the standard indigenous sedan. Or were they? It was hard to tell in the first few years because the rush was on to buy anything new and small. While the people were getting used to the new names, our friends, the excess engineers, were doing strange things with the definition of economy. The second generation compact cars were vastly more powerful and more luxurious. Americans loved them! It's hard to believe, but the cars were growing larger too! Yet, the popularity continued to increase, along with the size and the horsepower and the list of new names.

You'd swear we would have been tired of this pattern after being gorged by it in the late fifties. I think we were, but there are a couple of factors which came into play in the sixties that were not relevant the first time around. One such factor is actually a case of simple deception. Instead of disguising the size with chrome, as in the fifties, the engineers had us drooling over four-speeds and bucket seats. If you think Detroit's policy makers were pretty clever fellows to catch us twice with the same act, save your red cheeks for the part in the last chapter that tells you how they did it again! In any case, these examples demonstrate our various preoccupations over the years. It is an amusing, if not beneficial, lesson.

Oh yes, the other reason for the unchecked "intermediate" popularity — the war babies. They grew up in the sixties, and like their parents they had an insatiable thirst for power. Their hard-working guardians had seized the opportunity to turn America into the affluent society. Detroit was returning the favor by giving the youngsters what they wanted — and what they could afford.

It wasn't so bad in the mid-sixties. The mid-sized macho machines never out-stepped their territory. The large cars were still there, but were beginning to take on a symmetry of their own. By 1970, the big cars were actually starting to look good! At the other end of the spectrum there was already a new wave of smaller more economical cars, waiting for the next onslaught of padding and pooh-poohing to popularize them.

Locked away somewhere in Detroit must be a secret formula of success. If it exists, it should be called the theory of the ladder with the disappearing rungs. This image seems to depict the modus operandi of a group bent on producing a never-ending series of new car models, each escalating the previous limit of luxury. While the newcomer is being heralded as the standard of perfection, the oldest, most spartan name in the lineup is quietly dropped. Consider what Chevrolet has done with the Bel Air and Impala and what Plymouth did with the Fury, and so on. It's not so bad as long as you're climbing, but there's only one way down once you're up there. However, that is the story of the compacts of the seventies.

There was one other niche created in the sixties to round out the last separation by size. It was the "personal size" car and it really started with the 1958 Thunderbird. Thunderbird lost the handle with styling in 1961 before it could cash in on the image. So the credit for producing the first successful personal car goes to Pontiac's Grand Prix, a loner in 1962.* G.M. pursued the fortyish sport-luxury image the following year with the Buick Riviera. The competition grew from this point to include the usual number of glory-seeking mimes. Now that the customer had a full range of ideals to choose from for the very first time, we can safely say that Detroit was producing "all things for all people." What became of these things for the remainder of the sixties is a matter of nit-picking. The gamut of styling, power and luxury had been placed on the market. No matter how they shuffled the deck, the cards would still be the same. Maybe the names would be changed, but we already know about that.

What became of the people is more important. With all the options theirs for the picking, it is interesting to see how they reacted. No longer was it a case of wanting the missing piece of a puzzle, only to find it less than satisfactory. On a much larger scale the same was true of world events. By the time we reached the moon, it was an anticlimax; and by the time we got out of Viet Nam we had long since forgotten our purpose. What we got in those last years of the sixties was a firsthand look at all the pieces of this much larger puzzle. We found, as we did with our cars, that if you play with any one piece too long, no matter how tempting, it will grow out of proportion and lose its beauty and purpose. The deduction should have been that we live in a global community providing "all things for all people." Perhaps it would have come to that; but to be operable the premise required respect — respect for other people's choices as well as our own. We started out pretty well. The young people advocated respect for nature while the politicians brought growing respect for a person's color. Sadly, it was not the pieces that became distorted, but our new respect. When applied to law, it forced action in the name of ecology. When applied to ecology, it forced action against the automobile. When that happened, we found ourselves on the top rung of that disappearing ladder, staring at the horns of dilemma a goodly distance below! How could this happen in a nice place like America? Hang on and I'll tell you.

*Oldsmobile's Starfire cannot be included in this set because it was based on the longer 98 series body, even though the image was the same.

1960 Cadillac Convertible

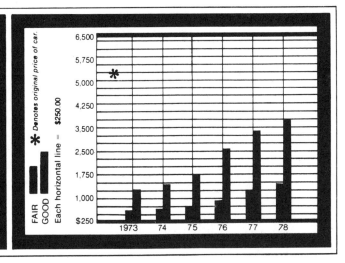

The 1960 Cadillac Convertible is sure to be revered one day, as any convertible will be in time. Especially any Cadillac convertible. While there are some more recent cars that have earned milestone recognition, the strength of their success is based on an outstanding individuality (Avanti), or on some conspicuous uniqueness (Lark Wagonaire). Any other car being collected that is less than 20 years old is sought because it has always been desirable. Hot-rodders have a knack for picking these cars while they're green. 1955-57 Chevys, 1962 Chevy Super Sports, 1965 Chevy Super Sports, to give a straight-line progression, are illustrative of this category.*

If you're wondering what happened to the 1960 Cadillac, so am I! It doesn't fit into any of these patterns. There weren't a lot of people who admired them in 1960, and most of those who didn't haven't changed their minds yet. No matter how clean it may be, it is difficult to justify recent prices ranging to $5,000 for a car that, timewise, should be dormant at the ebb of its value. I won't argue Cadillac quality and luxury and I have already admitted to the prestige of the name and the body type.

I won't even argue the fact that it is getting easier after only 15 years to observe how the 1959-60 Cadillac body style is graceful and beautiful. Why should I? Such words are nebulous because they evoke intangible concepts. It would be more

realistic to say that these Cadillacs have a gaudy arrangement up front, are smooth on the sides, and a little of both at the rear. They are so long and low that the unbroken lines of the sides become incisively subtle. The front is just plain incisive and the rear view is just subtle.

For those of you who feel as I do concerning the paradox of price, I offer the following explanation. If you can recall the recent attention given by the media to certain food shortages that seemed imminent, you will remember the panic it produced at the supermarket. The same thing happened with pennies. The warning became a self-fulfilling prophecy. The business facet of special-interest cars reflects such portents in the same way. As soon as someone sets a price that is out of sight or advertises a car that has not yet matured for the collector's market, the race is on. It seems unethical but it happens. As they say in Rome, caveat emptor!

There is one way to clear the air about this Cadillac. If you didn't guess the Chevys in the footnote, don't buy one. If you did, sell one to the guy who didn't!

*For those of you who can't guess, the continuing list of recent Chevrolets that will "become" valuable should read as follows: 1964-65 Chevelle Malibu SS, 1967 hardtop series of Camaros and Chevelles, followed in time by the Monte Carlos and one day the Monza 2+2.

SPECIFICATIONS

Wheelbase	130"
Tread; Front, Rear	61", 61"
Overall Length	225"
Overall Width	80"
Overall Height	54.9"
Weight, Lbs	4850
Tire Size	8.00 x 15"

ENGINE

Type	Overhead V-8
Bore & Stroke	4.000" x 3.875"
Displacement, Cu. In.	390
Compression Ratio	10.50 to 1
Horsepower @ RPM	325 @ 4800
Max. Torque @ RPM	430 @ 3100
Electrical	12 Volt, neg. grd.

TRANSMISSION

Type	Automatic
Available	—

REAR

Type	Hypoid, semi-floating
Ratio	2.94 to 1

TUNE UP

Spark Plug Gap	.035"
Point Gap	Adj. screw
Cam Angle, Degrees	30
Timing	5° B.T.D.C.
Firing Order	18436572
Tappet Clearances:	
Intake	Zero, hydraulic
Exhaust	Zero, hydraulic
Compression Pressure, Lbs	175
Idle Speed, RPM	480

BRAKES

Type	Hydraulic, int. exp.
Drum Diameter	12"

CAPACITIES

Cooling System, Qts	19.25
Fuel Tank, Gals	21
Crank Case, Qts	5
Trans.	10 Qts.
Differential, Pts	5

WHEEL ALIGNMENT

Caster, Degrees	0 to -1
Camber, Degrees	-3/8 to +3/8
Toe in, Inches	3/16 to 1/4

1961 Chrysler 300G

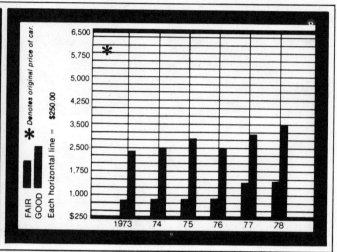

In this, the last year before Chrysler's 300 letter series became just another name, we have an excellent illustration of the strong character which earned it such success. To be worthy of triple or better the price of its brethren speaks well for the depth of the 300's reputation. Dedicated to the concept of a powerful, well-fitted road car, the 1961 version was secure in the image of its ancestors with a 413 cubic inch, 375 horsepower semi-hemi engine. This ramcharged powerplant had an unorthodox arrangement which placed its two four-barrel carburetors at diagonals to each other, atop the greatly extended plenum chambers of the intake manifold. It made the car fast and exciting and different. It was representative of the sophisticated mechanical achievement that had always typified the Chrysler 300's.

Torsion bars and a very strong torqueflite automatic transmission, which could be coupled to some absurd but interesting rear axle ratios,* insured that the power was not wasted. Inside, the driver was seated in the lap of luxury with fingertip control of all this brutish power. It was tempting to be ostentatious with its dispersal. But owners of Chrysler 300's were above that. They were gentlemen who, being already familiar with the varied forms of power, knew how to control their egos.

For 1961, the 300G was highlighted by long canted fins. It is fitting in a way that the car came and went with the era of the fins. Though many of Chrysler's wedge-shaped designs were less than inspirational, they always managed to be appealing on the 300 series cars. Maybe it's because only the two most pleasing body styles (hardtop and convertible) were offered in this line. I think it's more owing to the tremendous charisma generated by its spirit that no body could disgrace this master of the road. An excellent investment, any Chrysler 300 will reward its purchaser with the first ride home. Just to know the way it soft sells the feeling of exhilaration is worth the price of admission.

*For a few years, buyers could order ratios as numerically high as 6.17 to 1; about low enough to climb a wall.

SPECIFICATIONS

Wheelbase	.126"
Tread; Front, Rear	.61.2", 60"
Overall Length	.219.8"
Overall Width	.79.4"
Overall Height	.55.1"
Weight, Lbs	.4315
Tire Size	.8.50 x 14"

ENGINE

Type	.Overhead V-8
Bore & Stroke	.4.1875" x 3.75"
Displacement, Cu. In.	.413
Compression Ratio	.10.00 to 1
Horsepower @ RPM	.375 @ 4600
Max. Torque @ RPM	.495 @ 2800
Electrical	.12 Volt, neg. grd.

TRANSMISSION

Type	.Automatic
Available	.4 speed manual

REAR

Type	.Hypoid, semi-floating
Ratio	.3.23 to 1

TUNE UP

Spark Plug Gap	.035"
Point Gap	.017" - .021"
Cam Angle, Degrees	.27-32 each set
Timing	.5° B.T.D.C.
Firing Order	.18436572
Tappet Clearances:	
Intake	.Zero, hydraulic
Exhaust	.Zero, hydraulic
Compression Pressure,	
Lbs	.150
Idle Speed, RPM	.735

BRAKES

Type	.Hydraulic, int. exp.
Drum Diameter	.12"

CAPACITIES

Cooling System, Qts	.17
Fuel Tank, Gals	.23
Crank Case, Qts	.5
Trans. Pints	.21
Differential, Pts	.3.5

WHEEL ALIGNMENT

Caster, Degrees	.+¼ to +1¼
Camber, Degrees	.+⅛ to +⅝ (left) −⅛ to +⅛ (rt.)
Toe in, Inches	.³/₃₂ to ⁵/₃₂

1962 Continental Convertible

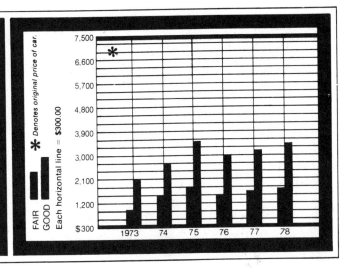

If you live near the shore long enough, you become familiar with nature; not only with the ocean and beaches that bound your existence, but with the clouds and the sky and a shift in the wind that signals foul weather. You can be aware of these signs anywhere. But in the city, too often the clouds of industry and the neon distractions overshadow this sense of oneness with nature. In urban areas the masses rely on the local T.V. meteorologist, backed by the latest technology, to predict the weather. As often as not, he is wrong.

The point of all this is that you can *feel* the synchronism of events, just as you can the weather. It is possible to pass by a car every day for years and think little of it. Then, one day in passing, something about it hits you. Suddenly, your biological clock tells you this car is ripe. The pendulum is on the upsweep. You can come to trust such intuition as surely as you do the coming of spring.

The wind of fate is constantly shifting over many old cars. It is a part of their cycle of existence. Sometimes the storm of their success leads to an early prognostication of prolonged high resale values. Sometimes a quirk in the character of an automobile can stir as much market activity as a tornado.

This brings us to the late Continental convertibles. The quirk in their chemistry is that they were the only four-door convertibles made in America since the Kaiser Virginian at the close of the nineteen-forties. This fact alone may not have made the "weatherman" jump the gun, but with such a strong name behind it, the extended forecast became immediate reality. Yes, 1961-65 Continentals have brought $5,000 at the auctions. They have been hot items for the last two years; hot before the pulse of time could ripen them. Doubtless, time will maintain the excellence of these Continentals. For now, though, there are only two ways to go. Either the storm will abate and prices will drop, or prices will remain consistently high. In the latter case, man again has triumphed over nature. This time by successfully incubating a prize snatched prematurely from her womb!

SPECIFICATIONS

Wheelbase	.123"
Tread; Front, Rear	.62.1", 61"
Overall Length	.213"
Overall Width	.78.6"
Overall Height	.53.7"
Weight, Lbs	.5528
Tire Size	.9.50 x 15"

ENGINE

Type	.Overhead V-8
Bore & Stroke	.4.30" x 3.70"
Displacement, Cu. In.	.430
Compression Ratio	.10.10 to 1
Horsepower @ RPM	.320 @ 4600
Max. Torque @ RPM	.465 @ 2600
Electrical	.12 Volt, neg. grd.

TRANSMISSION

Type	.Automatic
Available	—

REAR

Type	.Hypoid, semi-floating
Ratio	.2.89 to 1

TUNE UP

Spark Plug Gap	.035"
Point Gap	.015"
Cam Angle, Degrees	.27-29
Timing	.6° B.T.D.C.
Firing Order	.15426378
Tappet Clearances:	
Intake	.Zero, hydraulic
Exhaust	.Zero, hydraulic
Compression Pressure,	
Lbs	.180
Idle Speed, RPM	.465

BRAKES

Type	.Power hydraulic
Drum Diameter	.11.06"

CAPACITIES

Cooling System, Qts	.25
Fuel Tank, Gals	.21
Crank Case, Qts	.5
Trans. Pints	.23
Differential, Pts	.4.8

WHEEL ALIGNMENT

Caster, Degrees	.−¾ to −2¼
Camber, Degrees	.0 to +¾
Toe in, Inches	.1/16 to 3/16

1962 Studebaker Gran Turismo

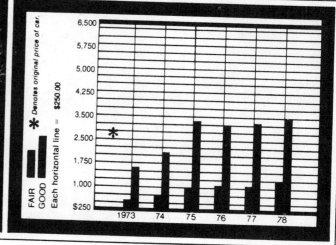

If you're collecting cars or driving them, the Studebaker Gran Turismos of the early sixties are a tantalizing temptation. They are good functional cars, consisting of the right combination of size and style. It is no wonder they have had superb resale value since their inception. Prevailing in these machines is a smartness of the kind that gets better with age.

It could be the power/weight ratio that makes the Studebaker GT a nimble car. Or it could be the proportions of its sculpted metal that make it feel so "right." It might even be the bucket seats and full range of driver-comfort accessories that puts the GT in these Studebakers. Most likely it is the combination of all these things plus the ageless beauty of the car itself that make it such a popular, enjoyable automobile.

The Gran Turismo is the gentleman's version of the Studebaker Hawks of the late 1950's. The refinement in image is obvious. Gone are the gilded fins of an ostentatious era. In their place are the more conventional lines of the subdued sixties. The racy looking front end was carried over to the GT because it was efficient looking and not bungled with meaningless afterthoughts. The manual plus overdrive transmissions that extolled the meaning of the Golden Hawk are far less frequent in the automatic equipped GT models. In a grand touring car, the object is effortless driving with a responsive attitude. The people in South Bend

discovered that the supercharger which bolstered the power of the original Hawk was an unnecessary addition in the GT. A normally aspirated engine could appease the power needs of all but the most lustful driver — and gentlemen are not lustful. And so it is, in its components and in its entirety the revised Studebaker GT filled the requirements of the driver of the sixties. In so doing, it became the double purpose car of the seventies. It is a bonus to find a car that can be used every day and then be sold at a profit when the novelty wears off.

SPECIFICATIONS

Wheelbase	121"
Tread; Front, Rear	57.375", 56.5625"
Overall Length	204"
Overall Width	71"
Overall Height	56"
Weight, Lbs	3230
Tire Size	6.70 x 15"

ENGINE

Type	Overhead V-8
Bore & Stroke	3.5625" x 3.625"
Displacement, Cu. In.	289
Compression Ratio	8.25 to 1
Horsepower @ RPM	225 @ 4500
Max. Torque @ RPM	305 @ 3000
Electrical	12 Volt, neg. grd.

TRANSMISSION

Type	Automatic
Available	3 spd. manual, overdrive, 4 spd. manual

REAR

Type	Hypoid, semi-floating
Ratio	3.31 to 1

TUNE UP

Spark Plug Gap	.035"
Point Gap	.016" - .017"
Cam Angle, Degrees	27-31
Timing	4° B.T.D.C.
Firing Order	18436572
Tappet Clearances:	
Intake	.024"
Exhaust	.024"
Compression Pressure, Lbs	150
Idle Speed, RPM	550

BRAKES

Type	Hydraulic, int. exp.
Drum Diameter	11" front, 10" rear

CAPACITIES

Cooling System, Qts	18
Fuel Tank, Gals	18
Crank Case, Qts	5
Trans.	9 Qts.
Differential, Pts	2.5

WHEEL ALIGNMENT

Caster, Degrees	−1¼ to +¼
Camber, Degrees	0 to +1
Toe in, Inches	1/16 to 1/8

1963 Avanti

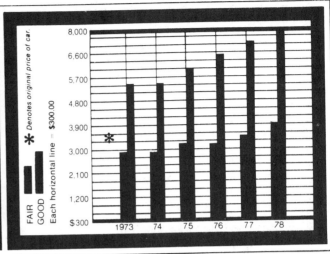

The 1963 Avanti is a rather unique example of motoring achievement. It shared its body with no other model or make and it was never available in a progression of later body styles. It was produced with two different (but excellent) drivetrains, though the second consisted of Chevrolet components assembled in Canada.

All Avantis are desirable. They never did get very low in price and, in fact, should rise in value at an accelerated rate. This is owing to the fact that they are almost always found in good shape because of the rust-immune fiberglass bodies. It is also due to the fact that they always were respected as a stylish, classy automobile.

To compare it to the Corvette, its intended competitor, would not be as accurate as likening it to the sporty Jaguar. In this way, the character of reserved elegance is better contrasted with the macho dominance of the Corvette. And, remember, the two were even available with the same drivetrain.

Appearing at the end of a glorious career, the limited Avanti was not enough to preserve Studebaker from going under. It was almost a self-fulfilling prophecy when Studebaker-Packard went out of business the following year. Once word got out that the empire was shaking, the people turned to alternatives with the reliability of continued parts and service. It should also be argued here that the new Corvette Stingray body was one of the best on the road — anywhere. It therefore provided ample competition for the money.

SPECIFICATIONS

Wheelbase	109"
Tread; Front, Rear	57.3", 56.5"
Overall Length	192.4"
Overall Width	70.4"
Overall Height	54.0"
Weight, Lbs	3148
Tire Size	6.70 x 15"

ENGINE

Type	Overhead V-8
Bore & Stroke	3.563" x 3.652"
Displacement, Cu. In.	289
Compression Ratio	9.00 to 1
Horsepower @ RPM	305 @ 5200
Max. Torque @ RPM	320 @ 4000
Electrical	12 Volt, neg. grd.

TRANSMISSION

Type	4 speed manual
Available	Automatic, power shift

REAR

Type	Hypoid, semi-floating
Ratio	3.73 to 1

TUNE UP

Spark Plug Gap	035"
Point Gap	017"
Cam Angle, Degrees	39
Timing	24° B.T.D.C.
Firing Order	18436572
Tappet Clearances:	
Intake	026"
Exhaust	026"
Compression Pressure,	
Lbs	160
Idle Speed, RPM	650

BRAKES

Type	Hydraulic, int. exp.
Drum Diameter	Disc., 11"

CAPACITIES

Cooling System, Qts	18
Fuel Tank, Gals	21
Crank Case, Qts	5
Trans. Pints	2.5
Differential, Pts	3

WHEEL ALIGNMENT

Caster, Degrees	−½
Camber, Degrees	+½
Toe in, Inches	3/16 to 1/4"

1963 Corvette Coupe

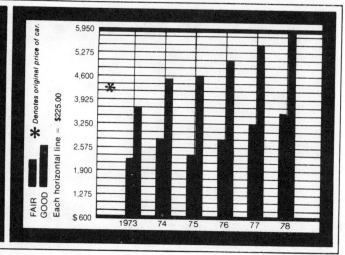

* Denotes original price of car.

FAIR GOOD

Each horizontal line = $225.00

5,950					
5,275					
4,600					
3,925					
3,250					
2,575					
1,900					
1,275					
$ 600					
1973	74	75	76	77	78

Five years ago you could buy a clean split-window Corvette for about $2500, if you could find one. Today the figure is much higher and the sight of a '63 Stingray Coupe is much less common. It's not that they rust away, being made of fiberglass, or that they end up in graveyards, because car buffs continually replace the drivetrain as it deteriorates. It is easier to liken this coupe to a rare bird that is protected by law and seen only at protected sanctuaries. In truth, the split-window is a rare species, a shark perhaps, but nevertheless pampered and selectively put on display.

The comparison to a shark is more than my own approximation. At the turn of the sixties, when Chevrolet was fiddling around with some wild creations to replace Corvette's aging body, one of them triggered the adrenalin of public response. It was called the Mako Shark and its offspring became known as the Stingray. Meanwhile, Jaguar was gaining favorable response of its own with the introduction of its new XKE series. This was 1962 and, noting similarities in the XKE Coupe and the forthcoming Stingray Coupe, G.M. had an excellent chance to sit back and measure the viability of its new product.

The rest of the story is history. Both cars set an envious pace of success. For the Corvette, which had always been a respected road car, a new twist was in the offing. The lithe new body, together with exotic engineering

refinements such as fully independent rear suspension, elevated its image from a macho brute to a sophisticated machine. While fuel-injection was offered in 1963 as a performance option, many Stingrays were sold more nominally equipped to a receptive crowd of class-conscious professionals. The benefit was mutual.

After twelve years, the testimony of time has revealed no fluke in the new image. It was the beauty, not the brawn, that kept prices high all this time. Compare the present value of a performance-equipped coupe with a docile street version and you will find little difference in price. Yet, if you evaluate the more common roadster version of the same year, you will find a marked discount in the figures. This is because the roadster does not have the continuation of graceful flowing lines found in the tapered roofline of the coupe. It has more of that macho appeal. Time is catching up to the roadster, though. It is being swept to a greater demand by the ever increasing popularity of its brother. Both are like money in the bank, and both are certainly more interest-bearing.

SPECIFICATIONS

Wheelbase	98"
Tread; Front, Rear	56.8", 57.6"
Overall Length	175.2"
Overall Width	69.2"
Overall Height	49.6"
Weight, Lbs	3130
Tire Size	6.70 x 15"

ENGINE

Type	Overhead V-8
Bore & Stroke	4.00" x 3.25"
Displacement, Cu. In.	327
Compression Ratio	11.25 to 1
Horsepower @ RPM	300 @ 5000
Max. Torque @ RPM	360 @ 3200
Electrical	12 Volt, neg. grd.

TRANSMISSION

Type	4 speed manual
Available	3 speed manual, automatic

REAR

Type	Independent 4 whl. susp.
Ratio	3.36 to 1

TUNE UP

Spark Plug Gap	.035"
Point Gap	.019"
Cam Angle, Degrees	30
Timing	4° B.T.D.C.
Firing Order	18436572
Tappet Clearances:	
Intake	Zero, hydraulic
Exhaust	Zero, hydraulic
Compression Pressure, Lbs	160
Idle Speed, RPM	500

BRAKES

Type	Hydraulic, int. exp.
Drum Diameter	11"

CAPACITIES

Cooling System, Qts	16.5
Fuel Tank, Gals	20
Crank Case, Qts	4
Trans. Pints	3.5
Differential, Pts	4

WHEEL ALIGNMENT

Caster, Degrees	0 to +2½
Camber, Degrees	+2 to +3
Toe in, Inches	⅛ to ¼

1963 Studebaker Lark Wagonaire

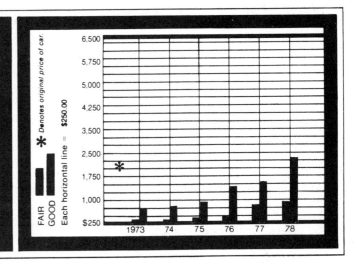

Yes, Larks are in! While they are still too recent for all models to have become valuable, the beginnings of the basic value hierarchy depicted in the Introduction are starting to become apparent. The Daytona convertibles are at least as collectible as the Wagonaire at this point, but indications are that time will favor the uniqueness of the roll-top wagon in much the same manner that the old "woody wagons" have enjoyed success. Presumably then, the two-door hardtops will soon be included in the ranks of the collectible Larks.

Again, the key word is unique. In this case, the individual attraction is the sliding rear section of the roof which can be rolled forward to create a reverse sun roof effect. Of course, the engineer's intention was to enable the owner to transport very large, bulky items, such as a refrigerator. Interestingly, these wagons could be equipped with almost the entire list of Avanti options, including disc brakes, tachometer and high-performance engines.

Produced for only three years, the 1965 and 1966 models were built in Canada and came equipped with Chevrolet engines. The short production run and non-extant insignia further add to the Wagonaire's value.

It is doubtful that a Wagonaire would win anybody's beauty contest. What style and continuity that exists in the hardtop is all but obliterated by the massive squareness of the roofline and fender-top placement of the taillights. However, individual interpretations of beauty are as varied as the range between the Willys Jeepster and the finned Chryslers of the late fifties. In this case, utility exempts any obligation toward beauty.

It seems incredible that a single company can offer the public such extreme variations as the Wagonaire and the Avanti simultaneously and find financial success in neither one of them. While these cars were excellent attempts to satisfy consumer extremists, Studebaker soon learned that the conservative middle market cannot be neglected. Sadly, it never seems to fail that the true value of such unique automobiles must be discovered in retrospect. Such is the case with the Studebaker Lark.

SPECIFICATIONS

Wheelbase	.113"
Tread; Front, Rear	.57.375", 59.5625"
Overall Length	.187"
Overall Width	.71.25"
Overall Height	.57"
Weight, Lbs	.3115
Tire Size	.6.50 x 15"

ENGINE

Type	Overhead V-8
Bore & Stroke	.3.563" x 3.625"
Displacement, Cu. In.	.289
Compression Ratio	.8.50 to 1
Horsepower @ RPM	.225 @ 4500
Max. Torque @ RPM	.305 @ 3000
Electrical	.12 Volt, neg. grd.

TRANSMISSION

Type	.3 speed manual
Available	.4 spd. manual, automatic, overdrive

REAR

Type	.Hypoid, semi-floating
Ratio	.3.31 to 1

TUNE UP

Spark Plug Gap	.035"
Point Gap	.017"
Cam Angle, Degrees	.39
Timing	.4° B.T.D.C.
Firing Order	.18436572
Tappet Clearances:	
Intake	.026"
Exhaust	.026"
Compression Pressure,	
Lbs	.185
Idle Speed, RPM	.650

BRAKES

Type	.Hydraulic, int. exp.
Drum Diameter	.11" front, 10" rear

CAPACITIES

Cooling System, Qts	.18
Fuel Tank, Gals	.18
Crank Case, Qts	.5
Trans. Pints	.3.8
Differential, Pts	.2.5

WHEEL ALIGNMENT

Caster, Degrees	.−1¼ to +¼
Camber, Degrees	.0 to +1
Toe in, Inches	.³/₁₆ to ¼

1964 Corvair Spyder Convertible

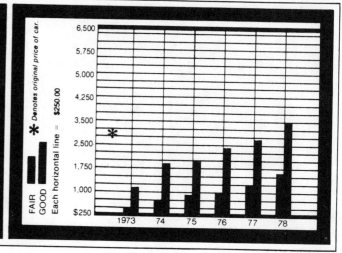

When Ralph Nader found the Corvair guilty of being unsafe, it was banished from the public mind. General Motors would soon have dropped its production anyway, because of convincing logic that "power for the people" meant horsepower. Horsepower was not abundant in the Corvair; neither was trunk space. But the problems that caused its consumer demise had been corrected before its death.

There it was in a state of limbo. The ignominy of defeat caused its reputation to sour, resulting in very low resale prices. A few people bought the car that nobody wanted because it was so cheap. Others found it better to hold on to their Corvairs rather than lose so much by selling. The cars kept running and they retained the elegance of their good looks; yet before long America was looking again for a sporty economy car. The alternatives were not good. Pollution devices and plastic had robbed the compacts of power and identity. And the people felt they were being robbed by the prices for these cars.

You guessed what happened next! Some joker drove by in a snappy convertible with a four-speed and the faintly reminiscent throb of a turbocharged engine. It had bucket seats and wire wheels and it got 20 miles per gallon. The looks, the handling and the room were suddenly better than the new compacts could offer.

Needless to say, the Corvair wasn't dead. It was too good a car, so it just hung around unnoticed until the people needed it. This has happened to several cars, but never so dramatically as with the Corvair. Each time, though, the price gets very dear the second time around. Hindsight is more expensive than foresight. It will get more expensive as time contrasts the character and quality of a past nobody wanted.

If you don't need the flamboyance, you can get around the prices by looking at the Corvair coupes, up to the last Corsa. By the time all the Vegas and Pintos have bucket seats and four speeds, the bench seats and automatic transmission will make a comeback. Kudos to Chevrolet, too, for producing a super clean car for nearly a decade without yielding to clutter and senseless gadgetry!

SPECIFICATIONS

Wheelbase	.108"
Tread; Front, Rear	.54.5", 55.1"
Overall Length	.180"
Overall Width	.67"
Overall Height	.51.5"
Weight, Lbs	.2555
Tire Size	.6.50 x 13"

ENGINE

Type	.Horiz. opposed 6 cyl.
Bore & Stroke	.3.438" x 2.60"
Displacement, Cu. In.	.145
Compression Ratio	.8.25 to 1
Horsepower @ RPM	.150 @ 4000
Max. Torque @ RPM	.232 @ 3200
Electrical	.12 Volt, neg. grd.

TRANSMISSION

Type	.4 speed manual
Available	.3 speed manual

REAR

Type	.Hypoid, semi-floating
Ratio	.3.55 to 1

TUNE UP

Spark Plug Gap	.035"
Point Gap	.019"
Cam Angle, Degrees	.33
Timing	.24° B.T.D.C.
Firing Order	.145236
Tappet Clearances:	
Intake	.Zero, hydraulic
Exhaust	.Zero, hydraulic
Compression Pressure, Lbs	.130
Idle Speed, RPM	.850

BRAKES

Type	.Hydraulic, int. exp.
Drum Diameter	.9"

CAPACITIES

Cooling System, Qts	.Air cooled
Fuel Tank, Gals	.14
Crank Case, Qts	.4
Trans. Pints	.3.75
Differential, Pts	.4.5

WHEEL ALIGNMENT

Caster, Degrees	.+1½ to +2½
Camber, Degrees	.−½ to +½
Toe in, Inches	.¼ to ⅜

1964 Pontiac GTO

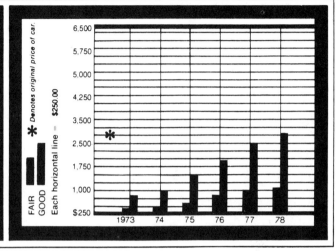

Let's face it! The sixties are not long gone and some of the memories are better left untouched. Nevertheless, it is amazing how quickly and totally the mood in America has changed in the last decade. The trend toward efficient economical cars in the seventies provides a good contrast with the muscle car philosophy of ten years ago. The progenitor of this breed of automobile was the 1964 Pontiac GTO. It turned out to be the surprise of the sixties.

The idea was simple enough. Pontiac engineers slipped the 389 cubic inch engine, already a proven performer in their full-size line, into the standard intermediate-size coupe and convertible bodies of their Tempest. The success of the Chevrolet Super Sport was apparent at this time, as was the fact that the sporty Corvair Monza had no room to grow. It seemed logical for Pontiac to combine the best qualities of each. The GTO was intended to transport four people in comfort and luxury — and as quickly as possible. Pontiac fulfilled this last qualification so completely that few people ever realized the letters GTO once stood for "gran turismo omologoto," intended as a reference to a touring sedan!

Loaded with pizzazz like trips* positraction and four on the floor, this little beastie could take you from a standstill to sixty miles per hour in less than six seconds. It took about five more seconds for your heart to arrive. No matter, the proof was on the

emblem. Symbolism has rarely spoken more clearly.

As with any good name, you must pay the price. The sobriety of the seventies has already made obvious the niche of the GTO, making its value accordingly high. In a few years, when we have plastic compacts to push us around, a lot more people will recall the inspiration of owning and driving a car with a name.

Muscle cars teach a lesson in life. Once an object comes along that exceeds the known limits of some category, it establishes a new standard which is both revered and desired by those who respect the category it defines. With the original GTO, the category is power. It is unwise to argue the necessity of such power. It is much easier to recognize that is exists and be secure in the awareness of its relative value as a salable commodity.

*Three two-barrel carburetors: hot-rodding's vanguard of performance and prestige goes as far back as the flatheat Fords.

SPECIFICATIONS

Wheelbase	115"
Tread; Front, Rear	58", 58"
Overall Length	203"
Overall Width	73.3"
Overall Height	53.5"
Weight, Lbs	2975
Tire Size	7.00 x 14"

ENGINE

Type	Overhead V-8
Bore & Stroke	4.09" x 3.75"
Displacement, Cu. In.	389
Compression Ratio	10.75 to 1
Horsepower @ RPM	348 @ 4900
Max. Torque @ RPM	428 @ 3600
Electrical	12 Volt, neg. grd.

TRANSMISSION

Type	4 speed manual
Available	Automatic

REAR

Type	Hypoid, semi-floating
Ratio	4.11 to 1

TUNE UP

Spark Plug Gap	.035"
Point Gap	.016"
Cam Angle, Degrees	30
Timing	6° B.T.D.C.
Firing Order	18436572
Tappet Clearances:	
Intake	Zero, hydraulic
Exhaust	Zero, hydraulic
Compression Pressure,	
Lbs	160
Idle Speed, RPM	500

BRAKES

Type	Hydraulic, int. exp.
Drum Diameter	9.5"

CAPACITIES

Cooling System, Qts	20.5
Fuel Tank, Gals	21.5
Crank Case, Qts	5
Trans. Pints	3.75
Differential, Pts	4.5

WHEEL ALIGNMENT

Caster, Degrees	−2 to −1
Camber, Degrees	−¼ to +¾
Toe in, Inches	0 to ⅛

1965 Rambler Marlin

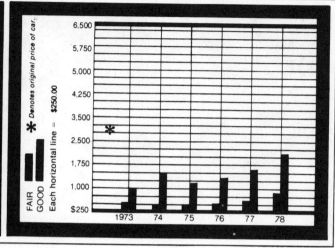

Surely, I must be joking! What is such a new car doing here, and a Rambler no less? If that isn't confusing, just try to find the beauty in this car. All too sadly, it must be reported that there is less beauty in the Marlin than uniqueness. To complicate things further, the car is not even very rare. Not "very" rare, but perhaps medium rare: a condition which, if one is to accept the verity of mortality tables, can only lead to the acuteness of this symptom.

It is one thing to realize this inevitability. It is another thing to realize that this is Rambler's only fastback (a condition from which it literally suffers). It is still another thing to combine these facts and conclude that the Marlin will have its day. And, you know, it's as plain as the handwriting on the wall.

There are two basic problems that obscure the prophecy. One is the fact that the car's measurements are not at all conducive to the assumed effect of fastback styling. That was the whole problem with the short-lived fastback revival of the mid-sixties. The other problem is that the car was pushed prematurely into its future role, creating the disparity of a double market and, consequently, undermining both the higher price structure and the credibility of its potential.

This has happened before and it will happen again. Cars, like water, will always seek their own level. They may be temporarily buoyed by optimism, but always they are left to sink or swim on their own accountability. This is why it pays to know how to spot beauty in the artfulness of the automobile. The alternative to a keen eye is the less precipitous reliance on the old equalizer, Father Time.

The paradox presented by the Rambler Marlin sheds light on another curious fact. Of the many variables that render a car collectible, perhaps no two are closer to being diametrically opposed than the factors of uniqueness and beauty. Sometimes the two can even be one and the same, but more often than not, a car's uniqueness (as in the case of the Marlin Fastback) is a wild card that exceeds in its value to the collector the artistic merit it warrants on its own accord. When this happens with a newer car, its value will ascend and decline rather sharply before gradually assuming its proper place. The car of beauty, on the other hand (AMX, for one), may rise in value early, but will tend to maintain a steady rate of growth. If you're smart, you can profit by either example. If you are less than certain, it's best to stay with older, proven cars.

SPECIFICATIONS

Wheelbase	.112"
Tread; Front, Rear	.58.6", 57.6"
Overall Length	.195"
Overall Width	.74.5"
Overall Height	.54.2"
Weight, Lbs	.2955
Tire Size	.7.75 x 14"

ENGINE

Type	Overhead V-8
Bore & Stroke	.4.00" x 3.25"
Displacement, Cu. In.	.327
Compression Ratio	.8.70 to 1
Horsepower @ RPM	.250 @ 4700
Max. Torque @ RPM	.340 @ 2600
Electrical	.12 Volt, neg. grd.

TRANSMISSION

Type	Automatic
Available	3 spd. manual, overdrive

REAR

Type	Hypoid, semi-floating
Ratio	.3.15 to 1

TUNE UP

Spark Plug Gap	.035"
Point Gap	.016"
Cam Angle, Degrees	.30
Timing	.5° B.T.D.C.
Firing Order	.18436572
Tappet Clearances:	
Intake	Zero, hydraulic
Exhaust	Zero, hydraulic
Compression Pressure, Lbs	.145
Idle Speed, RPM	.550

BRAKES

Type	Hydraulic, int. exp.
Drum Diameter	.10", (11.2" disc.)

CAPACITIES

Cooling System, Qts	.19
Fuel Tank, Gals	.19
Crank Case, Qts	.4
Trans.	11 Qts.
Differential, Pts	.4

WHEEL ALIGNMENT

Caster, Degrees	+¾ to +1½
Camber, Degrees	−¼ to +¼
Toe in, Inches	1/16 to 3/16

116

1966 Oldsmobile Toronado

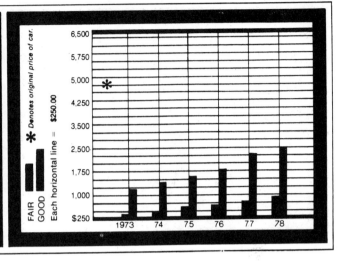

There are some things to be said of the American road machine. The 1966 Oldsmobile Toronado said most of them, and added a few ideas of its own. The result was a car that compressed history by turning up in collectors' circles before its tenth birthday. Other cars have done this, but for isolated reasons. The Toronado put it all together in one car.

America has the best network of highways in the world. It also has the most licensed drivers in the world. The great majority of these drivers do not understand the mechanics of a car. They turn the key and expect to drive away. Most of the time they find their car a willing servant, despite the way it is abused and neglected. In principle, there is a reason for this high rate of return.

With the overhead, oversquare V-8 engine came the advantage of less up and down travel for the reciprocating parts of the engine. This meant less inertia to tear at the vital components at the top and bottom of every stroke. The bigger bore allowed for larger pistons, which generated tremendous amounts of torque. This abundance of power made possible the use of lower numerical gear ratios, thus saving rpm's and allowing the engine to loaf at cruising speeds.

Contrast this theory with the popular European philosophy of a small displacement under-square engine of some in-line variety. The engine must work hard to find power from its small pistons, so it thrives on high rpm's with

a long stroke; the stress on the crank and its attached parts becomes terrific at high speeds, tending to tear itself apart. But the power is harder to come by, so higher numerical ratios are necessary to multiply the torque. Four- and five-speed gearboxes keep things spinning fast. That means more friction and a greater chance of failure in the drive-train. This is why so many exotic foreign cars are so fickle. On European roads, European cars are more effective. On American highways, there is no substitute for the big cruiser. It takes cubic inches and gasoline to make it work, but in 1966 there was plenty of each for the affluent American.

Look at the specs on this car. It had a monstrous engine capable of tremendous power. Yet it was quiet, controlled power, and it benefited from the stability of front wheel drive. It supplied enough power to run every option known to man and still could pin you to the seat under acceleration. All this for the average American driver who often couldn't even open the hood!

The original Toronado is a thoughtfully styled car. Its looks transcend a ruggedness capable of survival — no matter how demanding the test. It is a car that will be celebrated as one of the all-time greats. Judging from the way it's built, one suspects that it will be around for the party.

SPECIFICATIONS

Wheelbase	.119"
Tread; Front, Rear	.63.5", 63"
Overall Length	.211"
Overall Width	.78.5"
Overall Height	.52.8"
Weight, Lbs	.4496
Tire Size	.8.85 x 15"

ENGINE

Type	.Overhead V-8
Bore & Stroke	.4.125" x 3.975"
Displacement, Cu. In.	.425
Compression Ratio	.10.5 to 1
Horsepower @ RPM	.385 @ 4800
Max. Torque @ RPM	.475 @ 3200
Electrical	.12 Volt, neg. grd.

TRANSMISSION

Type	.Automatic
Available	.—

REAR

Type	.Hypoid, semi-floating
Ratio	.3.21 to 1

TUNE UP

Spark Plug Gap	.030"
Point Gap	.016"
Cam Angle, Degrees	.30
Timing	.7.5° B.T.D.C.
Firing Order	.18436572
Tappet Clearances:	
Intake	.Zero, hydraulic
Exhaust	.Zero, hydraulic
Compression Pressure,	
Lbs	.180
Idle Speed, RPM	.850

BRAKES

Type	.Hydraulic, int. exp.
Drum Diameter	.11"

CAPACITIES

Cooling System, Qts	.18
Fuel Tank, Gals	.24
Crank Case, Qts	.5
Trans.	.12 Qts.
Differential, Pts	.4.5

WHEEL ALIGNMENT

Caster, Degrees	.−1½ to −2½
Camber, Degrees	.−¼ to +½
Toe in, Inches	.0 to 1/16

1969 AMX

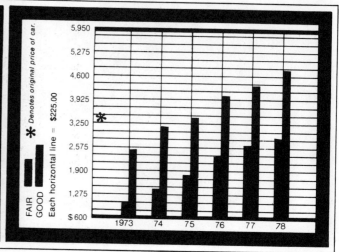

The inclusion of a car so new as the AMX is likely to meet with mixed impressions in a book dedicated to old cars. It is always harder to argue the case for valuable newer cars because of the mistaken importance most critics attach to a car's tenure. While age is certainly a valid criterion for judging a car's worth, the lack of it should not negatively influence the assessment of its objective merit. It is easy to study the great classics of the past and conclude that their value is attributable to the finesse of their form. It is more difficult, though, to project the logic of such observations in a way that applies the same pattern to present-day designs. This can be as risky as predicting the future, or as safe as finding the progression in a series of numbers. The difference is in *knowing* the classic's value, instead of agreeing to it after it has been popularly accepted.

The connection is, of course, that cars are objects of art, as well as objects of history. The life cycle of a car is very definitely affected by the timeless denominators of form and beauty. This brings us to the 1969 AMX. The AMX has a balanced, proportioned design that is neither cluttered nor clumsy. It is a delicate fusion of lines of power and lines of gracefulness. As in any good piece of art, there is a depth of character that reaches beyond the ephemeral. The car invokes, in an understanding observer, an instinctive response to its sense of meaning — a response which excites one's macho ego without disrupting the harmony of his aesthetic balance.

Conceived as an upper-middle priced compromise between power and luxury, the AMX gained by its appearance the maverick reputation of a car without class distinction. The nearest thing to it in looks was its brother, the Javelin, and the difference there was as marked as that between the original Mustang and the Mustang II!

The unique niche created among cars by the AMX and its untimely departure is responsible for its present high demand. You don't have to be a fortune-teller to predict a rosy future for the AMX; you just have to be fortunate enough to find one at an affordable price today.

SPECIFICATIONS

Wheelbase . . . . .97"
Tread; Front, Rear . . . . .58.4", 57"
Overall Length . . . . .177.2"
Overall Width . . . . .71.6"
Overall Height . . . . .51.7"
Weight, Lbs 3126
Tire Size . . . . .7.35 x 14"

ENGINE

Type . . . . .Overhead V-8
Bore & Stroke .4.17" x 3.57"
Displacement, Cu. In. 390
Compression Ratio . . . . .10.20 to 1
Horsepower @ RPM . . . . .315 @ 4600
Max. Torque @ RPM . . . . .425 @ 3200
Electrical . . . . .12 Volt, neg. grd.

TRANSMISSION

Type . . . . .4 speed manual
Available . . . . .Automatic

REAR

Type . . . . .Hypoid, semi-floating
Ratio . . . . .3.15 to 1

TUNE UP

Spark Plug Gap . . . . .035"
Point Gap . . . . .016"
Cam Angle, Degrees 30
Timing . . . . .T.D.C.
Firing Order 18436572
Tappet Clearances:
   Intake .Zero, hydraulic
   Exhaust . . . . .Zero, hydraulic
Compression Pressure,
Lbs 145
Idle Speed, RPM 650

BRAKES

Type . . . . .Hydraulic, int. exp.
Drum Diameter . . . . .10"

CAPACITIES

Cooling System, Qts 13
Fuel Tank, Gals 19
Crank Case, Qts 4
Trans. Pints 3.5
Differential, Pts 4

WHEEL ALIGNMENT

Caster, Degrees . . . .−½ to +½
Camber, Degrees . . . .−⅜ to +⅜
Toe in, Inches . . . . .¹/₁₆ to ³/₁₆

Crisis & Reasoning: 1970's

We were left suspended at the end of the sixties, caught in a vicious circle of conspicuous consumption of, and concern over, dwindling resources. For almost four years we hung on to that precarious pedestal in the sky, both fearing its collapse and causing its erosion. When 1974 greeted us with a gasoline crisis, it was the final precipitation of an overdue event. For years America had been living the life of Riley. So confident were we of our position that we failed to notice certain growing disparities. As we flooded the world with manufactured goods and spent our money on war, our need for raw materials increased while the demand for our products diminished. The world market was saturated. Suddenly, the relationship between dollars and resources reversed itself, with the dollar equating to something fixed and abundant and the resources becoming the common denominator. Then the Arabs forced a new exchange rate and fluid currency became the gold of the seventies. This is when we fell off the ladder. It was a hard fall, but a necessary one if we are ever to attain that mythical global community: for it was our own self-esteem that was the most distorted piece of the world puzzle.

Already we are making new friends and renewing old relationships. President Ford is wisely aware that an era of detente is necessary to the creation of a thriving world community. We are on the road to recovery. Let's go back to the last intersection, hop in our vehicle and continue our tour. The road looks pretty smooth ahead. If we don't get distracted, I think we can cover a lot of ground.

Yes, this must be it. The sign on the corner says 1970. The signs of the times confirm it. The cars are identifiable in a collective way as belonging to the seventies. In this decade the automobile came into its own. After exploring all the fads and fetishes in the fifties and all the sizes and shapes in the sixties, the automobile was left with a feeling of confidence — of maturity — as it entered the seventies. Early experiments with gas turbine engines and later ones with rotary engines revealed the adequacy of the modern overheads. Similarly, transistorized ignitions, radial-tuned suspensions and all sorts of refined power options combined to secure the position of the car as a commodity with merit. Time had given the car a certain wisdom by way of these experiences and provided a depth of character far greater than any superficial beauty of line. When this situation gelled we could accept virtually any role from the automobile, knowing it would be performed with all the charm of a mellowed actor and all the grace of fine ballerina.

The last few years have been drawn to a revival of classic lines, drawn to it as if by an instinctive urge to resume the business of art at the point when it was last known to flourish — a long, long time ago. Half-padded landau tops beckon the days of the great coachbuilders. We have not quite recaptured the craftsmanship of old, but the look of old is the current rage. Of course, it is done over in tastefully modern approach. Most of the larger new cars have some rendition of the classic free-standing grille. If it killed the Edsel, it's bowling them over in the seventies, another sign of the auto's coming of age.

Many new cars are being designed with sculpted streaks arcing over the front and rear wheels, highly reminiscent of the days when fenders brought flare to a car, unmindful of convention. You've got to admit it looks good to see the accent properly placed rather than distractingly tacked on as an afterthought. The days of the great chrome caper are over now, having yielded to an era of plastic and vinyl molding. This is actually better in the long run because it won't rust or ding over the years.

Another modern trend is toward ventless front windows and fixed rear windows. Flow-through ventilation made this possible, but cost-cutting advantages probably stimulated its implementation more than anything. It certainly hasn't hurt the sales of air-conditioning units, either. All of these trends will be with us for a while. As they climb toward a peak of development, they will be augmented by several new ideas and some not-so-new ideas revisited. Moving along on the road of the seventies, let us take a look at the latter half of the decade.

Always an area of great commotion, headlights are sure to unergo another industry-wide transition. In the fifties it was to quad setups and in the sixties there was a move to conceal the headlamps. In the seventies, the lights will become rectangular, à la the latest G.M. big cars. Stopgap catalytic converters will soon disappear in the wake of more efficient clean-burn measures. Lean-burning engines and stratified charge powerplants are much more effective in combating pollution at its source. When these improvements begin to make headway in the next few years, there will be a revival of powermania, with turbochargers returning to the limelight. We will get good mileage too in the cars of the future; it's in the law.

Just in case you haven't heard there's nothing new under the sun, Detroit will bring back an idea that was last popular in the fifties. Two-tone paint will accent the creases and bulges of almost all the new cars, creating recognition, but not necessarily in a positive way.

Obviously, there will be no more convertibles for awhile. We've just about stopped making them now. In a few years, when their absence has caused inflated prices and nostalgia, the clever Michigan minds will undoubtedly hail their revival as the modern version of the sunroof! And it will probably work!

A new (for America) size of car will make its presence felt in the next five years. The ultra-mini car will find a ready market due to the ever-increasing cost of gasoline. As it seeks a niche in our hearts, it is bound to expand a bit in size as well as decor. If Detroit ever decides to market a new type of engine, it is most likely to be found first in the mini. This is simply because there will be less to lose and more to gain by placing the unseeded reputation of a newcomer on the line. Odds are that diminishing resources will eventually force the gamble.

In the more distant future we might, perhaps, expect to see the modular car! Consisting of quickly replaceable front, middle and rear sections, it would virtually live forever. A tired engine would simply require the replacement of a prefabricated front or rear power unit, complete with (plastic) fenders and plug-in frame rails. A damaged core or passenger compartment could similarly be replaced with a matching unit of color-impregnated fiberglass, complete with molded seats and printed circuit dash ready to be popped into place.

Imagine the car that would last forever! Inexpensive disposable units would eliminate junkyards and costly damage repair bills. On the other hand, to bring the price down to a realistic level would mean standardizing the width and body contour at the cleavage points. This is no more difficult than standardizing the gauge of railroad track. In fact, once the junctures have been standardized, variations in length and design of the three modules that make up the car could afford combinations beyond their actual number. The substitution of a lengthier center section might be the ideal solution to the problem of the growing family.

Or perhaps replacing the rear, cargo module with a pickup unit would let the family car double as the work horse. The combinations are nearly limitless and quite exciting. Who knows, we may create the modular man before it's all over. We never did establish whether man dictates the course of the automobile or whether the car ushers the path for man. At any rate, it's a long way off. We have plenty of time to think about it — and lots of "Real Steel" to keep us busy.

Last Word

Real Steel was written for the connoisseur as well as the armchair hobbyist and everyone in between. The benefit you derive from it is up to you. To fully appreciate this book, you must allow yourself to frame it in the proper perspective; and, I think, you must be prepared for a good look at yourself.

This may sound strange to those of you who expected the book you bought to be a panacea for converting cars to dollars; but actually, you can only get as proficient in this art as your own intuitive awareness permits. For example, if you know coins or furniture or stamps, or even the stock market, you come to possess a kind of aesthetic appreciation of the intrinsic value of these items. You don't have to consult a guidebook because you can "feel" the value of the art form in that indefinable way that has enabled all art to endure since time began.

What's more, you come to appreciate all forms of art according to your own tastes and standards. All I have done in this book is expressed my personal reflections about how I perceive the common denominators of beauty and appeal in certain cars that are indicative of the range of the art form. The fact that values for these cars are high and steadily rising gives credence to my choices; that is, people support my decisions, or vice-versa.

However, if you have a "feel" for this kind of beauty, you will find it easy to venture apart from these "blue chip" standards and interpret the soul-appeal of any car — old or new — according to your own understanding of beauty, form and function. This is when you are an expert. And this is when you get your real reward, for you will have accomplished the most difficult task of converting the intangible quality of beauty to the very tangible measure of monetary success.

I hope, also, that you will protect and preserve the species as you pursue your pleasures through the automobile. Mostly I hope that if you become a true master at car selecting, you don't push the ante too high for the man with the little purse but big soul. Happy hunting!

Sources

Cars and Parts.
P.O. Box 299
Sesser, Ill. 62884
Subscription rate: $6.00/yr.

This is a monthy magazine devoted to old cars. It consists primarily of classified ads for all types of cars, including sport and foreign, and even motorcycles. It lists clubs and events and contains outstanding articles in every issue about the history of the automobile. There are sections devoted to "parts wanted" and "parts for sale." Its question and answer section should satisfy every type of car buff. A free ad for every new subscription is a generous offer. The results are excellent, as is the publication.

Chilton's Manuals.
Published by Chilton Book Company,
Philadelphia, Pa. Annually.

These comprehensive manuals have been available on a yearly basis for a long, long time. Each volume offers a complete specification and repair section for every American car produced during the year of the book's printing, as well as for several preceding years. A reprinted edition, covering the period from 1940 to 1953, was most helpful in my own research. Old issues of this and the similar **Motor's** manual are frequently seen floating around at swap meets. They are usually an inexpensive solution to an old car buff's statistical problems. Certainly, no reference collection is complete without several issues of this informative mechanic's guide.

Automobile Quarterly.
14 East 60th St.
New York, N.Y. 10022
Subscription rate: $28.50/yr.

Of all the publications that dealt with vintage cars, this is the most colorful pictorial available. Each issue is devoted to a few in-depth studies of the great cars of our past. You will find yourself impatiently awaiting each quarterly issue of this beautiful and factual booklet.

Hemming's Motor News.
Box 380
Bennington, Vt. 05201
Subscription rate: $4.75/yr.

Commonly referred to as **Hemming's,** this is the car lover's bible. It is similar in format to **Cars and Parts** but has only an occasional article on automobile highlights. The strength of this monthly magazine lies in its phenomenal ability to reach the old car market. If you want to buy or sell any car or part, no matter how rare, this is far and away the best bet. A thorough listing of services available should please any perplexed restorer.

Hot Rod Magazine.
6725 Sunset Blvd.
P.O. Box 3293
Los Angeles, Cal. 90028
Subscription rate: $9.00/yr.

Keeping in contact with cars involves being knowledgeable about every aspect of their development. **Hot Rod Magazine** is more than its name suggests. Topics range from performance to economy tips, from old cars to new, and from product research to the latest aftermarket developments. This monthly can be the backbone of a well-rounded automotive library. Were it not for my many years as a subscriber to **Hot Rod, Real Steel** would be much the weaker.

Motor's Manuals.
Published by Motor
250 West 55th St.
New York, N.Y. 10019 Annually.

Essentially the same as **Chilton's Manuals** in format and approach, **Motor's Manuals** are the equal of any available mechanic's guide. I firmly suggest a mixing of **Motor's** and **Chilton's** annuals as a healthy system of cross-reference. You'll be surprised at how they augment each other and relieve the frustration of not being able to find that one little fact that has you stumped.

Motor Trend Magazine.
8490 Sunset Blvd.
Los Angeles, Cal. 90069
Subscription rate: $7.50/yr.

Motor Trend has been around for a long time. You may question its value as a guide to older cars, but the truth is, much of **Real Steel** is the result of ardent reading about these cars when they were new. Naturally, **Motor Trend** supplied the information. No matter what car you read about, in time it will be an antique or special-interest auto. It is better to acquire information when cars are new so you can trace their development with great insight. **Motor Trend** will keep you abreast of the latest developments.

Old Cars.
Iola, Wisc. 54945
Subscription rate: $6.00/yr.

This is a unique publication for several reasons. Bi-weekly and in newspaper format, it includes the results of the latest old car auctions and shows. If you're in the business of old cars, this could well be your Wall Street Journal. In the rear of each issue is a classified section dealing with the usual old cars and related parts business. This publication is sprinkled with lively, diversified articles and always makes for interesting reading.

Old Car Value Guide.
Quentin Craft
El Paso, Texas
Subscription rate: $6.50/issue

For those who want to know the dollar value of just about any make or model of old car, this is an indispensable guide. Published yearly, it is continually being revised and improved upon. There are some pictures, but its strength is in its numbers! A hint: use the **Old Car Value Guide** as its name suggests, not as a fixed-figure source.

Special-Interest Autos.
Box 196
Bennington, Vt. 05201
Subscription rate: $7.00/yr.

Special-Interest Autos appears every other month. Over the last few years, since its introduction in 1970, this magazine has been unmatched in providing a wealth of information and illustrations to the automobile afficianado. More than any single publication, **Special-Interest Autos**, especially those issues produced under the direction of Mike Lamm, has revealed the full background and history of the automobile. Back issues are available and urgently recommended for the curious car nut.

Alphabetical Index

Snake

me

Inky

Bee

Name: Mackenzie

Class: 35

School: Muir lade School

Silent ‹b›

Write some silent ‹b› words in the lamb.

shin
bench
lame
come
thume
crumes
plummer
climming
mother
father

Choose a word from the list to fit each sentence.

I _Brush_ my hair every morning.

A baby sheep is called a _lame_.

The girls were _Planting_ the tree.

There are cake _clices_ on the table.

mother
mother
mother

father
father
father

Write the alphabet in capital and lower-case letters.

Aa Bb Cc _____

_____

_____

2

Alphabetical Order

Write the capital letters next to the lower-case letters.

A a B b C c D d E e

F f G g H h I i J j K k L l   m

N n O o P p Q q R r S s

T t U u V v W w X x Y y Z z

Put these sets of letters into alphabetical order.

D A B E   M L K J   U V T W

A B D C   J K L M   T U V W

J H G I   N A M D   P O Z Q

G H I J   A D M N   O P Q Z

Look up these words in the dictionary.
Write the page number and the part of speech beside each word.

stable

ark

chess

zebra

plate

kettle

3

chat
cash
<u>W</u>rite
_rist
_reck
<u>W</u>rong
ans_er
s_ordfish
sister
brother

Silent ‹w›

Write some silent ‹w› words in the shipwreck.

Choose a word from the list to fit each sentence.

She got the answer <u>wrong</u>.

Then she got the <u>anser</u> right.

I must <u>chat</u> to my pen friend.

He sprained his <u>wrist</u>.

sister
<u>sister</u>
<u>sister</u>

brother
<u>brother</u>
b<u>rothe</u>r

Put these words into alphabetical order.

clown
acrobat
tent
juggler

<u>acrobat</u>
<u>clown</u>
<u>Juggler</u>
<u>tent</u>

harp
oboe
trumpet
flute
drum

<u>drum</u>
<u>flute</u>
<u>harp</u>
<u>oboe</u>
<u>trumpet</u>

Sentence Writing

Write some sentences about the picture.

A mom and a kid is bilding a snowman
with carrot, butturs, tuot, sticks.
A kids are sleding and skieing.
A little girl is makeing a snow angre.

5

Silent ‹k›

song
trunk
_k_nee
_k_nit
_k_now
_k_nock
knight
pen_k_nife
grandma
grandpa

Write some silent ‹**k**› words in the knight's helmet.

Choose a word from the list to fit each sentence.

"Do you _____ the answer?" I asked.

The _____ wore shining armour.

Grandma will _____ a sweater.

Please _____ on the door.

grandma
grandma
grandma

grandpa
grandpa
grandpa

Write some sentences about one of your grandparents.
Then draw a picture of him or her.

_____

_____

_____

"Speech Marks"

Add the speech marks to these sentences.

Hello Snake, said Inky.
We have been looking for you, buzzed Bee.
Sssss, hissed Snake. Well, here I am.
Snake looked at the letter in Inky's hand. Is that for me? he asked.

Think what the three friends might say next, and write the words in the speech bubbles.

Now write out the speech as sentences.

REMEMBER Use speech marks, and explain who speaks which words.

_____

_____

_____

this
that
~~t~~aile
Wheat
_ _ip
_ _istle
_ _iskers
Whatever
aunt
uncle

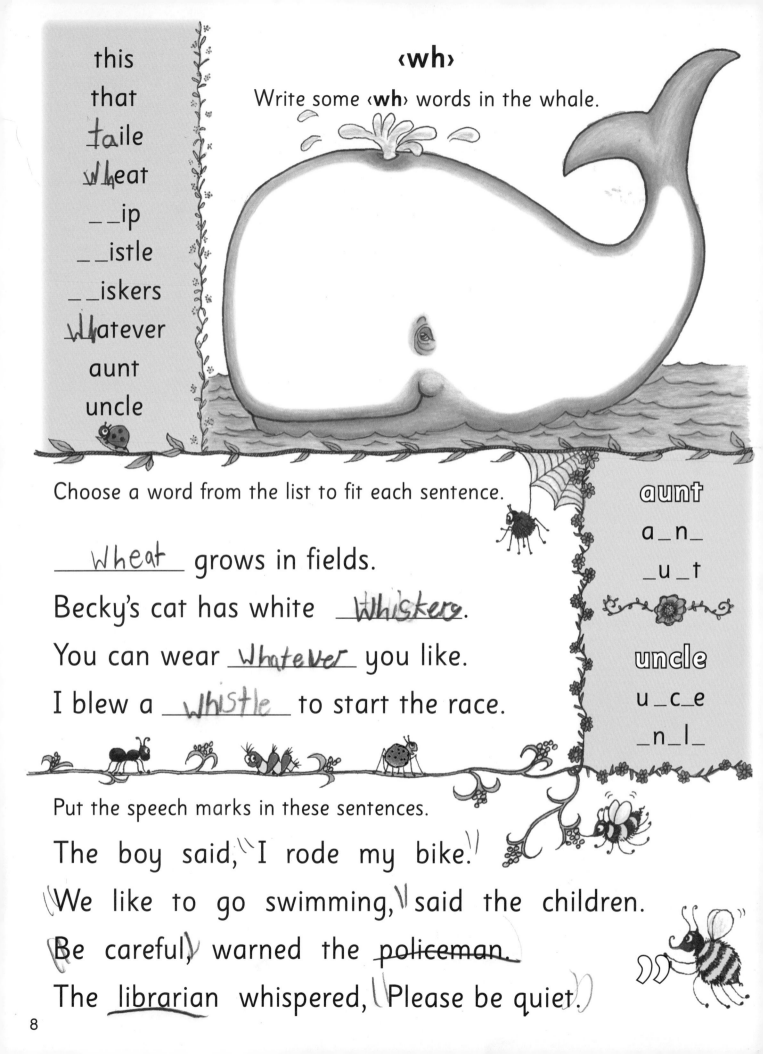

‹wh›

Write some ‹wh› words in the whale.

Choose a word from the list to fit each sentence.

Wheat grows in fields.

Becky's cat has white Whiskers.

You can wear Whatever you like.

I blew a whistle to start the race.

aunt
a _ n _
_ u _ t

uncle
u _ c e
_ n _ l _

Put the speech marks in these sentences.

The boy said, "I rode my bike."

"We like to go swimming," said the children.

"Be careful," warned the ~~policeman~~.

The librarian whispered, "Please be quiet."

8

Questions

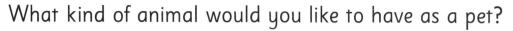

What kind of animal would you like to have as a pet?

bunny and Dogs are fun to Bunnys

Why? _There fun to play Wiith. Dog are active_

Bunnys are cute. Dogsare fun.

What? Why? When? Where?
Who? Whose? Which? How?

What questions could you ask to find out how to look after it properly?

1. _____

2. _____

3. _____

4. _____

Draw a picture of the pet you would like to have.

9

club
flag
_ _one
_ _oto
dol_ _in
ele**p h**ant
s_ _ere
al_ _abet
ne_ _ew
niece

‹ph›

Write some ‹ph› words in the elephant.

nephew
n_p_e_
_e_h_w

niece
n_e_e
_i_c_

Choose a word from the list to fit each sentence.

This is a _____ of my baby sister.

We can say the _____.

The _____ swam by the boat.

"_____ me tomorrow," said Tom.

Finish each sentence by adding a question mark or a period.

What time do we have to go to bed[8]

An orphan is a child whose mother and father are dead[.]

How old is Grandma[66]

Whose is this photo album[.]

10

Commas in Lists

We use commas to separate words in a list. Add commas to these lists.

Red **orange** yellow **green** **blue** **indigo** and **violet** are the colors of the rainbow.

Oak elm holly fir beech apple and chestnut are all trees.

On the farm there are cows dogs cats horses sheep and chickens.

Make lists to complete these sentences.

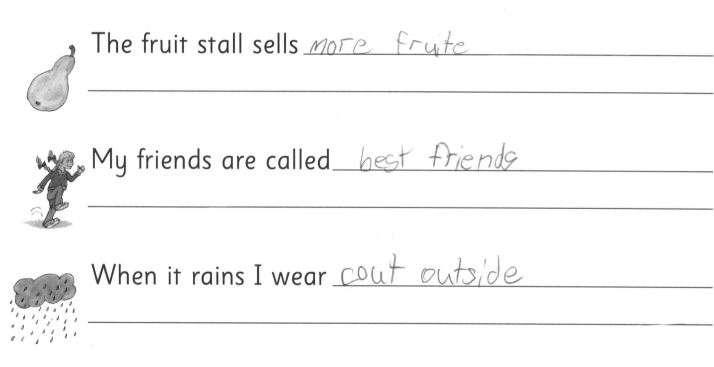

 The fruit stall sells _more fruite_ _____

My friends are called _best friends_ _____

 When it rains I wear _cout outside_ _____

My favorite games are _money_ _____

At the zoo we saw _a zebra,_ _____

REMEMBER Use commas and the word "and" to separate the words.

11

glad
plum
r_o_a_d
he_a_d
bre_a_d
we_a_ther
tre_a_sure
bre_a_kfast
cousin
friend

‹ea› saying the /e/ sound

Write some ‹ea› words in the loaf of bread.

Choose a word from the list to fit each sentence.

The _____ is sunny today.

Dad cooks _____ in the morning.

She found some buried _____.

I have _____ that book already.

cousin
c_ u_ i_
_o_ s_ n

friend
f_ i_ n_
_r_ e_ d

Add commas to these lists.

They went out to buy milk butter cheese and bread.

In my garden I grow carrots potatoes tomatoes beans and peas.

Squares circles triangles stars and rectangles are all shapes.

12

Exclamation Marks!

REMEMBER An exclamation mark shows that the person speaking or writing feels strongly about something.

What might you exclaim if you had these strong feelings?

Fill in the missing punctuation marks.

◻Stop◻◻ shouted the policeman◻

Tina went outside◻ ◻Brr◻ It is freezing◻◻ she said◻

◻Brilliant◻ That is just what I wanted◻◻ exclaimed Seth◻

13

mill
tell
i_e
dan_e
_ity
_ircle
poli_e
_ylinder
January
February

Soft ‹c› saying the /s/ sound

Write some **soft** ‹c› words in the circus tent.

ce
ci
cy

Choose a word from the list to fit each sentence.

A _____ is tube shaped.

I ate a vanilla ___ice___ cream.

The _____ arrested the robber.

We _____ to the music.

January
J_n_a_y
_a_u_r_

February
F_b_u_r_
_e_r_a_y

Fill in the missing punctuation marks.

◯Stop thief◯◯ shouted the man◯ ◯Call the police◯◯
The police arrived quickly◯ ◯What has been taken◯◯
asked the policeman◯
◯The thief stole two rings◯ a watch◯ a pair of earrings◯ and
a necklace,◯ the man explained◯

14

Alphabetical Order
Fill in the missing letters.

A _ C _ _ _   F G _ I J _ _ M   **B**

N _ _ Q _ S   T _ _ W _ _ _

Put these words into alphabetical order.

sheep   horse   dog   cow   **J**

F   cow   dog   horse   sheep

swing   bat   bike   toy   **O**

A   bat   bick _____

Tyrone   Sid   Ted   Billy   Tom   **U**

_____

Y   avocado   peach   cherry   orange   plum

_____

chin   clap   cake   cut   coat   crayon   **I**

_____

S   stop   scar   skin   second   sack   shell

_____

REMEMBER If more than one word starts with the same letter, look at the next letter in each word.

15

miss
cross
giant
magic
large
danger
orange
vegetable
March
April

Soft ‹g› saying the /j/ sound

Write some **soft ‹g›** words in the vegetables.

ge

gi

gy

Choose a word from the list to fit each sentence.

I ate a bowl of _____ soup.

Then I drank a glass of _____ juice.

Be careful! You are in _____.

The wizard cast a _____ spell.

March
M_r_h
_a_c_

April
A_r_l
_p_i_

Draw a ring around the word that would come first in the dictionary.

amber
acorn

raft
rook

gander
grammar

vowel
vixen

elk
expel

plural
penguin

Proper Nouns

The names of the months are **proper nouns**.
Write them in order on the calendar pages below, and
draw a picture for each month in the space.

REMEMBER Start each month with a capital letter.

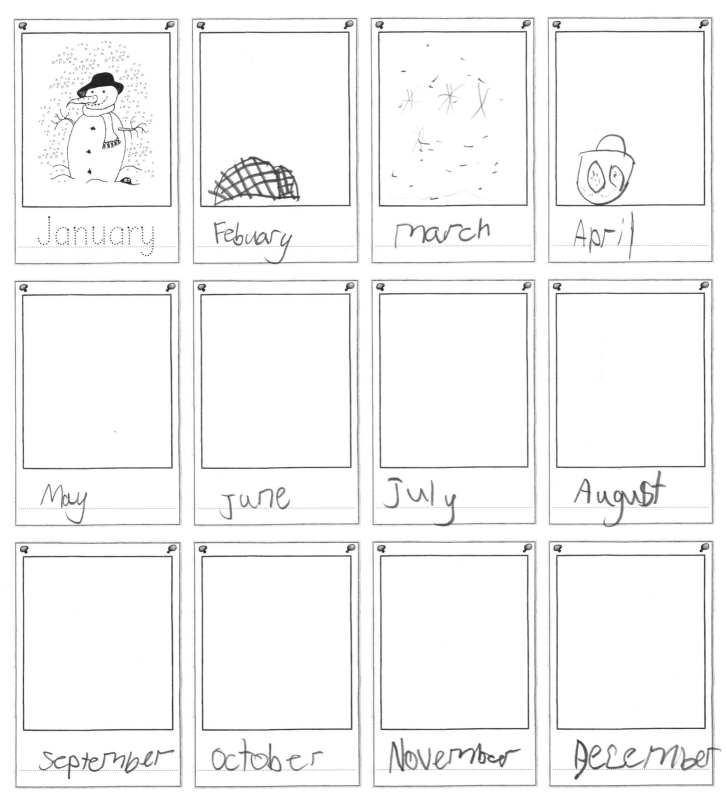

January

Febuary

march

April

May

June

July

August

september

October

November

December

duck
click
_ _nd
_ _sh
_ _sp
s_ _n
_ _tch
s_ _llow
May
June

‹wa› saying /wo/
Write some ‹wa› words in the swan.

May
M_y
_ a _
❀
June
J _ n _
_ u _ e

Choose a word from the list to fit each sentence.

My _____ says two o'clock.

She was stung by a _____.

We must _____ our hands.

A _____ is a big, white bird.

Read these **nouns**, and give each **proper noun** a capital letter.

england   michael   mrs swan   monday

wand   september   zack   flower

house   chair   watch   dog

mr brown   fire   hannah   new zealand

18

Adjectives

Choose a name for a planet
and write it on the line.

Action:

Touch the side of your
temple with your fist.

_____

Imagine an alien living on the planet.
Write an **adjective** to describe the alien's head in the first box, and draw
the head next to it. Then do the same for the alien's body and feet.

My alien has a

(any adjective)

ears

head...

...a butterfly

(texture adjective)

Green Schay

body...

...and some

(color adjective)

blue

feet!

19

thin
thick
t_ _ch
y_ _ng
d_ _ble
tr_ _ble
c_ _ntry
n_ _rish
July
August

‹ou› saying the /u/ sound

Write some ‹ou› words in the young birds.

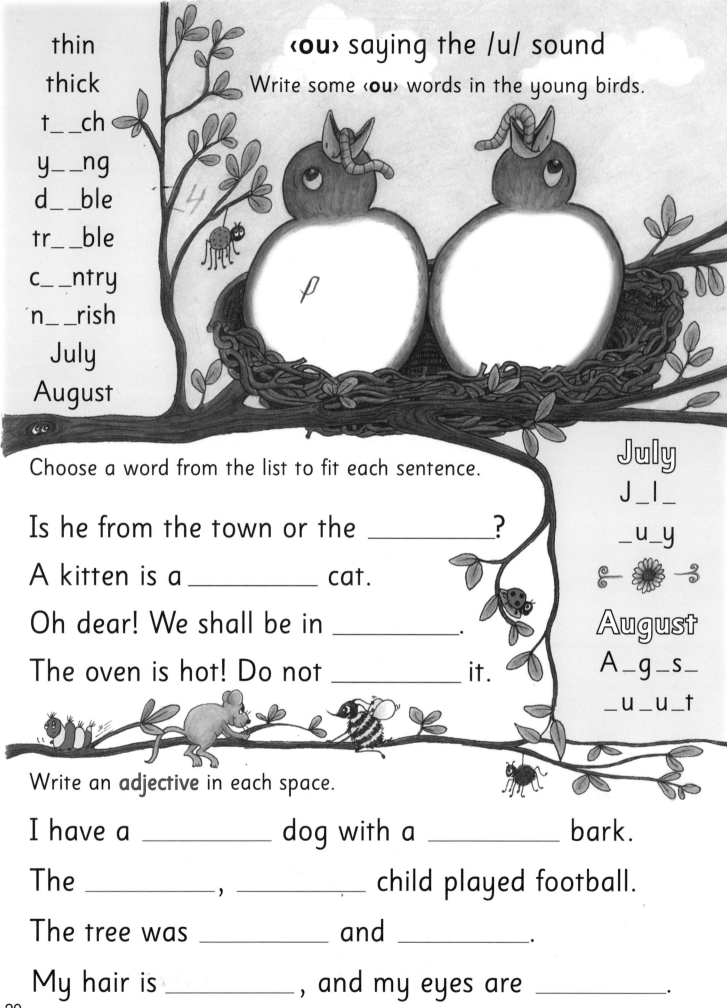

p

July
J_l_
_u_y

August
A_g_s_
_u_u_t

Choose a word from the list to fit each sentence.

Is he from the town or the _____?

A kitten is a _____ cat.

Oh dear! We shall be in _____.

The oven is hot! Do not _____ it.

Write an **adjective** in each space.

I have a _____ dog with a _____ bark.

The _____, _____ child played football.

The tree was _____ and _____.

My hair is _____, and my eyes are _____.

20

Draw more of each thing to make the pictures show plurals.
Write the plural **nouns** underneath.

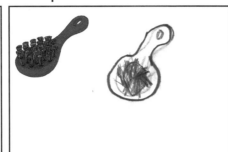

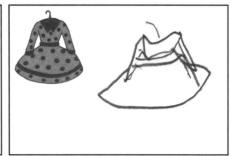

_____

_____

Write the word for each picture.

carotts

Boxs

churhs

chairs

Snakes

Boots

21

cliff
off
‹air› saying the /air/ sound

Write some ‹air› words in the hair.

___
h___
p___
st___
ch___
h___brush

September
October

Choose a word from the list to fit each sentence.

Her balloon floated up in the _____.

I brush my _____ with a _____.

The baby sits on a high_____.

He has a new _____ of shoes.

September
September
September

October
October
October

Give the plural for each of these **nouns** by adding ‹-s› or ‹-es›.

_____ _____ _____ _____

Possessive Adjectives

Action:

Touch the side of your temple with your fist.

Match each <u>pronoun</u> to its **possessive adjective**, and color the **possessive adjectives** in blue.

I   you   he   she   it   we   you   they

their   its   your   **my**   her   his   our   your

Choose the right **possessive adjective** for each sentence.

They put on _____ coats.

I put on _____ coat.

He puts on _____ coat.

We put on _____ coats.

She puts on _____ coat.

You put on _____ coat.

You put on _____ coats.

Choose a **noun** for each **possessive adjective**.

my   _____

your   _____

his   _____

her   _____

its   _____

our   _____

your   _____

their _____

Underline the **possessive adjectives** in blue.

Ben's friend, Sarah, came to visit. She brought her coloring books and pencils.

"Your books have lovely pictures in them," said Ben.

"This is my favorite book," replied Sarah. "If we share our colored pencils, we will have plenty of colors for that picture."

Ben fetched his pencils. He took them out of their box.

buzz

fizz

e _ _ o

_ _ oir

_ _ emist

stoma _ _

_ _ ristmas

_ _ aracter

November

December

‹ch› saying the /k/ sound

Write some ‹ch› words in the choir.

Choose a word from the list to fit each sentence.

I sing in the _____.

December 25th is _____ Day.

She was ill with a _____ ache.

The _____ sells medicine.

November
N _ v _ m _ e _
_ o _ e _ b _ r

December
D _ c _ m _ e _
_ e _ e _ b _ r

Complete each sentence with a **possessive adjective**.

your   its   their   our   his   your   my   her

The children took out _____ pencil cases.

The boy read _____ book.

My sister played _____ recorder.

We sang _____ favorite song.

24

Homophone Mix-ups

Choose the right word to complete each sentence.

there or their ?

They put on _____ hats.

Leave the parcel over _____ .

_____ he is, behind the tree.

The children rode _____ bikes.

_____ is no-one at home.

are or our ?

You _____ very tall.

_____ house has a red door.

They _____ all going to a party.

We put on _____ boots to go outside.

He likes _____ cat.

Write some more sentences containing there, their, are, or our.

_____

_____

_____

_____

next
quit
m_k_
p___
m__n
cl__
w__st
r__nstorm
half
quarter

The /ai/ sound: ‹ai›, ‹ay›, or ‹a_e›?

Underline the spelling you think is correct. Then use a dictionary to find the right answer, and put a check mark beside it.

wate
wait
wayt

ayt
ate
ait

day
dai
daye

name
naym
naim

traye
tray
trai

snake
snayk
snaik

Choose a word from the list to fit each sentence.

half (½)
h_l_
_a_f

quarter (¼)
q_a_t_r
_u_r_e_

She made a model from _____.

Is it free, or do we have to _____?

I got wet in the _____.

My jeans have a tight _____.

there or their?

_____ they are! Up _____.

_____ toys are over _____.

are or our?

We _____ going to visit _____ grandma.

They _____ all coming to _____ school.

26

A C Alphabetical Order

Write out the alphabet in the four groups.

1.____ ____ ____ ____ ____

2.

3.____ ____ ____ ____ ____ ____

4.____ ____ ____ ____ ____ ____ ____

For each set of three, decide which word comes first (1st), which word comes second (2nd), and which word comes third (3rd). If the words start with the same two letters, remember to look at the third letter of each word.

shell — 1st	hill — 2	crisp — 2
shop — 3rd	hive — 3	cross — 3
ship — 2nd	hidden — 1	crab — 1
pet — 3	rocket — 1	tree — 2
pen — 1	roof — 2	train — 1
people — 2	round — 3	trick — 3
march — 3	eat — 3	world — 3
magpie — 1	east — 2	wood — 2
make — 2	each — 1	wolf — 1
drink — 2	need — 1	knee — 1
dress — 1	nest — 2	knock — 3
drum — 3	next — 3	knife — 2

arm

shark

s _ _ n

thr _ _

s _ _ t

cr _ _ m

pl _ _ se

t _ _ nager

eleven

twelve

The /ee/ sound: ‹ee› or ‹ea›?

Underline the spelling you think is correct. Then use a dictionary to find the right answer, and put a check mark beside it.

bee
bea

leef
leaf

cheese
chease

streat
street

east
eest

dream
dreem

Choose a word from the list to fit each sentence.

I like strawberries and _____.

Eight plus _____ makes eleven.

We have _____ the new film.

_____ take care of my rabbit.

eleven (11)

e _ e _ e _

_ l _ v _ n

twelve (12)

t _ e _ v _

_ w _ l _ e

Which word would come 1st, which 2nd, and which 3rd in a dictionary?

green

grass   1st

grin

blue

black

block

smile

smell

small

skin

skunk

skate

allow

along

paper   also

paint

parrot

28

Are These Sentences?

Read each line. If there is a verb, underline it in red, and mark the sentence right with a check mark. If there is no verb, mark the line wrong with a cross.

The ducks swim on the pond. ☐   The cat watches the birds. ☐

A spotty dog. ☐   The park keeper sweeps up the leaves. ☐

A wooden boat with a blue sail. ☐   The tall tree. ☐

A bird sings. ☐   A spotty dog has a stick in his mouth. ☐

The boys play bat and ball. ☐   The rabbit hides from the fox. ☐

Write some more sentences about the picture.

_____

_____

_____

REMEMBER A sentence needs to have a verb, as well as a capital letter at the beginning and a period at the end.

snug
flex
fl_ing
s___t
s_d_
d__
br___t
sunsh_n_
thirteen
fourteen

The /ie/ sound: ‹ie›, ‹igh›, ‹y›, or ‹i_e›?

Underline the spelling you think is correct. Then use a dictionary to find the right answer, and put a check mark beside it.

bike
bighk
biek

ly
ligh
lie

sky
skigh
skie

ryd
ried
ride

bigh
by
bie

liet
light
lite

Choose a word from the list to fit each sentence.

They were _____ their kite.

Water the plant or it will _____!

The _____ is very bright.

I waved until she was out of _____.

thirteen (13)

t_i_t_e_
_h_r_e_n

fourteen (14)

f_u_t_e_
_o_r_e_n

Underline the **verbs** in these sentences in red.
There can be more than one **verb** in a sentence.

I fly my kite.
The big boat sails across the sea.
The dog barks and runs after the ball.
The children hop, skip, and jump.

Adverbs

Think of an adverb to describe each verb.
Write the adverbs on the lines to complete your poem.

Bang one fist on top of the other.

My Day

I wake ___up___,
I get out of bed ___Wash up___
I eat my breakfast _____,
I go to school _____,
I work _____,
I listen _____,
I play _____,
I speak ___up___,
I go home ___on Bus___,
I watch television _____,
I wash ___up___,
I go to bed _____,
I sleep _____, and
I dream ___about___.

Illustrate two lines from your poem. Write the lines underneath.

I get out of bed   I go home on bus

31

such
luck
h_m_
fr_z_
f__l
st_n_
t__st
sn__ball
fifteen
sixteen

The /oa/ sound: ‹oa›, ‹ow›, or ‹o_e›?

Underline the spelling you think is correct. Then use a dictionary to find the right answer, and put a check mark beside it.

broak
browk
broke

towd
toad
tode

bloa
blow
blowe

nows
nose
noas

coste
cowst
coast

elboa
elbow
elbowe

Choose a word from the list to fit each sentence.

A _____ is a baby horse.

They ate buttered _____.

I went _____ after school.

We had a _____ fight.

fifteen (15)

f_f_e_n

_i_t_e_

sixteen (16)

s_x_e_n

_i_t_e_

Underline the **verbs** in these sentences in red.
Write an **adverb** on each orange line.

She sings _____.

He dresses _____.

The cat plays _____.

We cut out the pictures _____.

Verbs

Action:

Move your arms back and forth at your sides, as if you are running.

"to be"

Fill in the verb "to be" in the present tense.

I _am_   we _are_

you _are_   you _are_

he/she/it _are_   they _are_

Write in the missing parts of the verb "to be."

You _are_ very tall.

She _atall_ a girl.

Today, they _its_ happy.

Ben said, "I _was_ six years old."

The car _is_ red.

We _won_ in the race.

Draw a bee around the part of the verb "to be" in each sentence.

It (is) a lovely day today.

She is in the (choir.)

The (bees) are busy.

The tree (is) tall.

"I am sorry," (he) said.

You are good at (dancing.)

sunk
book
h_g_
f_s_
resc__
que__
__e
_s_ful
seventeen
eighteen

The /ue/ sound: ‹ue›, ‹ew›, or ‹u_e›?

Underline the spelling you think is correct. Then use a dictionary to find the right answer, and put a check mark beside it.

cube
cueb
cewb

nues
news
nuse

argew
arguwe
argue

fewe
fue
few

refews
refuse
refues

tube
tewb
tueb

Choose a word from the list to fit each sentence.

A female sheep is called a _____.

They had to wait in a _____.

That fireman came to _____ us.

That whale is _____!

seventeen (17)

s_v_n_e_n
_e_e_t_e_

eighteen (18)

e_g_t_e_
_i_h_e_n

Write out the **verb** "to be."

I _____   you _____   he/she/it _____

we _____   you _____   they _____

Draw a bee around the part of the **verb** "to be" in each sentence.

It is quite cold today.   Today we are playing outside.

That elephant is very big.   "I am so tired," said Sam.

34

Verbs
Regular Past Tense

Add the right **verb** ending to the **verb** root in each mouse.
Now join each mouse to the right clock, and copy the **verb**
into the clock case.

Action:

Point backwards over
your shoulder with
your thumb.

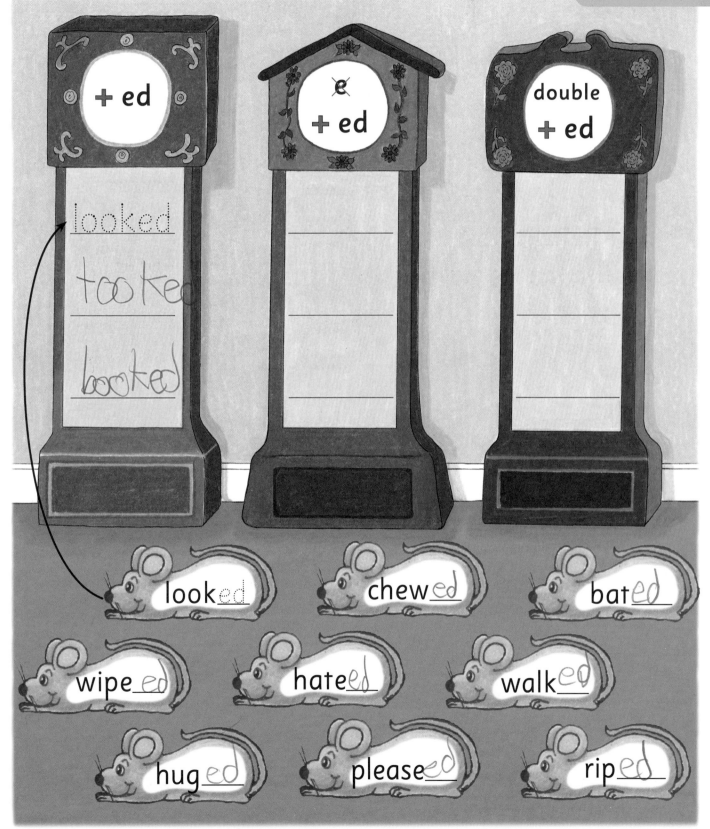

+ ed

ℓ̶ + ed

double + ed

looked
tooked
booked

looked

chewed

bated

wipeed

hateed

walked

huged

pleaseed

riped

35

hoo_
for_
ba_ _
bri_ _
de_ _
flo_ _
stru_ _
ba_ _pa_ _
nineteen
twenty

nineteen (19)
n_n_t_e_
_i_e_n

twenty (20)
t_e_t_
_w_n_y

The /k/ sound: ‹k› or ‹ck›?

Underline the spelling you think is correct. Then use a dictionary to find the right answer, and put a check mark beside it.

| duck | sack | forck |
| duk | sak | fork |

| sharck | oack | chick |
| shark | oak | chik |

| neck | boock | rocket |
| nek | book | roket |

| bicke | black | cacke |
| bike | blak | cake |

Underline the **verbs** in these sentences in red.
Then rewrite the sentences in the past tense.

I zip up my coat.

Yesterday, _____

He talks to his friend.

Last week, _____

36

Verbs

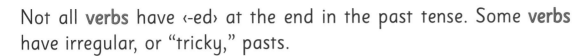

Irregular Past Tense

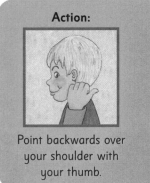

Action:

Point backwards over your shoulder with your thumb.

Not all **verbs** have ‹-ed› at the end in the past tense. Some **verbs** have irregular, or "tricky," pasts.

e.g. Today I swim. ——→ Yesterday I swam.

Match the present and past tenses of these **verbs**.

Present	Past
win	wrote
sing	won
drink	rode
get	dug
dig	drank
ride	sang
write	got

Now color the pictures.

Rewrite these sentences in the past tense.

We sing a song. _____

He rides his bike. _____

I write a letter. _____

You win a prize. _____

37

drip
plug
th__d
wint__
b__d
ov__
h__t
butt__fly
th__ty
forty

The /er/ sound: ‹er›, ‹ir›, or ‹ur›?

Underline the spelling you think is correct. Then use a dictionary to find the right answer, and put a check mark beside it.

gingir
gingur
ginger

pirple
purple
perple

girl
gerl
gurl

furst
ferst
first

bern
burn
birn

hirb
herb
hurb

Choose a word from the list to fit each sentence.

She fell and _____ her knee.

A _____ is a beautiful insect.

The snow was deep last _____.

I finished the race in _____ place.

thirty (30)
t_i_t_
_h_r_y

forty (40)
f_r_y
_o_t_

Each of these **verbs** has a tricky past tense. Write each past tense in the honeycomb.

run   sing   swim

dig   _____   ride   win

_____

Using a Dictionary

Use a dictionary to find out how each word should be spelled.
Write the word out correctly on the line, and illustrate the word in the box.

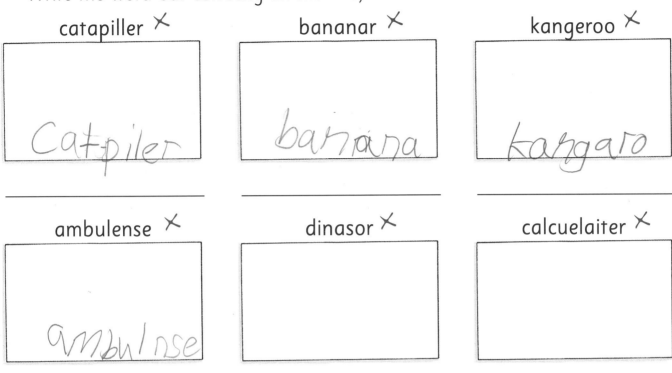

catapiller ✗

Catpiler

bananar ✗

banana

kangeroo ✗

kangaro

ambulense ✗

ambulnse

dinasor ✗

calcuelaiter ✗

Look up each word in the dictionary. Read the meanings, and illustrate each word.

hare

hair

ocean

ocean

blizzard

dolphin

dolphin

bouquet

aquarium

39

drag
trip
j_ _n
sp_ _l
p_ _nt
j_ _
r_ _al
_ _ntment
fifty
sixty

The /oi/ sound: ‹oi› or ‹oy›?

Underline the spelling you think is correct. Then use a dictionary to find the right answer, and put a check mark beside it.

coin
coyn

boi
boy

noise
noyse

annoi
annoy

loial
loyal

toilet
toylet

Choose a word from the list to fit each sentence.

Her pencil has a sharp _____.

Can we _____ your club?

The rain may _____ our picnic.

The nurse put _____ on his burn.

fifty (50)
f_f_y
_i_t_

sixty (60)
s_x_y
_i_t_

Look through the dictionary, and find two words that you did not know before. Copy out each word with its meaning.

1._____ _____

_____

2._____ _____

_____

Proofreading Sentences

Proofread these sentences. Write out the correct spelling above each misspelled word, and add in the missing punctuation.

1. Dolfins and wales live in the sea.

2. I saw some sheap with there lams on the hillsid.

3. it was mie berthday party

4. The dog ait the duc.

5. i wet on holiday with my muther father sister brother granma and grampa

6. Could I have a drinck pleas askt meg.

7. Whot is your naim sed the litle gerl.

8. Ouch i hit my thum wiv the hamer.

9. their are three yung Berds in the nest in are tree.

10. at the zoo we sor jiraffes elefants penguins and aardvarks.

Now color the pictures.

snap
swam
l_ _d
cl_ _d
f_ _nd
n_ _
cr_ _d
sunfl_ _er
seventy
eighty

The /ou/ sound: ‹ou› or ‹ow›?

Underline the spelling you think is correct. Then use a dictionary to find the right answer, and put a check mark beside it.

out
owt

broun
brown

shout
showt

toun
town

mouth
mowth

croun
crown

Choose a word from the list to fit each sentence.

She grew a tall, yellow _flower_.

He _found_ my lost watch.

A big _crowed_ gathered to watch.

The music was very _loud_.

seventy (70)
seventy
_e_e_t_

eighty (80)
e_g_t_
_i_h_y

Proofread these sentences.

I have made a cake for your birthday said mom.

Can you see the wite swon He asked.

the ducks kwacked lowdly as i threw them some bred.

She swimmed with dolfins last summir

42

Verbs

"to be"

Action:

Move your arms back and forth at your sides, as if you are running.

 Conjugate the **verb** "to be" in the present and past tenses.

Present	Past
I _am_	I _was_
you _are_	you _were_
he/she/it _is_	he/she/it _was_
we _are_	we _were_
you _are_	you _were_
they _are_	they _were_

Draw a bee around the part of the **verb** "to be" in each sentence. Then rewrite each sentence in the past tense. Underline the past tense part of the **verb** "to be" in red.

I (am) at school.
Yesterday ___I was at school.___

It is a beautiful sunny day.
Last Monday ___was sunny and bright___

We are happy.
Last week ___where happy___

They are good at football.
Last year _____

43

twig
from
c_st
w_ _k
j_ _
l_cket
str_ _
s_ _cepan
ninety
hundred

The /o/ sound: ‹o›, ‹al›, ‹au›, or ‹aw›?

Underline the spelling you think is correct. Then use a dictionary to find the right answer, and put a check mark beside it.

sal
sau
saw

folt
fault
fawlt

tawk
tauk
talk

dog
daug
dawg

boll
baul
ball

halk
hauk
hawk

Choose a word from the list to fit each sentence.

She always drinks through a _____.

We went for a _____ in the park.

He cooked rice in a big _____.

My dad gave me a pretty _____.

ninety (90)

n_n_t_

_i_e_y

hundred (100)

h_n_r_d

_u_d_e_

Conjugate the **verb** "to be" in the present and past tenses.

	Present	Past
I		
you		
he/she/it		
we		
you		
they		

Expanding a Sentence

① We can make a sentence more interesting by adding extra information to it. Read the simple sentence below. Underline the **noun** in black and the **verb** in red.

The dog barked.

Woof

② Now add an adjective to describe the **noun**.

The _____ dog barked.

③ Now add another adjective.

The _____, _____ dog barked.

④ Now add an adverb to describe the **verb**.

The dog barked _____.

WOOF!

⑤ Adding details can also make a sentence more interesting. What was the dog barking at?

The dog barked at _____.

⑥ Now write out the sentence, adding in all the details.

The _____, _____ dog barked _____
at _____.

Expand these sentences on the lines.

The boy laughed.

_____

_____

The rabbit hopped.

_____

_____

film
kept
ke**y**
hon**ey**
mon**ey**
donk**ey**
chimn**ey**
journ**e_**
thousand
million

‹ey› saying the /ee/ sound

Write some ‹ey› words in the honey pot.

Choose a word from the list to fit each sentence.

She set off on a long ___trip___ .

He locked the door with his ___keys___ .

Bees collect pollen to make ___honey___ .

I saved up my ___money___ to buy a toy.

thousand
(1,000)
t_o_s_n_
_h_u_a_d

million
(1,000,000)
m_l_i_n
_i_l_o_

Expand these sentences using **adjectives** and **adverbs**.

The ___fat___ horse jumped ___lazy___
over ___the fence___
Our ___little___ cousin played ___tenice lazy___
in the ___garden___

46

Conjunctions

Action:

Hold out hands palm up.
Move both hands so one
is on top of the other

There are many conjunctions,
but these are six of the most useful ones.

and but because or so while

Underline the **conjunctions** in purple.

Would you like an apple or an orange?

I did not tell anyone the news because it was a secret.

He fell over but he did not hurt himself.

We played games while we waited.

cats and dogs

It rained so she took her umbrella.

Match each sentence part on the left to one on the right. Choose a **conjunction**
to join them together, and write it on the line.

I was late for school   _____ the band played.

We went to the country   _____ is it too late?

Kim ran fast in the race   _____ I overslept.

Is there time to play   _____ he ate some oats.

The horse was hungry   _____ had a picnic.

They listened quietly   _____ she did not win.

Choose a **conjunction** to complete these sentences.

The children hid _____and_____ Dad counted to fifty.

Have you forgiven me, _____and_____ are you still angry?

My feet were cold, _____so_____ I put on my socks.

grip
milk
___
d___
y___
t___
sp___
___rings
zero
equals

‹ear› saying the /ear/ sound

Write some ‹ear› words in the earrings.

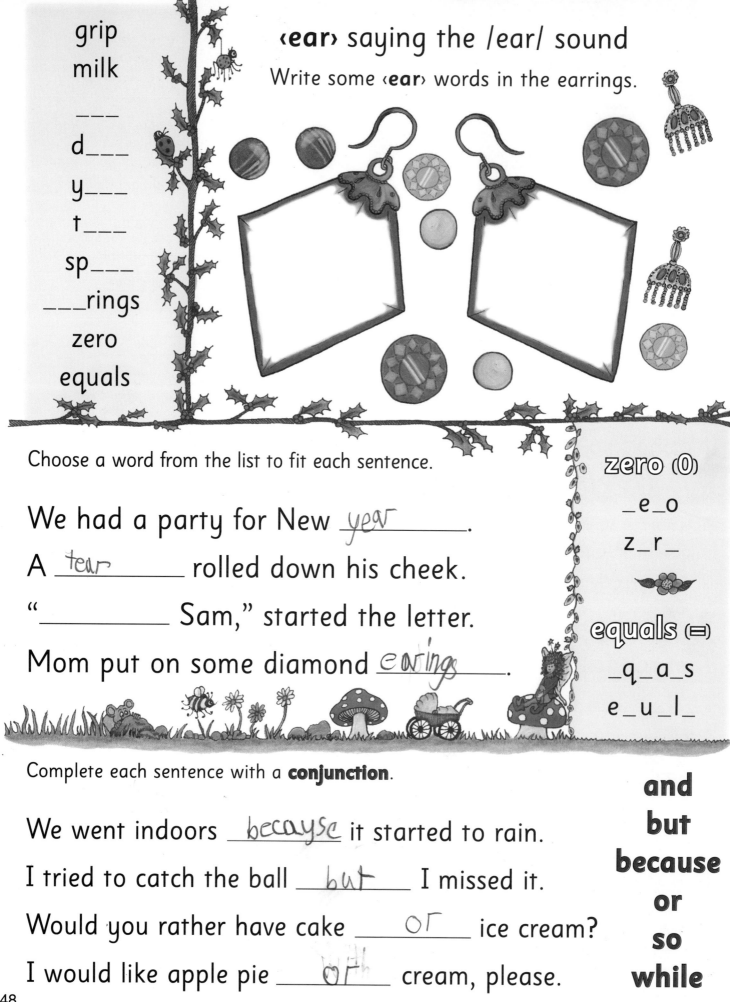

Choose a word from the list to fit each sentence.

We had a party for New _year_.

A _tear_ rolled down his cheek.

"_____ Sam," started the letter.

Mom put on some diamond _earings_.

zero (0)
_e_o
z_r_

equals (=)
_q_a_s
e_u_l_

Complete each sentence with a **conjunction**.

We went indoors _because_ it started to rain.

I tried to catch the ball _but_ I missed it.

Would you rather have cake _or_ ice cream?

I would like apple pie _with_ cream, please.

and
but
because
or
so
while

Plurals: ‹-s› and ‹-ies›

Write the plural for each word in the leaf. Then draw a picture for it in the daisy.

baby — babies

monkey —

daisy —

fly — flieys

berry — berries

donkey — donkies

boy — boys

teddy — teddys

lady —

Silent ‹h›

belt
farm
_our
g_ost
r_yme
r_ythm
_onest
r_inoceros
centimeter
meter

Write some silent ‹h› words in the rhinoceros.

Choose a word from the list to fit each sentence.

centimeter
c_n_i_e_e_
_e_t_m_t_r
meter
m_t_r
_e_e_

Poems often _____.

The train leaves in one _____.

I trust John because he is _____.

A _____ is a wild animal.

Write the plural of each **noun** on the leaf, and draw a picture in the daisy.

star

pony

toy

fairy

50

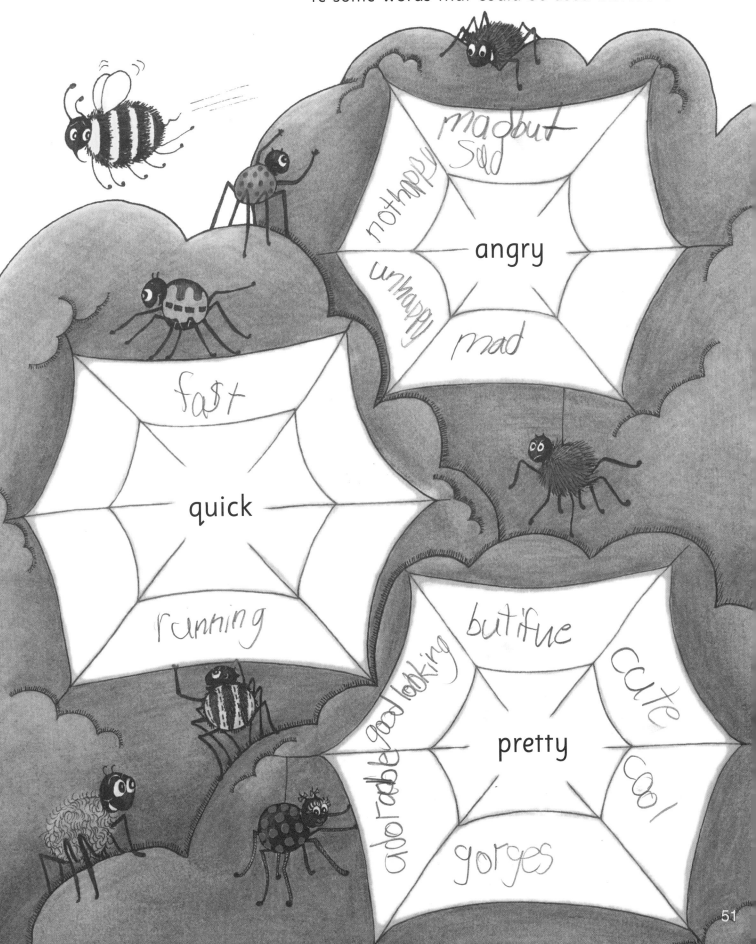

madbut
Sad
nothappy
unhappy
angry
mad

fast
quick
running

butifue
adorable good looking
cute
pretty
cool
gorges

land
quiz
s_ene
s_ent
mus_le
s_ience
s_issors
cres_ent
gram
kilogram

Silent ‹c›

Write some silent ‹c› words in the crescent moon.

Choose a word from the list to fit each sentence.

The moon can be a _____ shape.

I cut the paper with my _____.

Those flowers have a lovely _____.

We do experiments in _____.

gram
g_a_
_r_m

kilogram
k_l_g_a_
_i_o_r_m

In the spaces in each word web, write some words that could be used instead of the word in the middle.

cold

freeze

excited

happy

sad

upset

52

Proofreading a Story

REMEMBER After writing something, it is a good idea to read it through to make sure there are no mistakes.

This is the beginning of a story. Read it through, correcting the spelling mistakes, and adding in the punctuation marks and capital letters.

farmer brown has lots of animals on his farm he has rabits chickens cows horses a donkee and a goat the goat has a very bad temper and butts his horns against the tree trunc wen he is angry it wos munday morning and farmer brown was feding his animals good morning, he called to the horses here is your hai he gave the goat a big bag of oats just then a little robin flew down and started peking at them those are mine showted the goat

There are 13 missing capital letters, 9 missing periods, 5 missing commas, 6 missing speech marks, 1 missing exclamation mark, and 10 spelling mistakes! Snort!

What do you think might happen next? Continue the story on the lines.

_____

_____

_____

_____

_____

_____

kiln
wept
h___
c___
sh___
sc___
squ___
nightm___
milliliter
liter

‹are› saying the /air/ sound

Write some ‹are› words in the hare.

Choose a word from the list to fit each sentence.

Tim takes ___care___ of his pets.

We must ___share___ the sweets fairly.

A ___hare___ is bigger than a rabbit.

She woke from a frightening ___nightmare___.

milliliter
m_l_i_i_e_
_i_l_t_r

liter
l_t_r
_i_e_

Proofread this story.

The goat was very angry that the robin had stolen some of his brekfast. He snorted and stamped his hooves. The robin floo up into the oak tree and started singing. The goat was so angry that he charged the tree Crash! a large branch fell on top ov him, Oh dear, exclaimed farmer Brown i shall have to go and get my tractor to get you owt.

54

Prefixes

There are many prefixes, but these are four of the most useful ones.

un-   dis-   mis-   im-

Choose a prefix to go in front of each of the base words, and write it on the line. Then see how the meaning of the words and sentences has changed.

It was ___*im*___possible to walk along the path.

I really ___*dis*___like writing stories in school.

Mom ___*im*___packed the holiday suitcases.

Jason ___*mis*___understood what he had to do.

Choose a prefix to go in front of each of the base words in the fish bodies, and write it on the line in the fish's head.

un happy	*im* patient	*Un* lucky
dis appear	*mis* behave	*Un* lock
un do	*mis* take	*dis* agree
un dress	*im* possible	*Un* comfortable

drip
silk
b____
t____
p____
w____
sw____
underw____
weight
volume

‹ear› saying the /air/ sound

Write some ‹ear› words in the bear.

Choose a word from the list to fit each sentence.

I shall _____ my new shoes.

The _____ was green and juicy.

Be careful not to _____ the paper!

I like to cuddle my teddy _____ .

weight
w _ i _ h _
_ e _ g _ t

volume
v _ l _ m _
_ o _ u _ e

Make new words by joining up the prefixes and base words below.

tri-   tele-   scope   angle   cycle   vision

telescope _____ _____ _____

56

Apostrophe ‹s›

An apostrophe ‹s› shows that something belongs to someone.

     ## Belonging Poem

Think of a person's name for each letter of the alphabet. Then think of something that the person might own, which begins with the same letter as their name.

REMEMBER Use an apostrophe ‹s› after each name to show that the next word is something belonging to that person.

Anna's apple,   N _____

Ben's book,   O _____

C _____   P _____

D _____   Quentin's _____

E _____   R _____

F _____   S _____

G _____   T _____

H _____   Usain's _____

I _____   V _____

J _____   W _____

K _____   Xander's _____

L _____   Y _____

M _____   Zoe's _____

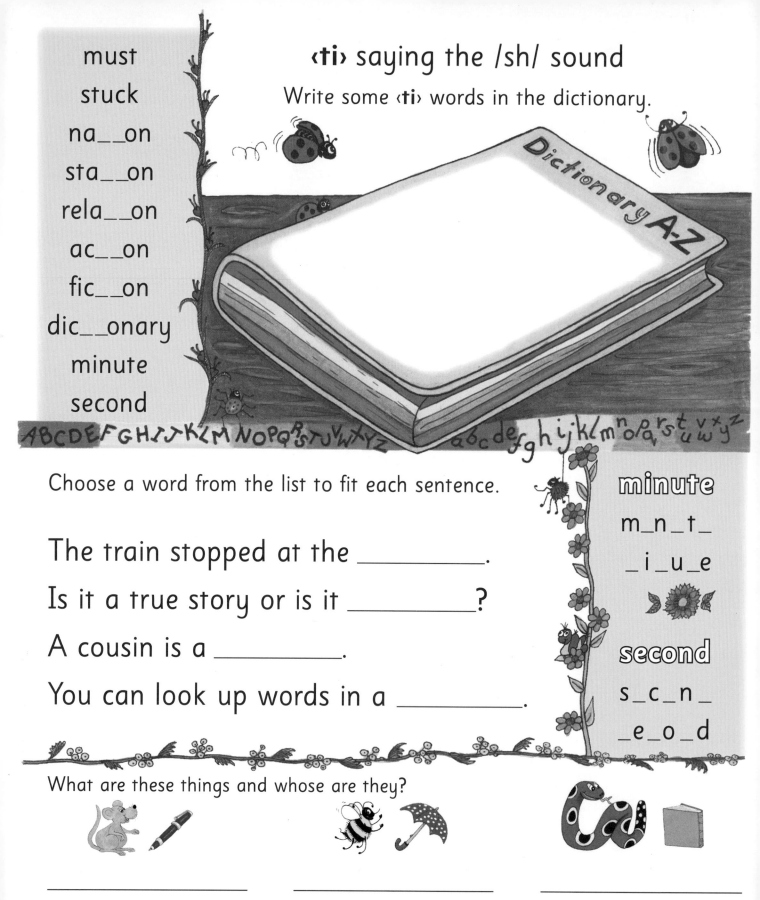

must
stuck
na__on
sta__on
rela__on
ac__on
fic__on
dic__onary
minute
second

ABCDEFGHIJKLMNOPQRSTUVWXYZ

‹ti› saying the /sh/ sound

Write some ‹ti› words in the dictionary.

Dictionary A-Z

abcdefghijklmnopqrstuvwxyz

Choose a word from the list to fit each sentence.

The train stopped at the _____.

Is it a true story or is it _____?

A cousin is a _____.

You can look up words in a _____.

minute
m_n_t_
_i_u_e

second
s_c_n_
_e_o_d

What are these things and whose are they?

_____   _____   _____

There is an apostrophe ‹s› missing from each of these sentences. Write them in.

Bee went to Inky house on Saturday morning.
Inky liked Bee new red boots.

58

Contractions

We sometimes shorten pairs of words by joining them together, and leaving out some of the letters. We use an apostrophe to show where the missing letter, or letters, used to be. These shortened words are called **contractions**.

Write out each contraction in full, as two words and with no letters missing.

couldn't _____ ____   didn't _____ ____

haven't _____ ____   mustn't _____ ____

don't _____ ____   I'm _____

I shall ➡ I'll

Write out each pair of words as a contraction by joining them together and replacing some of the letters with an apostrophe.

I shall ___I'll_____   we shall _____

you will ___you'll_____   you will _____

he will _____   they will _____

she will _____

it will _____

I'm winning!

REMEMBER We use contractions when we speak. They should not be used in writing except when writing direct speech, or in a friendly note.

59

fist
best
occa**si**on
divi**si**on
revi**si**on
inva**si**on
explo**si**on
televi**si**on
fraction
estimate

‹si› saying the /sh/ and /zh/ sounds
Write some ‹si› words in the television.

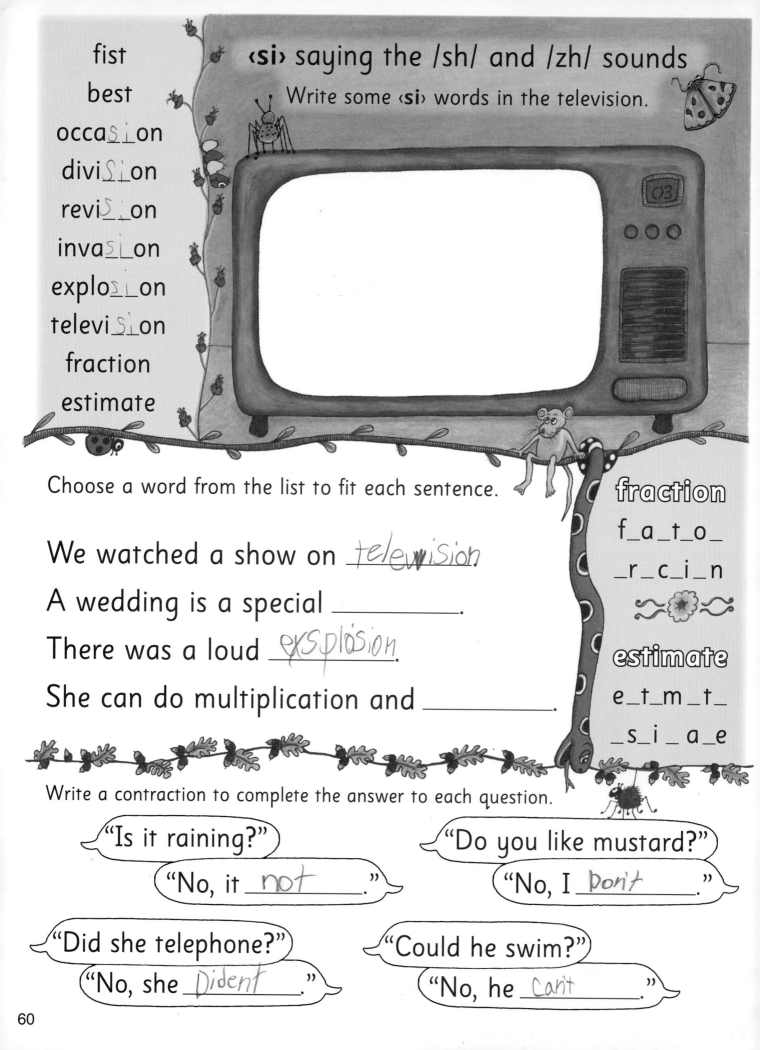

Choose a word from the list to fit each sentence.

We watched a show on _television_

A wedding is a special _____.

There was a loud _exsplosion_.

She can do multiplication and _____.

fraction
f_a_t_o_
_r_c_i_n

estimate
e_t_m_t_
_s_i_a_e

Write a contraction to complete the answer to each question.

"Is it raining?"
"No, it _not_."

"Do you like mustard?"
"No, I _Don't_."

"Did she telephone?"
"No, she _Dident_."

"Could he swim?"
"No, he _Can't_."

60

Prepositions

Choose a **preposition** to write in each gap. There can be more than one correct answer.

Action: 
Point from one noun to another.

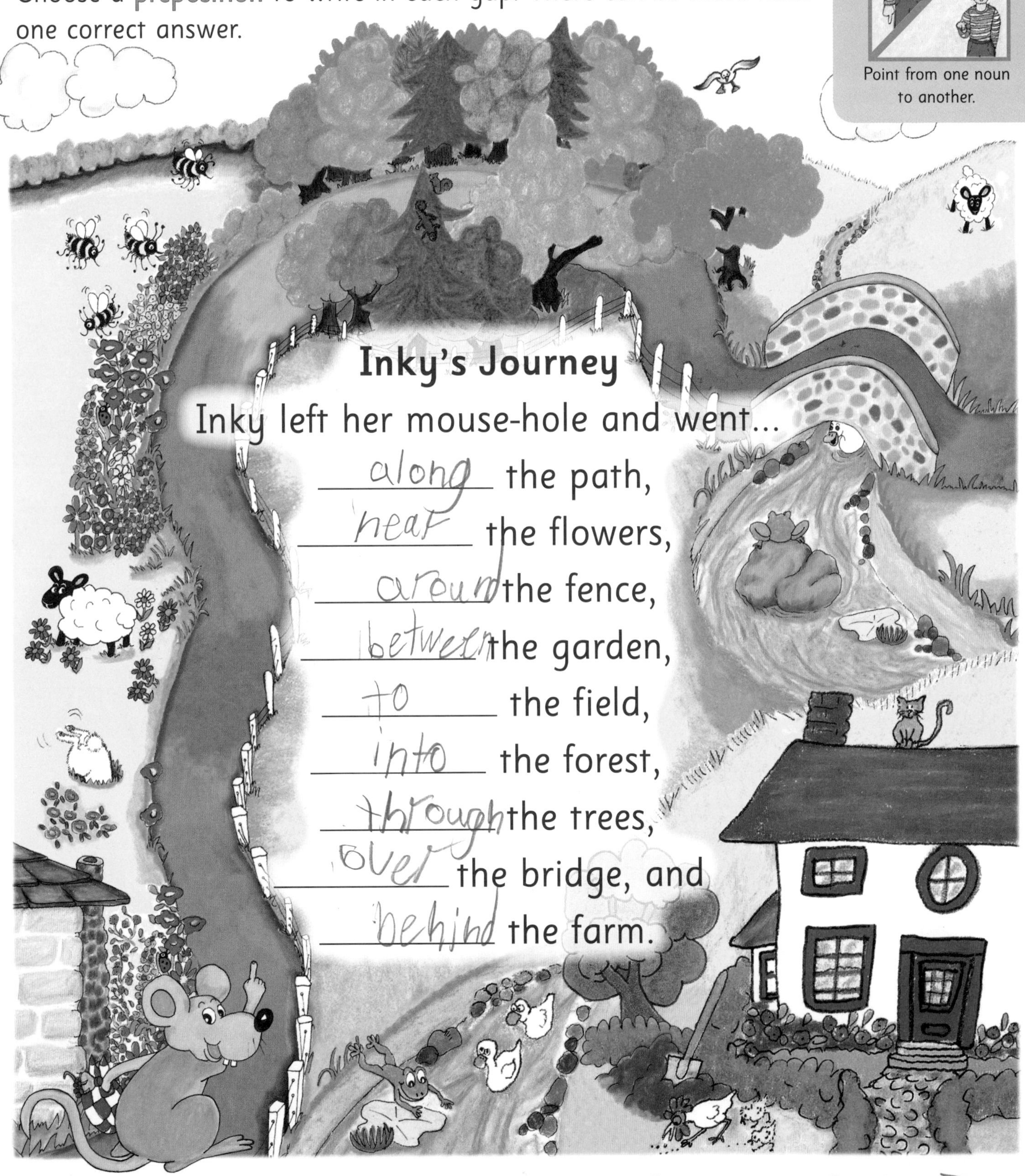

Inky's Journey

Inky left her mouse-hole and went...

_____along_____ the path,

_____near_____ the flowers,

_____around_____ the fence,

_____between_____ the garden,

_____to_____ the field,

_____into_____ the forest,

_____through_____ the trees,

_____over_____ the bridge, and

_____behind_____ the farm.

across under along down up towards among between to
from near into behind through in around over past beside

61

grub
slug
_ _ _ _ t
_ _ _ _ teen
_ _ _ _ ty
w _ _ _ _
r _ _ ndeer
n _ _ _ _ bor
child
children

‹ei› and ‹eigh› saying the /ai/ sound

Write some ‹ei› and ‹eigh› words in the reindeer.

Choose a word from the list to fit each sentence.

Four plus four equals _____.

Eight tens are _____.

She is our next-door _____.

A _____ has antlers.

child
c _ i _ d
_ h _ l _

children
c _ i _ d _ e _
_ h _ l _ r _ n

Complete each sentence with a preposition.

I want to sit _____ my best friend.

Kayla climbed _____ the ladder.

We read _____ left _____ right.

Grandpa keeps his keys _____ his pocket.

up from
to in
beside

Finding the Meaning

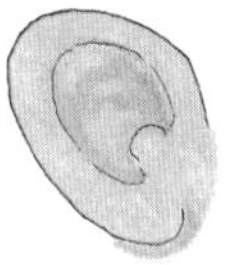

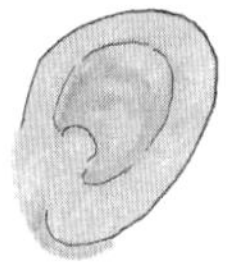

REMEMBER Homophones sound the same, but have different spellings and meanings.

Use a dictionary to find out which word has which meaning. Write the meaning of each word on the line beside it.

beech _____

beach _____

flour _____

flower _____

right _____

write _____

wait _____

weight _____

whole _____

hole _____

meet _____

meat _____

sea _____

see _____

hear _____

here _____

Choose the correct word to complete each sentence.   **where or wear ?**

"_____ are we going?" asked Kelly.

I want to _____ my favorite sweater.

63

ark
clever
gl_ves
s_n
fr_nt
d_zen
m_nkey
s_mebody
woman
women

<o> saying the /u/ sound
Write some <o> words in the glove.

Choose a word from the list to fit each sentence.

There are twelve eggs in a ___*pan*___ .

I put on my hat, scarf and ___*boots*___ .

The _____ was swinging by his tail.

He has two daughters and a _____ .

woman
w_o_m_a_n
_wo_ma_n

women
w_o_m_e_n
_wo_me_n

to, too, or two ?

I have ___*two*___ cats called Micky and Minnie.

We went ___*to*___ the mountains for our holidays.

There were ___*too*___ many of us ___*to*___ squeeze in the car.

I must go at ___*two*___ o'clock. Do you want to come ___*to*___ ?

64

Verbs

Suffixes: ‹-ing›

-ing

One of the most useful suffixes is ‹-ing›.
Make new words by adding ‹-ing› to the **verb** roots, and write them on the lines.

talk

talking

ride

rideing

look

looking

run

runing

clap

clapin

fly

flying

hope

hoping

swim

swiming

sneeze

sneezeing

jog

jogging

copy

copying

arrive

arriveing

shook
often
pic*ture*
fu_____
na____
crea____
frac____
adven____
mouse
mice

‹ture›
Write some ‹**ture**› words in the picture frame.

Choose a word from the list to fit each sentence.

She painted a beautiful _____.

A dragon is a fantastic _____.

They had an exciting _____.

Tomorrow is in the _____.

mouse
m _ u _ e
_ o _ s _

mice
m _ c _
_ i _ e

Add the suffix ‹-ing› to each **verb** root, and write the new word on the line.

make _____   cook _____

stop _____   raise _____

jump _____   try _____

swing _____   whine _____

Comparatives and Superlatives

Suffixes: ‹-er› and ‹-est›

Action:

Touch the side of your temple with your fist.

Two of the most useful suffixes are ‹-er› and ‹-est›.

Make **comparatives** and **superlatives** by adding ‹-er› and ‹-est› to the adjectives in Est-er Elephant and her friends.

big

strong

rare

tall

angry

quit
sweet
field
piece
chief
thief
shield
belief
library
computer

‹ie› saying the /ee/ sound
Write some ‹ie› words in the shield.

Choose a word from the list to fit each sentence.

I ate a ___piece___ of pie.

The sheep grazed in the ___field___.

The ___theif___ stole the jewels.

The knight had a big ___shield___.

library
library
library

computer
computer
computer

Use a **comparative** or a **superlative** to complete each sentence.
Underline the **adjectives** in blue.

This drink is sweet, but that drink is ___sweetest___.

I am slim, he is slimmer, and you are the ___slimest___.

All four dogs are wet, but our dog is the ___wetest___.

Kelly was friendly, and Ann was even ___freindlyer___.

Interesting Words

We use some words too often. Think of a more interesting word to replace each of the underlined words, and write it on the line. Use a different word in each sentence.

ran

The spider <u>ran</u> across the floor. _running_

Tommy <u>ran</u> all the way home. _runnd_

Their dog <u>ran</u> after our cat. _ran_

nice

It was a <u>nice</u> day. _cool_

We had a <u>nice</u> lunch. _awsome_

Everyone was very <u>nice</u> to me. _kind_

good

The adventure park was <u>good</u>. _cool_

The rides were <u>good</u>. _crazy_

I had a <u>good</u> time. _fun_

said

"Sh! The baby is asleep," <u>said</u> Dad. _whisperd_

"Stop!" <u>said</u> the policewoman. _yelled_

"Come over here," <u>said</u> the boys. _says_

get

I want to <u>get</u> new shoes. _have_

Please <u>get</u> me a glass of water. _grab_

They will <u>get</u> angry. _be_

swung
spring
m**ore**
w**ore**
st**ore**
sn**ore**
bef**ore**
seash**ore**
English
language

‹ore› saying the /or/ sound

Write some ‹ore› words in the seashore.

Choose a word from the list to fit each sentence.

She ___wore___ a blue coat yesterday.

Please may we have some ___more___ ?

I found a jellyfish on the ___seashore___.

Did he arrive ___before___ or after you?

English
English
English

language
language
language

Think of a more interesting word to replace each of the underlined words, and write it on the line.

She wore a <u>red</u> dress. ___yesterday___

The dinosaur gave a <u>loud</u> roar. ___loud___

It was a <u>cold</u> morning. ___cold___

He caught a <u>small</u> fish. ___small___

70

Commas in Speech

REMEMBER A comma is needed between the spoken words and the rest of the sentence.

Add the missing commas and speech marks to these sentences.

1. My favorite color is blue said the little girl.

2. The policewoman put her hand up and said, Stop!

3. Hello said Uncle John. How are you today?

4. I know the names of all the dinosaurs said Toby and I've got a book about them at home.

REMEMBER A new line is needed each time someone different starts to speak.

Read this conversation, and rewrite it correctly underneath.

Hello Bee called Inky. Hello Inky replied Bee, waving her antenna and flying over to her friend. Did you have a good time at the adventure park yesterday? asked Inky. Oh yes sighed Bee it was brilliant. I went on all the rides and we stayed all day. Did everyone from the hive go? wondered Inky. Yes said Bee and then she paused. Everyone who wanted to she corrected herself.

_____

_____

_____

_____

_____

_____

_____

_____

damp
stand
apple
table
little
middle
bottle
syllable
continent
world

‹le›

Write some ‹le› words in the apple.

Choose a word from the list to fit each sentence.

He asked for a _____ of lemonade.

My _____ sister is only two.

She laid the _____ for dinner.

I baked an _____ pie.

continent
continent
continent

world
world
world

Fill in the missing punctuation marks.

◻Do you want to come and play at my house◻◻ asked Josh◻
Tammy replied◻ ◻I◻ll have to ask my dad first◻◻
◻Look◻◻ exclaimed Josh◻ ◻There is your dad now◻ Why
don◻t you ask him◻◻
◻I will◻◻ Tammy agreed◻

72

Parsing

Identify as many of the different parts of speech as you can, and underline them in the correct colors.

Nouns   **Verbs**   **Pronouns**   **Adjectives**
Adverbs   **Prepositions**   **Conjunctions**

Inky's Necklace

It is a sunny morning. Inky and Bee are in the garden. Inky proudly shows Bee her birthday present, a silver chain. It glitters in the sunlight. Suddenly, a magpie swoops to the ground, and grabs the chain.

"Stop!" shout Inky and Bee, but the naughty magpie escapes with it. Bee flies after the magpie. Inky runs quickly along the road below her friend. She follows the magpie and Bee into the forest. She sees Bee at the bottom of a tall tree.

"The nest is at the top of the tree," pants Bee. "I can't get the chain because the magpies are bigger than me." At this moment, an empty nutshell lands beside Inky.

"I am sorry!" calls a squirrel from the tree.

"It doesn't matter," Inky replies. "Could you help us?" She explains that the magpie took her chain. The squirrel scampers nimbly up the tree, and fetches it from the nest.

Spellings

Spelling Test 1

1.
2.
3.
4.
5.
6.
7.
8.
9.
10.

Spelling Test 2

1.
2.
3.
4.
5.
6.
7.
8.
9.
10.

Spelling Test 3

1.
2.
3.
4.
5.
6.
7.
8.
9.
10.

Spelling Test 4

1.
2.
3.
4.
5.
6.
7.
8.
9.
10.

Spelling Test 5

1. club
2. flag
3. phone
4. photo
5. dallp
6. elephant
7. sphere
8. alphbet
9. nephu
10. ness

Spelling Test 6

1. glad
2. plum
3. read
4. Head
5. bread
6. Wheather
7. thresher
8. brekfist
9. cusin
10. freind

74

Spellings

Spelling Test 7 _____

1. _____
2. _____
3. _____
4. _____
5. _____
6. _____
7. _____
8. _____
9. _____
10. _____

Spelling Test 8 _____

1. _____
2. _____
3. _____
4. _____
5. _____
6. _____
7. _____
8. _____
9. _____
10. _____

Spelling Test 9 _____

1. _____
2. _____
3. _____
4. _____
5. _____
6. _____
7. _____
8. _____
9. _____
10. _____

Spelling Test 10 _____

1. _____
2. _____
3. _____
4. _____
5. _____
6. _____
7. _____
8. _____
9. _____
10. _____

Spelling Test 11 _____

1. _____
2. _____
3. _____
4. _____
5. _____
6. _____
7. _____
8. _____
9. _____
10. _____

Spelling Test 12 _____

1. _____
2. _____
3. _____
4. _____
5. _____
6. _____
7. _____
8. _____
9. _____
10. _____

Spellings

Spelling Test 13

1. _____
2. _____
3. _____
4. _____
5. _____
6. _____
7. _____
8. _____
9. _____
10. _____

Spelling Test 14

1. _____
2. _____
3. _____
4. _____
5. _____
6. _____
7. _____
8. _____
9. _____
10. _____

Spelling Test 15

1. _____
2. _____
3. _____
4. _____
5. _____
6. _____
7. _____
8. _____
9. _____
10. _____

Spelling Test 16

1. _____
2. _____
3. _____
4. _____
5. _____
6. _____
7. _____
8. _____
9. _____
10. _____

Spelling Test 17

1. _____
2. _____
3. _____
4. _____
5. _____
6. _____
7. _____
8. _____
9. _____
10. _____

Spelling Test 18

1. _____
2. _____
3. _____
4. _____
5. _____
6. _____
7. _____
8. _____
9. _____
10. _____

Spellings

Spelling Test 19	Spelling Test 20	Spelling Test 21
1.	1.	1.
2.	2.	2.
3.	3.	3.
4.	4.	4.
5.	5.	5.
6.	6.	6.
7.	7.	7.
8.	8.	8.
9.	9.	9.
10.	10.	10.

Spelling Test 22	Spelling Test 23	Spelling Test 24
1.	1.	1.
2.	2.	2.
3.	3.	3.
4.	4.	4.
5.	5.	5.
6.	6.	6.
7.	7.	7.
8.	8.	8.
9.	9.	9.
10.	10.	10.

Spellings

Spelling Test 25

1. _____
2. _____
3. _____
4. _____
5. _____
6. _____
7. _____
8. _____
9. _____
10. _____

Spelling Test 26

1. _____
2. _____
3. _____
4. _____
5. _____
6. _____
7. _____
8. _____
9. _____
10. _____

Spelling Test 27

1. _____
2. _____
3. _____
4. _____
5. _____
6. _____
7. _____
8. _____
9. _____
10. _____

Spelling Test 28

1. _____
2. _____
3. _____
4. _____
5. _____
6. _____
7. _____
8. _____
9. _____
10. _____

Spelling Test 29

1. _____
2. _____
3. _____
4. _____
5. _____
6. _____
7. _____
8. _____
9. _____
10. _____

Spelling Test 30

1. _____
2. _____
3. _____
4. _____
5. _____
6. _____
7. _____
8. _____
9. _____
10. _____

Spellings

Spelling Test 31	Spelling Test 32	Spelling Test 33
1.	1.	1.
2.	2.	2.
3.	3.	3.
4.	4.	4.
5.	5.	5.
6.	6.	6.
7.	7.	7.
8.	8.	8.
9.	9.	9.
10.	10.	10.

Spelling Test 34	Spelling Test 35	Spelling Test 36
1.	1.	1.
2.	2.	2.
3.	3.	3.
4.	4.	4.
5.	5.	5.
6.	6.	6.
7.	7.	7.
8.	8.	8.
9.	9.	9.
10.	10.	10.

A B C D E F G H I J K L M N O P Q R S T U V W X Y Z

Nouns
- A noun is something we can see, or hear, or touch.
- The color for all types of noun is black.

Proper Nouns
- A proper noun is the name of a particular person, place, or thing.
- The action for a proper noun is to touch your forehead with your index and middle fingers.

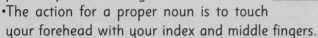

Common Nouns
- A common noun is any noun that is not a proper noun.
- The action for a common noun is to touch your forehead with all the fingers of one hand.

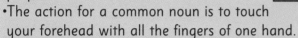

Pronouns
- Pronouns are the little words used to replace nouns.
- The color for all pronouns is pink.
- The actions for pronouns are:

    For **I**, point to yourself.
    For **you** (singular), point to someone else.
    For **he**, point to a boy.
    For **she**, point to a girl.
    For **it**, point to the floor.

For **we**, point in a circle, including yourself and others.
For **you** (plural), point to two other people.
For **they**, point to the next-door class.

Adjectives
- An adjective describes a noun or a pronoun.
- The action for an adjective is to touch the side of your temple with your fist.
- The color for adjectives is blue.

Verbs
- A verb is a doing word.
- The action for verbs in general is to clench your fists and move your arms backwards and forwards at your sides, as if running.
- The color for all types of verb is red.

Past Tense Verbs
- The action for the past tense is pointing backwards over your shoulder with your thumb.

Present Tense Verbs
- The action for the present tense is pointing towards the floor with the palm of the hand.

Verbs in the Future
- The action for verbs that describe the future is pointing towards the front.

Adverbs
- An adverb describes a verb.
- The action for adverbs is to bang one fist on top of the other.
- The color for adverbs is orange.

Conjunctions
- A conjunction is used to join parts of a sentence.
- The action for conjunctions is to hold your hands apart with palms facing up. Move both hands so one is on top of the other.
- The color for conjunctions is purple.

Prepositions
- A preposition relates one noun or pronoun to another.
- The action for prepositions is to point from one noun to another.
- The color for prepositions is green.